THE HOUSE THAT
JACK BUILT

2011 Anne Punton
To Patti

God bless. Lovely
to see you after all
these years. So much
to catch up on. So
many blessings
to share. With love
from Anne (Aug 2014)

THE HOUSE THAT
JACK BUILT

Anne Punton

To order additional copies of this book, contact:
Xlibris Corporation
1-888-795-4274
www.Xlibris.com
Orders@Xlibris.com
106964

CONTENTS

Acknowledgments 11

Preface 13

Chapter 1   WINNING THE JACKPOT orHOW I MET JACK 15

HOW I arrived in the small Yorkshire town of Snaith and met Jack. A bit about me.

How, courtesy of God and a dog, a fifty-four-year-old woman, in a wheelchair with multiple sclerosis, marries a fit, youthful, handsome, and still eligible widower of eighty.

Chapter 2   THE YOUNG JACKANAPES or
              OUR JACKY ENTERS THE WORLD 41

A WIDOW'S STRUGGLES to rear six children. Wielding saws in the clog mill and "tatie scratting" and so on.

HOME, QUAINT HOME with its amenities. The copper, the tap in the yard, the privy, and ashpit.

POOR BUT SECURE and very happy. Food, clothes, school, fun and games, pleasures and pastimes, pranks, and peccadilloes.

Chapter 3   JACK AND THE BEANSTALK or
              HOW JACK BEGINS TO MAKE HIS WAY IN LIFE 63

WORK: Joiner's apprentice. The clog mill.

PLAY: Dramatic and musical talents of a sought-after young bachelor.

SPIRITUAL: Acquiring a faith for life.

GENERAL: Within context, descriptions of local customs, the historical market town of Snaith, the ancient parish of the Peculiar of Great Snaith, the language of the bells, and a lost joke on the church clock.

Chapter 4   JACKBOOTS ON THE MARCH or
                HOW JACK SPENT THE WAR.......................................86

METHODIST CONNECTIONS and growth of personal convictions.
WAR ISSUES affecting Snaith in general and Jack in particular.
PACIFICISM—its cost and outcome.
THE NCC two tribunals and life in the Non-Combatant Corps according to Jack.

Chapter 5   JACK OF HEARTS or
                HOW JACK FINDS ROMANCE....................................109

DIDCOT: Blackout encounter in the bushes.
CORNWALL: The exigencies of a wartime wedding.
YORKSHIRE: Six kids in ten years. Early family recollections. Struggles and a mum who manages on "nothing." Forays into fostering. Romance survives the treadmill of toil and routine.

Chapter 6   JACK AND JILL or
                HOW JACK AND HIS JILL
                CLIMBED THE FAMILY HILL....................................134

HOME LIFE: A Christian foundation, Christmas and summer holidays, school discipline, pets, Margaret's breast cancer.
THE CARING ETHIC: Bringing the old and needy into the home and two tramps. Relating to disadvantaged people in a local institution.
FAMILY FORTUNES: Where everyone is today.

Chapter 7   JACK OF ALL TRADES or
                HOW JACK MADE A LIVING..161

GOING IT ALONE as a painter and decorator with a bike and borrowed brushes.
THE DAY OF THE AUCTION when Jack bought a dilapidated property for a song and set up his DIY shop and undertaking business.
COUNTRY UNDERTAKING then and now. Clients dead and alive. The art of grave digging and tales of the grave and the not so grave.

Chapter 8   JACK THE WALKING MAN or
             HOW JACK TOOK TO THE ROAD..............................189

1977 AND ON: Margaret dies when Jack is sixty-four. John joins the business, and his dad finds a new interest.

SPONSORED WALKING: How it began and where it led. Of feet, thirst, weather, routes, and places. Of kindness, hospitality, donations, and people. Trips down memory lane.

INTERLUDES: Hills alive (literally) with the sound of music. Completing the Los Angeles marathon against the odds.

Chapter 9   JACK THE GIANT KILLER or
             JACK'S PHILOSOPHY OF LIFE.....................................217

A FIGHTING SPIRIT in a mild, peace-loving man.

CHRISTIAN FAITH in action, municipal matters, green issues, charitable concerns, personal relationships. Humour, compassion, strength, public speaking

ALL ILLUSTRATED with such stories as the German POW, the egg-and-spoon race, and what happened when the Duke of Norfolk opened Snaith chapel fete.

Chapter 10   WELL DONE, JACK! or
             JACK'S LAST WALK..248

THE VOICE FROM BEHIND: Amsterdam and Snaith High Street.

THE BEST-LAID PLANS: Training for the New York Marathon. Cancellation. A special day. Sudden death.

A PANORAMA OF THOUGHTS: Instantaneously glimpsed but described in several pages.

THE FUNERAL and my God-given comfort at home from the Song of Songs, a book for brides and weddings.

JACK PUNTON (1913–1999): The well-deserved accolade, "Well done, Jack!"

INDEX 273

DEDICATION

This book is dedicated to Jack and Margaret, their six children, numerous grandchildren, a few great-grandchildren, and future generations of the Punton clan.

ACKNOWLEDGMENTS

So many people have talked to me about Jack and answered questions that I could not possibly mention each one by name, even if I could remember them all. He was very widely known and loved. Some people, however, were particularly helpful.

Margaret Barker, Ron Christian, and Bill and Dot Ramsey all loaned me books about Snaith and its history. Jerry Horner, Norwood Howard, Mary Law, and Harry Poeschke wrote long letters in response to queries. All Jack's children passed on personal memories and sorted through old family photographs for illustrations. Sally spent long hours typing the manuscript. Jane allowed me to quote extensively from a wonderful record of her early family life which she had written for an entirely different purpose. I thank everyone for their invaluable help, and that includes my brother Laurence who prepared the manuscript for publication and carried the project through to completion.

Above all, my greatest debt is to Jack himself who shared so much of his life and feelings with me. If some of you who knew Jack longer than I did feel that I have not got everything quite right, please be tolerant. I have to emphasise that this is my story about Jack as I understand it. I have done my best to write a true and good story with some literary merit. After all, only the best is worthy of such a special man—of Jack.

Anne Punton, October 2011

PREFACE

This is the story of an ordinary man. He even had an ordinary name, for he was christened JACK, not John. His mother was a widow with five other children to rear. He lived through two world wars in a world that changed unimaginably during his nine decades within it. He worked hard to raise his family, then lost his beloved wife shortly before he was due to retire. Never one to sit back and bemoan his lot, he developed challenging new interests, including the acquirement of a second wife.

Many people could summarise their lives similarly. So why write about them? Is there an epic of quiet heroism to tell? Are there some complex grounds of motivation to explore which explain a person's actions? Has someone lived through a period of significant history? Is this person what we call "a character"? If so, however ordinary they be, they have a story to tell.

Mostly the detachment of familiarity or the very anonymity of ordinariness means that the story never gets told—until a stranger comes to town and sees the possibilities. As far as Jack was concerned, I was the newcomer to town who saw and responded to the potential for a good tale. I head this introduction to my efforts "Jack High." In a game of lawn bowls, the bowl which reaches the same level on the green as the jack is said to be jack high. If this account of Jack succeeds in catching the imagination and highlighting the extraordinary qualities of an ordinary man, it too will have reached the hoped-for level of "Jack High."

CHAPTER 1

WINNING THE JACKPOT
or
HOW I MET JACK

In the Beginning

This is the story of Jack. Why then do I begin it by talking about me? The answer is simple. Although I only knew this man for seven years, my account is very personal. Somehow I feel that you will appreciate it more if you know a little about who I am as well as how I came to meet Jack and eventually acquired the right to tell you his story.

Imagine, therefore, a scene. It takes place in the entrance hall of a charactered old Church of Scotland manse. Standing in a circle, arms entwined, is the manse family—father, mother, thirteen-year-old daughter, and eight-year-old son. They hug each other tightly. Kerry, the dog, barks and pushes against their legs. Never one to be left out, he wriggles into the centre of the group and leaps to lick his humans' faces. I treasure the memory. It totally summarises the love and warm security of my childhood in a home where Jesus was loved and served. Such a home my brother and I had.

I was born in 1939 in Dovercourt near Harwich where my father, William Dexter, was a pastor in the Methodist Church. In Dovercourt my parents saw "Dunkirk" happen although only later did they learn what all the activity had been about. When they moved to Scalloway in the Shetland Isles in 1940, they were again in a strategic zone for the sea defences of the nation. There they saw the "Shetland Bus" in action—gun running and espionage between occupied Norway and Britain carried out by Norwegian fishermen in the course of their workaday duties. A family in my father's congregation owned the marine engineering business that serviced the fishing boats involved.

Young though I was, I have many vivid memories of those years, including things learned about the Christian faith through Bible and missionary stories and the daily routine of manse life.

Our next move in 1944 was to Tetney in Lincolnshire where two significant things happened. My brother Laurence, who is one of the most important people in my life, was born; and something occurred which determined the course my life would take.

Now Mum was a local preacher, and I was used to going everywhere with her. While she took a service I would sit at her feet in the pulpit playing with my toys. There are still folk around who tell me how I would occasionally poke my head out to survey the congregation below and, I regret to say, even pull faces at times. On this occasion, however, I was in the pulpit with Dad whilst Mum was at home with the new baby. My toys were ignored as I enjoyed the challenge of finding the hymns and singing the words for even at the age of five I could read well. In fact, I was most upset when the Sunday school of this same church had given me a "baby" book at the prize giving. I realise now that it was perfectly suitable for my age, but I was looking forward to a "proper" book such as the older children were receiving.

My dad announced hymn 801, "From Greenland's Icy Mountains." The imagery thrilled me. I could see those snowy peaks, wide rivers, hot golden sands, and palm-fronded islands lapped by sun-sparkled seas. I wondered about the people who lived in such far-off lands and who, according to the hymn, had never heard about Jesus. Doubtless, my understanding of the gospel message was simple. Nevertheless, I knew with complete clarity that God wanted me to be someone who would go and tell others about Jesus. Such was my call to be a missionary. It never left me.

Milestones along the Way

We moved to Wales, to Leeds, and, when I was eleven, back to Shetland. This time round Dad was with the Church of Scotland and ministering in an isolated community in Cullivoe on Yell, an island in the far north.

By then I had already passed the scholarship exam in Leeds, and so arrangements were made for me to go to the Anderson Educational Institute, the only senior secondary school in the islands and the equivalent of an English

Grammar School. The institute was in Lerwick, Shetland's capital and fifty miles from Cullivoe. It might have been five hundred. The journey involved three twenty-seater buses and a rough sea crossing in a minuscule launch no bigger than one of the buses. It took most of the day, and in bad weather the boat could not sail.

Accordingly children from such a distance away who went to the institute stayed in either the girls' or boys' hostel or in lodgings. As my parents wanted me to be in an actively Christian home, they arranged for me to live with Bob and Mina Moore, members of their former church in Scalloway.

Scalloway was convenient being a mere seven miles and daily, school bus journey away from Lerwick. Bob, by the way, was the younger son of the marine engineering family who serviced the Shetland Bus boats.

The Moores were staunch Methodists and very special people. They treated me like their own daughter, and I learned things from them that I would not have done from my own parents, wonderful as they also were. Their daughter and only child was Kathleen. Years back we had started infant school together. We soon became close friends and remained so until she died when I was doing some of the final editing of this book.

In my first year at the institute I did badly for I fell between the English and the Scottish educational systems and was a year younger than my classmates. Happily, the school gave me a second chance, and I repeated the year. By this time Kathleen had joined me, and from then on we went through school together. At home we shared a bedroom and all our leisure interests, most of which centred round the local Methodist chapel.

The chapel was lively with a good youth work, excellent ministers, and sound Bible teaching. During this time Kath and I committed our lives to the Lord. Two of the chapel members were particularly influential in our lives. One was John Thomson who later married Kathleen, and the other was John Macdonald, the Sunday school superintendent. The two Johns and Kath and I regularly went out hymn singing to the sick and elderly. If I say that many of these people died soon after our ministrations, I trust you will understand. They really were old and ill; and we certainly hoped that our time with them eased, rather than speeded, their departure.

One day Dad said to me, "If God has called you to be a missionary, why don't you ask him to show you where he wants you to go?"

Plenty of time for that later, I thought. I was only thirteen. However, I knew Dad. He was persistent and would one day say, "Did you ever do what I suggested?"

It was better to comply, then I could tell him, yes, but there was no response. I was neither rebellious nor sceptical. I genuinely felt that there was time and to spare for all that in the future. Accordingly, I went to bed one particular night, and to please Dad I prayed a rather perfunctory prayer.

"Dear Lord, where do you want me to go as a missionary? It would be nice to know even though it isn't necessary yet—and you know what Dad is like."

I slept. Much later I awoke. In the blackness I heard a masculine voice, right above me in the room, twice saying, "The Jews! The Jews!" I heard it with my ears. It was not inside my head.

So that was that. God had, in a fashion, called my bluff. Surely he has a sense of humour! In some way he wanted me to work amongst Jewish people. Even at that age I realised that Jesus was Jewish and that many of his own nation had opposed him. I had met a few of my father's Jewish friends in Leeds and knew that they still did not accept Jesus. I recalled hearing how my paternal grandfather had once sheltered an old Jewish lady from an anti-Semitic mob—in his church of all places. I also remembered the excitement in our home when the State of Israel was declared and how Mum had tried to explain the significance of the event in terms an eight-year-old could understand. Everything came together in my mind and suddenly clicked. "Of course," I said to myself, "Jewish people need to trust in Jesus as their Saviour the same as anyone else." I turned over and went to sleep, but from that moment the distant path ahead took direction.

A Privileged Childhood

Although I was away at school for most of my teenage years, it remains true to say, both for my brother and myself, that our lives centred round our parents. We did things together. In summer there were long walks along the cliffs or over the hills where the streams, though peaty, were so clean you could safely drink the water. In winter Laurence and Dad made working models with a meccano set whilst Mum and I tackled crosswords and jigsaws. A Christmas Day tradition was for my mother and me to share a jigsaw and a box of chocolates between us. If it was not finished by Boxing Day lunch (the jigsaw I mean, the chocs always were), the tablecloth went over it with the meal on top. In the evenings we played pencil-and-paper and board games. When we could not afford a Monopoly set we made our own. As we lived in Glasgow by then we adapted it to Glasgow place-names which made it much more fun. Our house was full of books, and Laurence and I were advanced readers from an early age. Even when television became common we never had one, and we never wanted one. Yes, we had a radio and listened to the news and a few favourite programmes, but mostly we entertained ourselves, and we preferred it that way.

Above all we really communicated with each other as a family. We talked all the time and would confide in our parents and ask them almost anything.

Some of the simplest pleasures we shared are now precious memories. Take, for instance, Mum and Dad's bedroom in Shetland which faced due north. One midsummer night when it never gets properly dark at such a latitude, we stood at their window and watched the sun just dip below the westerly edge of the northern horizon. A magnificent sunset spread across the northerly sky, slowly to merge into an equally spectacular sunrise as a short while later the sun reappeared on the eastern rim of the same horizon.

Naturally schooldays and Scalloway were different, but Kathleen and I shared a similar happy security with Bob and Mina. We did not know at the time how blessed we were.

After I left school we moved to Glasgow where we took up fell walking, youth hostelling, and cycling, much of it still as a family. Laurence joined his school rowing club. Regatta days saw us down at the Clyde shouting for his crew. He played the viola in Glasgow Schools' Orchestra, and so naturally we attended all the concerts in the St Andrew's Halls. Sadly, the halls burned down a few years later.

For the sake of balance and honesty, I also have to say that if ever there was a row in our house, it was usually when Laurence and I were slack about our Saturday cleaning duties; and sometimes it was because I had a tendency to answer back when ticked off. Dad was the one to be cross. Mum was milder.

There is one more important childhood influence to tell you about. Our paternal grandmother was full of fun and a woman who served God. She was a great inspiration to me and many others. When Laurence was a toddler we lived in Leeds for two years. Granny took me to the Salvation Army where the meetings were lively, and everything I saw about the Christian faith was bright and attractive.

And it worked! For instance, Granny prayed and saw results. Some of her prayers took courage, but the answers came and still challenge me. Granddad had a stroke while shaving one morning. Before attempting to call a doctor Granny prayed. He recovered instantaneously. Important keys went missing. Everyone laughed when in a dream Granny saw them in the grating of the local swimming baths—but they were there. One of the youngsters in the family had taken them and had lost them when he went swimming. I put my hand through the rollers of the electric wringer on her old-fashioned washing machine. In seconds the hand was blackening, swollen, and useless. She anointed it with what was probably cooking oil and in the name of Jesus made the briefest of petitions. When we opened our eyes and removed the tea cloth she had put over it, the hand was perfect.

Throughout my childhood I grew up knowing God. Dare I say it without sounding irreverent? In all the activity and happiness of our home, God was as much a natural part of the family as were the cat and dog, only they moved around at our feet whereas God was somewhere above and unseen. Even so, he was important and real and somehow made us feel safe.

At the Crossroads

In Glasgow my parents pastored an independent church, the Grove Street Institute. It was well known in the city and had been founded a century before to minister to the needy, both spiritually and socially, in the rough Cowcaddens district of the city. At Glasgow University I took an MA in English and history followed by a certificate in social science. For a year I then worked in Stobhill General Hospital in the Almoners' Department, as it was called. All along, my main interest was still in Christian things, and in the Grove Street Church we had a thriving establishment with plenty happening for young people.

Early on I acquired a boyfriend, a gifted young man with an active faith. He was Seth and son of evangelist parents, Seth and Bessie Sykes, who were well known in their generation, especially in Scotland. They wrote "Thank you, Lord, for Saving My Soul" and other catchy choruses which were popular in beach missions and gospel meetings. Seth senior had already died before I met his son, but Bessie carried on their evangelistic work alone into her old age.

Seth and I were together for about five years, but although we considered marriage, somehow I always held back. I never felt that we were right for each other, and he never pretended to have a missionary call or an interest in things Jewish. About four times we broke it off, but we really did care for each other and it was hard. Invariably we came together again and always I knew it was wrong.

Eventually, in the final year at university, I began exploring openings into Jewish work, and not only in Israel. There are Jewish people all over the world. Where did God want me to go? Despite my efforts all doors remained firmly closed, and I knew why. It is the main principle of divine guidance. Why should God show us the next step when we have not shown him that we are ready to take it? He would never reveal his plans until I had given up Seth and proved myself free to go forward. I was at a crossroads, and my whole future depended on my choice of path—Seth or God.

Each new year Methodists reconsecrate themselves to God in a covenant service. The covenant statement is solemn and not lightly avowed.

I am no longer my own, but yours. Put me to what you will, rank me with whom you will; put me to doing, put me to suffering; let me be employed for you or laid aside for you, exalted for you or brought low for you; let me be full, let me be empty; let me have all things, let me have nothing; I freely and whole-heartedly yield all things to your pleasure and disposal.

We used this covenant service in our church too. That year, as I repeated those awesome words, I said to God in my heart and with complete sincerity, "I want your will for my life. I've tried to put you first and failed. I can't do it. Please do it for me. If you break this relationship I promise I'll accept it."

Within days Seth told me he had met someone else. If I would not commit myself fully to him, he wanted to be free. I went home and cried and cried and deep inside I rejoiced in the utter relief and freedom that I suddenly felt. Mum dried the tears and took me out. We finished up laughing in Lewis's department store and eating huge knickerbocker glories.

An Open Door

Immediately God took over and a totally unlooked-for door began to nudge ajar. It started when a speaker came to our church who just happened to know a Glasgow lady who was shortly going out to work in Israel with an Anglican society. He put us in touch, and thereby I met Janette Ross who later became a lifelong friend and colleague. I liked Janette, but I was not keen on working with the Church of England. For I had the prejudiced notion that not many Anglicans were proper Christians. It was probably something to do with my Scottish background as it was not an idea that came from my parents. Politely but definitely I turned my back on CMJ, the Church's Ministry Amongst the Jewish People—until one day I received a letter. The Reverend Ted Yorke, CMJ's home secretary, was coming to Glasgow. "Could we meet?" It was the least I could do even if privately I felt it was a waste of time. We met. Before we parted Mr Yorke said, "Shall we pray together?"

I cannot tell you what he said. I can tell you that the Holy Spirit radiated from his words. Mr Yorke's prayer caused me to change direction. If this man, I reasoned, can pray so beautifully, then the society he represents must be all right. I felt urged to investigate CMJ more closely. CMJ, I discovered, ran a summer conference each year to bring staff and supporters together. Obviously I ought to go, but I could not really afford the fees. There and then I put a silent feeler out to God.

"Lord, if I'm invited for the week, costs paid, I'll take it as a sign that CMJ might be for me."

The invitation came, and I went. There I met other impressive people and, incidentally, changed my view about Anglicans. Still I hesitated. Would God confirm in just one more way that this society was his choice for me? He did. I read my mother's text calendar for the day. It quoted Isaiah 22:22.

And I will place on his shoulder the key of the house of David; he shall open, and none shall shut; and he shall shut, and none shall open.

It was all there—the house of David representing the Jewish people, a key, closed doors I was unable to open, and now a door opening wide before me which I could not close. Only a few months later I met the Candidates' Committee in London, not wondering if they would approve of me but confident that they could not reject me. An open door stood ahead.

Through the door lay Oxford, not the university but a women's theological college called St Michael's House. Here CMJ sent its female recruits for training. At this juncture would you once again envisage a scene. It takes place early in 1963 at this same St Michael's House.

A young lady has arrived for the weekend to be interviewed for a place as a student. At dinner she sits at a table with a mixture of staff and students. It is all very staid and proper. Conversation proceeds somewhat as follows:

"Have you travelled far today?"

"Yes, from Glasgow."

For reasons you will discover, the young lady is not keen to continue the topic but cannot muster the conversational skills to change the subject.

"That is a long way. Did you drive down?"

The young lady neither drives nor has a car. Someone else pursues the question. It is not an interrogation, only a polite interest in a guest. Nevertheless, the said guest begins to feel slightly harassed.

"I suppose you came by train then, or coach?"

For a moment the future theological student is almost tempted to tell a lie before moral rectitude and a touch of bravado prevails.

"No, I hitchhiked."

The table fell silent. In those days the casual lifestyle of modern times was only beginning to emerge. Folk might hitchhike on holiday, but not to attend an important interview. My fellow diners were definitely shocked but with hasty politeness endeavoured to fill the conversational hiatus with safer subjects. Only much later did I realise that the principal, a Ms Dorothy Barter Snow, who was widely recognised to be "a character," was much more of a free spirit than most of her staff and students. If I have misjudged anyone I happily apologise. I can only say that the overall reaction to my mode of transport was such that I truly believed I might have jeopardised my chances of being accepted as a student. This was not something I had foreseen.

Fortunately, far from counting against me, the episode delighted Ms Snow. Here, she reasoned, was the true missionary spirit enjoying adventure, finding ways and means, prepared to rough it or do the unexpected. Actually, it was not so commendable as that. I simply had no money to spare on expensive fares and neither did my parents, but I was used to hitchhiking. In such fashion, Laurence and I made the trip together. On arrival in the city we found the railway station. In the ladies' room I changed into a sedate "costume" with a hat and accessories. Laurence then took my casual clothes and made for the youth hostel. I, meanwhile, equipped with a small overnight bag, arrived at the college on the Banbury Road optimistically hoping that nobody would care about my journey there.

All my life I had looked forward to Bible college. Truth to tell, when I got there I found the all-female environment and atmosphere of "properness" rather daunting. It probably shows how much I needed the social polish of such a place. Furthermore everything was so "spiritual." This, of course, is a hazard of any Bible college; but it irked me. I once bought a women's magazine. Someone saw it and said "Oh!" as if I had indulged in a feminine equivalent of *Playboy*. These were minor irritations. The expected tensions of sharing bedrooms and college discipline posed no problems. It was in the unexpected that my greatest difficulty lay.

The trouble was that I was not well, and some of the physical symptoms, such as tremor in my hands, were hard to hide. I had no idea that I was coping with the early symptoms of an illness that would only be diagnosed many years later. I used to ask myself, "Am I heading for a nervous breakdown or becoming a hypochondriac?" Neither seemed in character. Either way I refused to give in. Only my family knew of my struggles as I plodded on. Those eagerly anticipated years at Bible college were tough. Having said all that, I was very happy, met some great people, and learned a lot. I took the interdiocesan certificate which qualifies one to be an official parish worker in the Anglican church and also a diploma in theology externally with London University. In my second year I became senior student which was both a burden and an honour.

Clear Road Ahead

At last the great day came. In September 1965 I sailed into Haifa Bay, thrilled to be in Israel even though my call was to a people not a place. I was appointed to be housekeeper at a newly opened conference centre called Stella Carmel. Stella was (still is) a beautifully arched and balconied Arab mansion sited on almost the highest part of the Mount Carmel ridge. We were on the outskirts of Isfiya, a Druze village, nearly two thousand feet above sea level and ten miles from downtown Haifa. Our views and climate were fabulous.

In the sixties Israel was still a vibrant, pioneer country full of hope and exuberance. At the same time it was also a shelter for many weary refugees from war and holocaust in Europe and from persecution in Arab lands. Scattered amongst these hurt and hurting people was a handful of "Hebrew Christians," as they were then called. Emotionally and physically scarred by past experiences they were now discriminated against because of their faith in Jesus. Many were also isolated from Christian fellowship. Over the years some of their erstwhile pastors or missionary leaders also arrived in Israel. They sought out those members of their former flocks who still survived.

At this juncture CMJ saw the need for a house of fellowship and retreat for such people. To this end they purchased Stella Carmel, a one-time Arab hotel. The place was ideal, peaceful, and cut off from mainstream Israeli life. In those days the only road to Haifa was still a dirt track. When I arrived the centre was only just beginning to function. The groups who came to us arranged their own programmes while we looked after them behind the scenes. Let me tell you about a few of them.

There were the Bulgarians led by Jo Isakoff who, apart from being a pastor had also edited a newspaper in Bulgaria and had been imprisoned by the Communists for his faith. Jo now nurtured his scattered congregation with benevolent authority, and they loved him. Then there was Huguette Harari, an Egyptian Jewish believer. She gathered together French and Arabic-speaking Hebrew Christians who had come from places like Egypt, Tunisia, and Morocco. Her great gift was Bible teaching. The Romanians came with Pastor Solheim, a Norwegian, Lutheran missionary who had built up congregations in Romania and who also had been imprisoned under the Communists. One of his members was a frail gentleman who had come to faith when he shared a prison cell with the well-known Pastor Wurmbrand. His body was broken by daily beatings, but his faith was bright. How vulnerable these men and women were! The older ones would never be comfortable with Hebrew or integrate fully into Israeli society.

Not so another group of our guests who were of a younger generation and who called themselves "Messianic Jews." If not born in the state, they had arrived in its early years in a spirit of idealism as pioneer immigrants and mostly from free countries. Settled predominantly in Jerusalem, Tel Aviv, and Haifa, they had formed Messianic Assemblies on the Brethren style. And yet, for them too, life was not easy because of their faith in Jesus. We therefore found ourselves hosting young family house parties, marriage guidance weekends, youth and children camps. This was truly an indigenous group. However, growth was slow and mostly in terms of birth rather than evangelism. Not until the early eighties did a move of the Holy Spirit lead to Jewish people all over the world coming to Jesus and the eventual founding of congregations in virtually every town in Israel.

And what about the Arabs? Most Israeli Arabs are Muslims. A small percentage are Greek Catholic or Orthodox Christians, and only a few hundreds are of Protestant persuasion such as Baptist, Episcopal, or Church of the Nazarene. Christian Arabs are disliked by the Muslims and often harassed, and they have always faced peculiar problems vis-à-vis the Palestinian question. Gladly we widened our ministry to embrace them. We welcomed Arab youth weekends, various conferences, and congregation days plus clergy retreats. One young clergyman from those days was Riach Abu El Assal, who later became Riach, Episcopal bishop in Jerusalem. After the Six-Day War, Arab Lutheran pastors from the West Bank territories began bringing their congregations to us for various activities. They too needed much encouragement and comfort.

In addition we saw tourists, expatriates, and a steady stream of secular Israelis who loved the tranquillity of our house after the "push and shove" attitude of Israeli society. They joined us (voluntarily) for family prayers, went mountain walks with our staff members, invited us to their homes, and often asked questions about our faith. Some of these were able, thinking people—a university lecturer, a professional musician, a beautician, an amateur art collector—yet underneath they were spiritually needy.

What a privilege it was to be there. I met people of such diverse cultural and religious backgrounds and from all over the world. I shared life with the inhabitants of the land as a resident and not a tourist. I went through the crises of the 1967 Six-Day War and the 1973 Yom Kippur War with my Israeli friends. In quieter times there was chance to explore the country and to see and feel the environment in which Jesus lived and most of the Bible is set. Without realising it, I learned things that enabled me to move into the next phase of my life and eventually to write two books, *View the Land* (under my maiden name of Dexter) and *The World That Jesus Knew* (under my married name of Punton). How I loved Israel and my friends there. Never did I envisage anything other than spending my working life there and, if possible, retiring there when that time came.

The Turn in the Road

What happened to change my planned direction? Initially the health concerns of Bible college days cleared up. They quickly returned in other forms and always accompanied by a relentless fatigue that no one else seemed to experience despite the fact that we were often short staffed and overworked. Often I suspected a neurological illness, but it seemed a far-fetched notion, and

I would pull myself together and battle on. Not until a dropped foot sent me to the doctor yet again was I correctly referred to a neurologist. He immediately put me on three weeks' bed rest and steroid injections and then told me I had multiple sclerosis.

It was a shock but, paradoxically, no real surprise to learn that it was serious, and yet, oh the relief of knowing what I was up against at last. Now I could focus my energies on fighting a real foe instead of struggling against the unknown. Above all I never doubted that God was in control. In the days that followed I saw the world with new eyes. Nature was beautiful and joyous. Colours, scents, and sounds were intensified; and God was everywhere. We sang a modern hymn which has since disappeared into oblivion. Based on Lamentations 3:22 and 23, it felt so apt.

> *New, every morning it's new,*
> *The love of God to me is wonderfully new.*

The MS was diagnosed in summer 1975. In April 1977 I returned to the UK. Life in Israel was finished.

I returned home fully expecting that CMJ would gently ask me to leave. Not so! Quite fortuitously they had plans to open a centre in North London for training new workers and teaching churches about the Jewish roots of our faith together with the place of the Jewish people in God's purposes and our responsibilities towards them. Would I help with this? Thus, in February 1978 I moved to North Finchley. Whilst the Reverend Gordon Jessop, who was in charge of the scheme, dealt with property matters and organised a programme, I spent time reading and investigating Jewish life around me. It was all so different from Israel, and there was much to learn. Eighteen months later Gordon returned to parish life. I could not handle all his projects, but I offered to do the training of staff in a home-based setting. Everyone was delighted.

My home was the ground floor flat of a CMJ house. Upstairs was a three-bedroom flat where trainees could stay. We seldom had more than three or four at a time. For lectures I used my own sitting room. Each course was adapted for those attending. I might have one person for a week or six people for four months or a couple for one weekend per month for half a year and so on. Nor should you imagine that our trainees were raw recruits fresh from college. They were all experienced men and women such as teachers, clergy, and other professionals, some of whom were appointed to top positions in CMJ. Lectures covered subjects related to Jewish studies and Israel background in greater or lesser detail as appropriate. We also examined issues such as mission, culture, and personal relationships. I arranged visits to synagogues and other places or events, and students joined our outreach team in street witness.

Despite my limitations I established a busy schedule. I made a number of Jewish friends and went to a weekly Hebrew class for many years as well as serving on various CMJ committees and becoming joint editor of our magazine. Inexorably, however, the MS made its slow, insidious inroads into my strength. From managing with a walking stick I graduated to a manual wheelchair and then an electric one. I spent evenings and weekends resting on my bed.

In 1988 Dad died. Mum sold the family home in Glasgow where she and Dad had ministered for thirty years. She moved to Yorkshire to be near relatives and rented a house in Swinefleet. How I longed to take early retirement to be with her, but God had taken me into CMJ. Only he would take me out. By 1991 I was not well. God held the key to the door, and he had to act soon.

A Closing Door

Came the day when I sat talking to colleagues in my comfortable sitting room. Despite the homely atmosphere we had a day of official business ahead, and the day's agenda was paramount. During the first session, and unconnected to anything under discussion, an unexpected sensation of insight suddenly entered my mind. It came like a beam of directed light at a diagonal slant from without and above. It penetrated my forehead. "This is your time to go."

Guests and working sessions came and went all day. I had no time to think. I did not need it. As soon as I was alone I phoned my mum. The door was closing. I could retire. Within twenty-four hours three passages of scripture randomly and confirmed my decision. I needed confirmation, and it was good to have it.

Immediately I wrote to my CMJ boss. My letter arrived on the very day he had determined to come and see me. Due to financial difficulties my society was making staff cutbacks. With a heavy heart he was coming to tell me that the council felt my time to go had come. In so far as my pride was concerned, I am always glad that I received my marching orders from God first and council second.

Naturally I had ideas about the timing and planning of my retirement. What in fact happened was that God overruled and speeded the process along at every stage. Within two weeks my mother found a bungalow suitable for us to buy. A long time before, I had booked for a course in a centre near Doncaster and had planned to spend the weekend with my mother. In one of God's foreordained coincidences I saw the bungalow at the same time. There and then we made an offer. Three months later Mum moved in.

It took me another four months to sort out my affairs, but in June 1992 I joined her and we squeezed, literally, into our new home. I was two weeks short of my fifty-third birthday and thrilled to be retired and with my mum at last. Six weeks later I had to call a strange doctor in the middle of the night. My mother was rushed into hospital for an emergency operation. In all the trauma we saw God's perfect timing in our lives.

New Start in Snaith

Our bungalow was in Snaith. As few people have ever heard of the place, a little background information is in order. Start with York which most people can find on the map. Some fourteen miles south of York lies Selby with its mediaeval abbey. Seven miles south of Selby you come to Snaith. If you then turn east, another seven miles will bring you to Goole, the most inland port of the British Isles. Goole is on the Ouse, already by that stage a wide river swelled by the streams of the many other Yorkshire rivers which join its lower reaches. A few miles downstream the Ouse itself flows into the mighty Humber estuary. Large ships berth in Goole docks. For its size it is one of the busiest ports in Britain.

I like Goole. It is a down to earth, red brick, working town with no frills or pretensions. It is not very big, and the people are friendly. It has its seamy side. What town does not, especially a port? Apparently it is also one of the chief drug centres of the country. Going in to shop or on business the less salubrious aspects of life are not obvious. Administratively Snaith is closer to Goole than Selby. Historically Snaith is older than Goole which, in its present form, is a relatively new town of some one hundred and fifty or so years' growth.

The area around Snaith is mainly agricultural. Over by Selby there are a few mines left, despite the pit closures of recent years. Nearer at hand unexpected pockets of industry, such as the chemical works in Rawcliffe Bridge, sit comfortably camouflaged by fields and trees. We were not overly keen about the close proximity of three power stations, Drax power station being the largest in Europe. If what one hears is true, Drax is also the biggest single air pollutant in Britain. Apparently the acid rain killing off Scandinavian pine forests originates largely from our Drax and its neighbours.

Such drawbacks aside, what pleased us when we moved to Snaith was its convenience. Although it is no more than a village in size it is officially classed as a town and has everything, and sometimes more than one of the same amenity. There is a health centre, fire station, bank, library, vet, chemist, optician, hairdresser, florist, newsagent, post office, estate agent, take away food shops, small supermarket, haberdashery, electrical shop, butcher, chippy, garages, and a DIY shop and undertaking business, both of these latter being owned by our Jack and now by his son, John.

As if this is not enough, and I may well have missed something, there is a railway station where nowadays only few trains stop. This is compensated for by an hourly bus service that sandwiches in Snaith between Selby and Goole. Then we have two schools, a residential nursing home, a brewery, five pubs, two churches, and a sewage farm. The pubs did not concern us greatly, the churches did. As for the sewage works, the smell from that had me worrying about our drains for a long time until I learned about its existence. Above all, the area was flat, an important consideration for a wheelchair user and the pusher.

Enter Jack

Wherever in the world Christians go they can make instant friends by attending a local church. By the time I arrived my mother had already received a warm welcome at the Methodist chapel. I wanted to retain some link with my Anglican connections as well but had no realistic choice. The parish church had no toilet and inadequate heating. The Methodist church had both. One such commonplace but, for me, crucial criteria was my decision made to transfer membership to the chapel and back to my childhood roots. Snaith suited us, and we settled speedily.

"You know," said my mother one day, "I met a really unusual man recently. He's nearly eighty, but he still does long distance, sponsored walks and has raised thousands of pounds for children's charities."

The word "walk" caught my attention. Many of our family holidays had been spent fell walking and youth hostelling. Nine months before Dad died at the age of eighty, he and Mum had taken their usual summer break carrying their tent and equipment on their backs. Mother continued, "He's walking round Scotland right now. The local radio stations and papers were all full of it when he set off. They call him Jack, the walking man."

I was interested but not overly excited. It was just a piece of local news, and if he came from Goole, as I thought, I was not likely to meet him. Mum had not specified where she met him, and I did not think to ask.

Next Sunday at chapel a prolific display of wild flowers dominated the front. After the service a lady approached us.

"What a beautiful flower arrangement," I said, making conversation.

"Would you like to take them home?" she responded.

To my shame I felt and sounded less than gracious as I refused.

"It's not easy to manage such a big bouquet when you're in a wheelchair. I need both hands to hold on."

It was true. Mum was pushing me, and the pavements were rough. I was also feeling a bit weak and not too well. I tried to explain and hoped to overlay my initial tone of incivility.

Throughout this exchange a fit, sunburned gentleman stood nearby. Someone then told me that he always put wild flowers in chapel in July in memory of his late wife. The magnificent arrangement was his. Had he heard me refusing his blooms so lovingly gathered? I felt ashamed. As it happened and as I later learned, he was slightly deaf and had heard nothing. When we got home the flowers were there on the doorstep, brought round by car. As for the tanned gentleman, it was only after we were home that Mum told me that he was Jack the Walking Man.

Mr Jack Punton was a longtime chapel member and a local preacher. He lived here in Snaith in a green colour-washed house directly on the High Street and diagonally opposite the parish church. He had his own DIY shop and undertaking business at the end of the High Street in Market Place, and everybody knew him.

A New Friend

Meanwhile, the news about my mother was bad. She had bowel cancer and an estimated six months to live. I was devastated. We had looked forward so much to being with each other. I asked God for one thing.

"Please give us one year together with a reasonable quality of life for Mum."

Mum had her operation on the twenty-third of July 1992. She died one year later on the twentieth of July. God's timing was accurate. In spite of increasing pain and weakness she was able to shop and do light household tasks until three weeks before her death. God granted my request, and we were both grateful.

During that year we lived quietly and happily. We had some adaptations made in the bungalow for my disabilities. We involved ourselves in chapel activities and thereby made many new friends. We both knew that I would be well supported when Mum went.

Every so often Jack called along to see us, usually on a Sunday afternoon on his way home from a chapel service which he used to attend in a nearby village. I do not think he was lonely, even although he was a long-standing widower. He was too involved with living for that, and he had his family. He also still worked full time in his own business except for when he was off walking. At the same time he loved company and preferred to be out and about rather than by himself at home. Busyness and involvement had helped him through the hard years after he lost his wife. They still helped him and so, in an unobtrusive way, he gently included us in the circle of his friends.

Two things stood out for me about Jack's visits. First, he was so friendly and outgoing that I was surprised to discover how quiet and unassuming he really was and with no great conversational fluency. Get him going on the right topic, and he was fine. Leave him to initiate a subject or fill a pause in the discourse, and there would be silence. This apparent contradiction in his character interested me and still does. Was this man who offered such an extrovert surface to the world really a little shy and possibly an introvert? Most people show a mixture of both tendencies in their personalities, generally with one side predominating. If by introvert you happen to think of someone withdrawn, taciturn, or pessimistic, then Jack was certainly no introvert. If, on the other hand, it simply means a person who is quiet, self-contained, not showy or pushy, perhaps a little shy and yet still able to relate to the world around with warmth and energy, then that, as I soon discovered, was Jack.

Second, I had not realised that a man of eighty, as Jack was then, could be so attractive. I was surprised at my own reaction. He stood tall and well proportioned. He looked fit and smart. He was intellectually alert with nothing doddery about him, either physically or mentally. He even had an ample supply of hair. (We will not dwell on the subject of teeth at this stage.) True, his hair had turned silver, but that made him handsome and distinguished. How such a man had stayed a widower for fifteen years was hard to explain.

One Sunday in late May Jack dropped in. My mother suddenly said to him, "I don't have long to go now. Will you look after me at the end?" She added, "And will you look after Anne too?"

Jack, as an undertaker, knew exactly what my mother meant. Even so he was taken aback. He had not realised how ill she was. Few people did. After a lifetime of public Christian ministry she automatically pulled herself up to face people and situations with a smile, no matter how she felt inside. A month later she suddenly deteriorated and rapidly weakened. A further three weeks and she died in Pontefract Hospital.

Jack and his daughter Ruth took me once to visit Mum in the hospital. When we left Jack had a prayer with her. As he kissed her good-bye she confided, much to his surprise, "What a comfort you are to me."

Leaving me was her great worry. Otherwise she was glad to go. She saw that he was already looking after her precious daughter, and it helped her. As far as the funeral was concerned he would make things as smooth for me as possible. Afterwards he would continue to support me as a caring friend.

The Day of the Dog

It would be wrong to give the impression that I stood alone at this time. Ever since my father's death his brother and sister-in-law, Frank and Ronnie, had supported my mother beyond measure. Although they lived in Leeds, they were there for me throughout those difficult days. Laurence and Sheena came over from Canada too. Regarding the future, I felt confident enough. I could no longer walk much but so long as I had proper help in the house, and with shopping I could still care for myself. I was accustomed to living alone. I had lots of sedentary interests, and I had plans to write. I expected to cope. My big worry was the dog, Sally. Mum got her for company after Dad died. She chose her from the kennels because of her gentle face and appealing eyes.

"What am I doing with a young dog at my age?" she asked.

"Don't worry! If anything happens to you I'll look after her or make sure she goes to a good home," I assured her.

I wanted to keep Sally. She had brought us a lot of happiness. The trouble was exercise. We did not know her antecedents, but we had no doubt from her shape and behaviour that she was part whippet. She could run, and she loved to run, and for me to give her even a little walk was impossible.

A gentleman opposite who took his own three dogs out four times a day offered to include her. We called him Mr Lucy after the name of one of his dogs. He was actually a Mr Smith, but we did not know his real name for a long time. Unfortunately Sally was scared of other dogs. From the safety of the garden or sitting room window, no animal could bark a fiercer challenge at passing canines. Sharing a walk with them terrified her. She began to wet when Mr Lucy came and hurled herself on me for protection. Two neighbours were willing to take her out. She protested. If she was on the lead, she choked herself pulling to get home and worked out of her collar. If she was off the lead, she merely trotted the few yards to the corner of the street then headed back determinedly for the garden gate. Sally would be neither cajoled nor forced. Then Jack arrived.

He came along one evening to see how I was getting on. Even before I told him of my doggy dilemma he asked, "Would Sally like a walk?"

"You can try." I felt sceptical.

He did try. She went with alacrity and unquestioningly, if that is the right word. He came the next night. It was drizzling, but he offered again. The beast who had to be pushed outside, even for her toilet functions, in the slightest bit of damp made no demur. She set off, ears high and tail aloft.

It now became a habit. Jack turned up most days after tea, and Sally stood at the window watching for him. It was not enough to wag her tail when he came in view, her whole hind half wriggled violently as well. Truth to tell, her mistress felt much the same only she had no tail to wag. Jack and Sally then went for their daily jaunt while I had a cup of tea ready for when they returned.

I was a bit concerned about these outings. Jack had celebrated his eightieth birthday in February. In honour of that milestone he had planned to walk from John o'Groats to Land's End in the spring. He had already done it the other way and joked that this time it would be downhill and easier. During the winter he began training. Almost at once he experienced chest pains before he had gone any distance. To his dismay the doctor diagnosed mild angina. The pains grew worse until even the few hundred yards from his house to his shop were difficult. Fortunately his son, John, handled the day-to-day running of the business, but Jack took a daily, active role as well.

Then came a day when he had a funeral. He went home for a quick snack before changing into his black clothes. He felt unwell and used his spray for the pain, expecting it to ease. It did not. Time passed. Eventually he phoned John.

"Look, I'm not well. Can you close shop and do this funeral for me?"

It was a come down to admit defeat, but he then phoned the doctor. He knew he needed help. By the time John returned from the funeral Jack was in hospital. The way he left the house was typical.

"Where's the patient?" called the ambulance men as they came through the door.

"Here!" said Jack walking towards them.

"Sit down," said Dr Sim as he prepared to hand his charge over and leave. "Sit down! These men will look after you now."

"What's that for?" asked Jack, still walking to the door and pointing to the stretcher.

"It's to take you out on. You shouldn't be on your feet in your condition."

"You're not taking me anywhere on that thing. I'll go out on my own two feet." He almost added, "Or in one of my own 'boxes.'" (Euphemism for coffin.)

Jack stayed in hospital for ten days having tests and at first on complete bed rest. He soon felt better, sufficiently so to ban the nurse from the bathroom when first allowed a bath. By the time he came home he was almost well, but he knew he must come to terms with the fact that his long-distance exploits were over. It was a blow, but it brought out his resilience and pragmatic approach to life.

All the spring and summer of 1993 Jack's health improved. To help John in the business they took on Jack's nephew, Nicky, who had recently become redundant. Jack soon began to go in regularly again, but they were no longer so dependent on his presence. Constantly in this time of adjustment he asked God what he should do next and to give him some useful purpose in life. He had no intention of vegetating. Just at the right time my need for extra support dovetailed with his need to be a help.

I need not have worried about Jack's walks with Sally. As long as they went steadily he had no problems. He even began to go out longer and further afield as his confidence came back. Already he was again handling a good workload each day for John was on holiday and Nicky was still settling into the new job. Also during this time he was obviously well enough to invite me out for a car ride round the villages one lovely summer evening. He looked fit, and his energy was returning.

Invitation to Afternoon Tea

Our friendship grew. He brought his son, Simon, and his family to meet me when they were down from Stockton. Simon and Jayne had been to Israel which gave us something in common. One Sunday afternoon he took me to his daughter's home. Kevin and Sally own a garden centre outside Hull. I had already met another daughter, Ruth, who lives near Bath. We were in the vestry after Sunday morning service when, there amongst all the others, Ruth suddenly gave her dad a big hug. Jack's family were my kind of people, I knew at that moment. Strangely, I do not remember when I met John and Jean who live in Snaith and Jane and Joyce were, of course, in America.

Before long Jack invited me to his house for afternoon tea and to view his canaries in their aviary at the bottom of the garden. Seldom have I entered a house so welcoming and comfortably lived in. True, some of the furnishings were a bit worn. I soon realised that Margaret, his wife, had made many of the things around. Understandably he had no desire to change what they had so happily shared together. Family photos covered the walls and knick knacks from grandchildren stood on shelves. What a close-knit clan it all portrayed. Everything was clean and cared for and Jack, alone for so many years, had somehow kept the atmosphere of a happy family home.

How long does a guest politely stay for afternoon tea? That question exercised me on my visit, especially because I depended on my host for transport. I saw the canaries and established who was who in the pictures on the walls. We had tea and cake using Jack's best china, and Sally made her acquaintance with the garden. It was on the tip of my tongue to say that I ought to be making a move when Jack got in first.

"Come on, Sally, let's go for a walk."

They left me with a pile of photograph albums and newspaper cuttings of Jack's walks. They came back, Jack apologetic and Sally in guilty delight.

"I took her on the riverbank—the cows were there—I'm sorry."

Say no more, I thought. *I could both see and smell it.*

Jack and Sally headed for the bathroom, emerging sometime later with a less malodorous but exceedingly wet dog who was straightway banished to the garden to shake herself dry in the sun. I could not possibly depart immediately. Give it fifteen minutes or so, Jack must need a rest after his exertions.

Again I was about to announce my departure. Again my host got in first. "Are you ready for tea?"

Out came the best tea service once more. It was a treasured possession, though no longer complete, because Jack and Margaret had chosen it together. He produced sandwiches and other nice things, all beautifully made. Obviously he had it all arranged.

Never think that I was not enjoying myself. I was, but I was afraid of outstaying my welcome. Therefore for the third time I was on the verge of making my departure only to be beaten to it, this time by three faces at the window. Because Jack's house fronted onto the High Street visitors often announced themselves in such fashion. Jack had invited our minister and two friends who were up with her on holiday, to come for the evening. Followed some chatting, singing round the piano, and more of the best tea cups. I got home at 11:00 p.m. after a delightfully memorable afternoon tea.

Just as You Thought

Is there any need to prolong suspense? In October 1993, Jack and I announced our engagement. To most people it was a surprise. On learning the news one lady remarked, bluntly and with, I think, a hint of regret, "I'd no idea he was on the market."

Other folks expressed it to me in equally inelegant terms.

"He could have had his pick at any time."

Even Jack, who was a modest man, accepted that the statement was not entirely inaccurate.

Truth to say, we ourselves were surprised at how things had developed. Jack had been very happy with Margaret and had never wanted to remarry. He was not looking for a wife. As for me, although I had never lost hope of finding a suitable husband, I knew that a middle-aged woman in a wheelchair and with a progressive illness had limited chances. Neither was I seeking someone in Jack's age group. These very factors caught us both out. By the time we became aware of what was happening, it had happened and neither of us wished to draw back. More than one of Jack's old friends appeared not so much to congratulate as to commiserate with us, saying solemnly, "Ah well, it's nice to have a bit of company—better than being alone."

We laughed, especially at the lugubrious tones that invariably accompanied this pronouncement. We were marrying for love, not company. Above all we knew that God had brought us together.

Twice in my life I have received a word from God in advance. Having no inkling of the circumstances in which it would be required, it made little sense at the time. Nevertheless, I knew that God had spoken. The first time this happened is not part of our story, the second is. Shortly after Mum's passing, my daily Bible reading centred on the story of Joseph. When Joseph interprets Pharaoh's dreams and warns of future famine, Pharaoh decides to appoint a man to prepare Egypt for the coming catastrophe. He looks at Joseph and makes up his mind.

"Where," he asks, "can we find such a man as this in whom the Spirit of the Lord is?"

Do not ask how, but with total surety I know that this verse was for me and that it applied to Jack. The only sense I could make of it all was that God, in his goodness, was confirming something I already knew, namely that Jack could become a good friend and support to me. It was nice of God to say so but not really necessary. Only as our association grew closer did the full significance of God's word become clear. At each milestone in our relationship the Joseph theme was repeated in unlooked-for ways. Undergirded by this assurance I made, quite uncharacteristically, one of the most important decisions of my life with the minimum of heart searching. Jack was God's man for me. I agreed to marry him.

Unlike his new fiancee, Jack was not an introspective person. Faced with the big moments of life he "had a word with God" about them. He then thought matters through carefully and made up his mind. Thereafter he put all his energies into making things work. He seldom made a wrong decision on any crucial matter, and he rarely spent time analysing the whys and wherefores of his decisions, once made. He too had no doubts that we were meant for each other. Our marriage would work.

We fixed our wedding for April 2, 1994. When my new text calendar arrived I looked up the text for the great day and was disappointed that it said nothing appropriate. When Jack came round later he did the same. I had made an inexplicable mistake. The verse for April 2 proclaimed, "Where shall we find such a man as this, in whom the Spirit of the Lord is?"

It All Works Out

We were fully aware of apparent drawbacks. Apart from my MS and the wheelchair, there was an age gap of twenty-six years, and Jack was eighty. Would we not be sensible to remain good friends and share part of our lives but stay single? No! We wanted more, and we loved each other. In some ways we knew very little about each other, either past history or present characters.

Here God's word about Joseph reassured both of us. We knew enough to go ahead with confidence.

I was concerned about the depth of my feelings. It was easy to be attracted to the man Jack was then. He neither looked nor behaved like an old man. What if he suddenly began to age and change? A wife of many years has a lifetime of learning to love her husband in a way that the frailties of age cannot erase. Could a few months only of togetherness bear the strains of change and decline? Five years later I knew that I need not have worried. He was precious for himself; and weakness and wrinkles, sickness, and even senility would never alter that, whatever other havoc they might wreak. Jack too wondered about my health. Would I one day need nursing when he was unable to care for me? Later when I became ill and he had to do everything round the house, I asked, "Did you really know what you were letting yourself in for when you took me on?"

"I'd a good idea."

"Do you ever wish you hadn't done it?"

"Never. I'm very happy."

"And so am I!"

We had no regrets, and from the start we faced the uncertain future day at a time.

Regarding Jack's heart, we were much encouraged even before our marriage. Both his daughters in California, Jane and Joyce, are nurses. They took it upon themselves to phone Jack's doctor from America to ask about the possibility of an angioplasty to relieve the angina. Dr Sim was impressed by their concern. He was willing to refer Jack to a good cardiologist in Hull. The ensuing tests were extensive. The conclusion was that "this man does not have angina although he has angina-like pains."

A change in medication was prescribed, and Jack immediately felt fitter and began to extend his physical activities. Just over a year later he made a walking comeback. Simon and his family were down for the day. We were having a meal together when suddenly Jack stated, "I'm going to walk to York to raise money for the new sports centre in Snaith."

His son was taken aback then quickly rallied. Too quietly for his dad to hear, he said to Jayne, "I'd better go with him."

None of us would seriously have tried to dissuade him, for he was not irresponsible, but I was glad that he would have company.

Returning to the angina issue, Jack subscribed to a runner's magazine. One day, and this was also later in our marriage, we read a question-and-answer page. There was this young runner suddenly experiencing chest pains while running and wondering if his heart was all right. The answer, without discounting a heart problem, suggested that it sounded more like something which many athletes commonly come up against. I do not have the article and cannot recall the exact details, but it had something to do with muscle spasms and chest cramps. It was not dangerous or associated with the heart, and it had a proper medical name. For Jack it made sense. He had felt similar chest pains on exertion way back as a young man during the war. The MO said his heart was fine, and after a while the trouble disappeared. We knew that something to do with his heart had put him into hospital, but rightly or wrongly, this correspondence in his magazine finally put our minds at rest about some aspects of his health. Above all we always believed that Jack's health was under God's control.

However, all this came later. For the time being our engagement weeks were a period of welcome recovery of strength and stamina for Jack. Thus we moved towards our April wedding.

Wed at Last

Looking back I think we had a funny wedding. It was simple and, because it was unrehearsed, slightly ad hoc. It suited us. Simon and Jayne's daughters, Katie and Jessica, were bridesmaids. I had no one on my side to ask until I bethought me of Lorna. Lorna is my sister-in-law's niece. As she lived in Selby and was of an age with Jessica, she was an ideal choice. Ross, Simon and Jayne's son, was a pageboy. He chose his own outfit of red shirt and shoes, brightly striped shorts, and yellow waistcoat. I gasped when I first saw it then revelled in the gaiety that it would bring to the proceedings. Our wedding would be different. It was.

Being in a wheelchair, I wanted my bridesmaids and pageboy to precede me, Ross leading and carrying the ring. The chapel aisles were short. As we entered and the incidental music merged into "Here Comes the Bride," my pageboy saw Grandpa Jack in front and rushed forward to reach the security of his smiling welcome. The girls followed suit. We were all there before the first few bars of the bridal music were over. Jack's arms went round my little retinue, then he looked at me and moved to kiss me as if we had been apart for months. Eventually we sorted ourselves out.

During the ceremony Lorna and Jessica, who were only five and who had never met, made themselves acquainted with smiles and surreptitious nods and nudges. Then there was the moment when the minister formally asks the congregation to declare any known impediment to the union. Jack, to his everlasting embarrassment since, turned round and with an admonitory finger and smile said, "Don't anyone dare!"

The only three decorous members of the party were Simon and John, Jack's best men, and my uncle Frank who gave me away; and even he got muddled about seating arrangements.

I was glad that our minister, the Reverend Julia Pellett, had gone through the service privately with Jack and me the week before. While all was quiet around us, that was when I consciously made my vows and truly married Jack before God. During the wedding itself I was too tense, concentrating on all that was happening around me, to do more than repeat my vows by rote.

I could talk about our reception. It was not in any posh hotel but in the relatively new and pleasant village hall in East Cowick. In the subsequent videos, you can hardly hear the speeches for the sound of small children running round on the wooden floors. Moreover, I took the risk of issuing a blanket invitation to any of my past CMJ colleagues in London who wanted to come. Eleven accepted and therewith received official invitation cards. If all thirty or so had responded, we would have had to rearrange the venue.

I might further talk about where we decided to live. My bungalow was small but adapted to my disabilities. Jack's lovely large house needed a lot of work to make it suitable. We therefore chose to live in the bungalow whilst keeping Jack's house for visitors. We developed the routine of spending Saturdays and Sundays in our "town house" but always slept in the "country residence"! There was only ten minutes' walk between them. Jack went down every day to keep things nice or simply to sing and play his piano. Finally, and when we could afford it, he installed central heating, and we built an extension on the back and moved to live there permanently. It meant so much to Jack, and I wish I had pushed to do it earlier.

There is one last question. How easily did we adjust to married life? Jack, of course, had done it all before and was naturally easygoing and accommodating. This was just as well when I, following the pattern of a lifelong lived single, sometimes made decisions without consulting first. My greatest problem was getting used to my married name. The phone would ring, and I would respond, "Anne Dexter speaking," whilst more than one cheque with the wrong signature had to be torn up and rewritten. Overall we both agreed that we settled into our new circumstances pretty easily.

The purpose of this chapter is now complete. I have explained how I met Jack and why I am able to tell his story. At this time when lottery fever touches all our lives, everyone knows what it means to hit the jackpot. When Jack and I found each other we both felt that, by God's grace, we had done exactly that. If the following story of his life proves to have any value or interest then, in a different sense, this book will hit the jackpot too.

Wedding Day, April 1994. Isn't he a handsome guy? (Photo: Mike Scorbie)

Jack and Anne engaged thanks to Sally the dog, October 1993 (Courtesy of the Selby Times)

CHAPTER 2

THE YOUNG JACKANAPES
or
OUR JACKY ENTERS THE WORLD

Enter Jacky

The dictionary defines a jackanapes as an impertinent young man. It can also mean an organ-grinder's monkey—something which was still a feature of life when our Jacky was a boy. When the appellation is affectionately applied to a child of tender years it generally refers to a mischievous but lovable youngster. On February 2, 1913, yet another lively little lad entered the world—our Jackanapes Jack. He joined the family after Jimmy Punton had died leaving his widow to rear their five other children alone.

When my husband was in his eighties, he began to write the story of his childhood and youth. Originally I planned to quote from that record in this book but regretfully had to conclude that it was inadequate for my purposes. To begin with, his efforts were short and unfinished. He told me so much more about his early life than ever he committed to paper, and I want to include these extra details to make the story fuller. Also he tended to write as the memories came, with the result that there is no real logical or chronological progression. Even so, although I cannot use Jack's words directly much of the flavour of the following narrative comes from him.

A Significant Discovery

One day, when Jacky was about eight, he noticed his mother's birthday book on the table. He picked it up. Yes, his brothers and sisters were all neatly entered. There was his mother's birthday—Ada, May 13, 1877. Now for the father he had never known. Here he was, Jimmy Punton. But what was this? Young Jacky checked again to make sure. Beside her husband's birth date Ada had written, "died 1910." Although on Jack's birth certificate Jimmy Punton is declared to be his father, he understood the significance of the entry, even at that early age. His mother came in and saw the book in his hands. She made no comment, only took it from him as she sharply sent him out to play.

I write this in a generation where anything goes. It was not so at the beginning of the twentieth century. Then people still preached a clear morality and denounced any lapse from the given code. Therein, of course, lay a paradox. The society that condemned also sinned and, perforce, had to accommodate itself to the shortcomings of its members. This was especially so in any close-knit country place like Snaith and for three reasons.

To begin with, many people are related by blood and marriage. We are all more tolerant of the failings of those close to us than of strangers. Also, in a small community everybody knows each other, faults and virtues alike. No one dares be too judgmental. Finally, in a self-sufficient, interdependent system such as prevailed in Snaith ninety years ago, it is better that people affirm rather than exclude each other.

Of course, such a charitable picture is one-sided. Even in the best of situations the stigma of being born out of wedlock could cloud one's childhood and later limit job opportunities, friendships, and much more, including choice of marriage partner. With all this in mind I asked my husband, "Did it ever affect you adversely?"

Jack's reply was reassuring.

"I was surrounded by love from the moment I was born and all through my life. I was a grown-up before I understood all the implications of my birth and parentage. I don't think I was ever discriminated against because of it although in my young days illegitimacy was widely held to be a disgrace."

There is no doubt, however, that Jack was sensitive about the issue. Many years later one of his daughters asked,

"Dad, you always talk about your mother a lot. Why don't you ever mention your father?"

"I never knew my father."

The reply was uncharacteristically curt. It closed the subject. Later the mother explained the situation to her daughter. She added, "Dad doesn't like to talk about it."

That was in the early sixties. By then attitudes had already changed considerably, and yet they were still narrow compared with how we see things today.

Jack never spoke of his birthday book discovery to anyone. Neither did his mother ever mention the matter until 1944 when he announced his intention of getting married. Only then did she write to tell him the facts. When Ada died nine years later he overheard one of his sisters saying, "Somebody ought to tell Jack." Another responded, "He already knows. Mother told him when he got engaged."

Nobody in the family ever raised the subject with him. By the time I got to know him the whole climate of opinion had changed so radically that he genuinely no longer seemed to feel it was a problem. Rather he had begun to wish he knew more about his own father and Ada's relationship with him. It was too late. Who was there left to ask?

John, Jimmy, and Ada

"Did you ever meet your proper father?" was my next question.

"Never. I know very little about him other than that he was a gardener at some big house, and his name was John Mellor Bower. I presume I'm called after him though my given name is Jack and not John. I have no idea where he came from or what happened to him. He may have died early."

As Jack spoke he was searching through a box of old photographs and eventually produced a tiny snap of a slim man in a greenhouse. It was all he had. I could not see any family likeness but then, it was so small. Obviously it was also precious. He continued, "When I was very little I remember someone used to come to the door every so often with 'a little present for Jacky.' I like to think it was my father."

As for Ada, she once told a friend that John Bower was the only man she ever truly loved. Does that explain why Jack sensed that she always had a special feeling for him too?

When I decided, shortly after our marriage, that I would one day write my husband's life story, I asked him if he would prefer that I leave the birth part out. He thought briefly before he spoke with certainty,

"No! It happened a long time ago. Things are different now. I don't suppose there's anyone left alive who knows the facts. It's time they came into the open."

"What about Jimmy Punton?" I then asked. Jack knew more about him though not a lot.

"Jimmy was a travelling insurance salesman. He was musical and played well. We had his piano. I think he drank a bit. Why he died I don't know. Lots of folk died young in those days from minor illnesses."

"Were the Puntons a local family?"

"No! My so-called grandfather came from Aberdeen to be Snaith's first police inspector although they had a constable here for years. They built a new police station for him with a courthouse and cells. You can still see the building in Court Road with the inscription and date, 1898, carved above the door."

At the time of writing this property is a private residence owned by some art teachers. Apparently they have left the cells in their original state and use them as galleries for their painting collection.

Once, when we were near Aberdeen on holiday, we checked the phone book for Puntons. Not one! We are told the family originates from Haddington near Edinburgh. As far as I am aware Jack never knew the Punton grandparents.

And Ada? She hailed from a pretty village, Little Smeaton, situated in the hills some twelve miles south west of Snaith. Did she meet Jimmy when he visited her house selling insurance? We can only speculate. I believe that Jack did meet his maternal grandparents when he was small, but they lived too far away for regular contact and may also have died relatively young.

Ada, Lone Breadwinner

Ada Punton struggled to provide for her children. She may have been eligible for help from the parish. Never, ever, would she have asked for it. For many years she worked in the clog sole mill, which was situated at the edge of the town as you go out to Selby. The mill was a flourishing industrial concern that gave welcome employment to many local people, including women like Ada as well as men. Sometimes Ada operated a circular saw and at other times the band saw which cut the clog sole shapes from the wood. It was hard, dangerous work. Did she, one asks, take home the same pay for her labours as the men?

For twenty-five years she was also caretaker of one of the town's two schools. The Wesleyan establishment, opened in 1849, was at the east end of Snaith behind the present Methodist chapel. The Church of England place of learning which Ada cared for was on the west side and only a few convenient yards from her home. It boasted the grandiose but, in modern terms, misleading title of grammar school. Both buildings still exist, the grammar school plain to see on the right side of the Pontefract road as you leave Snaith to the west.

It is a squat square red-bricked edifice, now used as a day care centre. Do not confuse it with the Old Grammar School, founded in 1626 for the education of a select few scholars. That more ancient building is tucked away in the northwest angle of the churchyard wall. It ceased to function as a school in 1877 when the new larger premises opened. It is now the church hall.

The grammar school had three classrooms, each with a coal fire. Early in the morning Ada went across to light the fires. At the end of the day, after the rigours of the mill, she returned to clean out the grates and lay the coals ready for lighting next morning. As Jacky got bigger she taught him how to help her as he recalls.

"We filled coal scuttles, tidied, swept, and dusted. Three times a year my mother scrubbed the wooden floors. All the family had to help, and we hated it."

No wonder! This was no sloppy, mop-and-bucket performance but an on-the-knees job with scrubbing brushes, soapy water, and an abundance of elbow grease. The only good part was to see how clean and white the wood looked at the end.

At certain seasons the farmers took on casual labour for such tasks as "tatie scratting" (digging up potatoes) and pea pulling. Ada and her family were there. Says Jack, "We earned nine old pennies for four stone of shelled peas. That was just less than one-third of our week's rent. Have you any idea how many peas it takes to make four stone, or what long back-breaking work it is?" With the aid of a conversion table I found that four stone is almost 25.5 kg.

In addition, and at all times of the year, Ada took in washing, another laborious enterprise. Indeed, one wonders how there were enough hours in a day to do all she did. Obviously the older children learned to help, but it is not surprising to hear Jack say, "My mother was always busy. I never saw her sitting down and relaxing, even of an evening."

The washing was done in an outhouse in the stone copper. This was a built-up brick structure in the corner. It had place for a fire underneath and a bowl shape hollowed out of stone above. Ada arduously filled the bowl with cold water, all of which had to be carried from the one and only tap they had, situated in the yard outside the back door. She lit the fire below and kept it stoked until the water was hot. Only then could she turn her attention to the process of washing each item separately and by hand. She rubbed heavily soiled articles up and down on the ridged surface of a scrubbing board. Later she emptied the copper and collected fresh water for rinsing. Some things had to be bleached with a kind of whitener known as a dolly blue which gave a blue tinge to the rinsing water. Some articles were starched.

With no synthetic fabrics, Ada also had to iron everything. Three heavy metal irons stood on top of the kitchen range heating up. When one cooled down as it was used, there was always a hot one to replace it. No one with arthritis could have handled those old irons. They needed a strong wrist. As lightweight electric irons did not exist, there was no alternative. No wonder, considering all she accomplished, that Jack described his mother thus, "She was a well-made woman with great strength and stamina. She was pleasant and kind, with a good sense of humour. Everybody loved her."

I could see what Jack meant when I saw his old pictures of Ada. What a lovely face she had! Her character showed in every line. She must often have found life hard and felt tired or anxious. If so, she never bemoaned her lot or grew bitter. Despite her own struggles she was generous to everyone. Even passing tramps, of whom there were plenty, called at her door knowing she would treat them courteously. Jack explained this to me too.

"There was a real community of the road when I was young. These men took up seasonal work all over. At certain times of the year we would see them camping out under Carlton bridge. They were mostly decent and honest, and the farmers depended on them. As they moved from place to place they left signs for each other and marked houses where they would not be turned away. I'm pretty sure that our house had a tramp mark."

We shall never know what traits of character Jack inherited from his father. In his cheery good nature, patience, respect for others, and capacity for work and endurance, he surely emulated his mother.

The Sibling Setup

A new baby in a family, dependent solely on the mother for support, greatly strained resources, for there was no welfare state with its child allowances, pensions, social services, and free health care. It was opportune, therefore, that Lizzie, aged fifteen and the eldest, went into service with the local doctor at this time. He and his wife treated her like a daughter. They gave her toys and clothing for her brothers and sisters from their own children. She went with them when they moved and eventually married from their home. Apparently Lizzie did not like John Bower, which is hardly surprising. She was old enough to know what was happening and probably felt jealous or threatened.

Lizzie's daughter, Jean, was a beautiful singer and active all her life in amateur operatics. Jack kept in touch and often stayed with her and her husband, Alan, when his walks took him through Somerset. It was to Jean that Jack wrote when he tried to find out more about his father. He wondered if Lizzie might have talked about him to Jean at some time. We were both disappointed, but she knew nothing. After a long illness Jean died only a few weeks after her uncle Jack.

Mary came next. She was eleven when Jack was born. After leaving school at fourteen and spending a period in the clog mill she went to work in neighbouring Howden. There she helped to build airships which were a popular form of transport at that time. For the interest of any aficionado of the genre, she worked on the R29, R33, and R34 models. Mary's marriage ended in divorce when her bus driver husband took up with his conductress. Kenneth, her son, had a stroke in later life. Until Jack himself died he regularly visited his nephew in a nursing home near Selby.

Billy was ten years older than Jack. At about twenty he started his own painting and decorating business. He also showed an aptitude for car mechanics and was thrilled when he could afford to buy a small Jowitt car. Jack looked up to his clever big brother. He told me his story.

"Billy got married and had three children, but sadly he developed diabetes. It was a death sentence then, without insulin injections. The doctor put him on a diet and told him to eat an orange a day. It was easier said than done. Oranges were hard to come by and expensive if you did find them."

Billy had a great spirit. As he could not serve in the army when the war came he applied to become a special constable with the police. Perhaps they were desperate for recruits as they made no enquiries about his health, and Billy offered no information. They accepted him. Nevertheless, and despite a brave fight, he died during the war, and Jack came home from the south of England for the funeral. He felt his grief keenly.

When I got to know Elsie, Billy's widow, she was in her late eighties. Two or three times a week she still walked into the centre of Snaith for her shopping and then visited John and Nicky in Punton's DIY store. Now Elsie was not a lady you took liberties with, but her two nephews had some measure of dispensation. They always dared to tease her as they sat her down, gave her coffee, and then drove her home. It was Elsie's daughter, Margaret, who lives in Surrey, who made our beautiful wedding cake when Jack and I married.

I often wondered how Elsie felt about me. After all, she had known Jack since his boyhood. Was I somewhat of an interloper? One day I was aware that she was giving me a keen look. Suddenly she remarked brusquely, "I suppose we're sisters-in-law." Elsie had accepted me.

We were not long married before Elsie began to fail. Jack went round each day to help her. One afternoon the warden of the sheltered houses where she lived called the doctor who sent her to hospital. Jack saw her that evening. She was ill but stable. Early next morning her daughter, Margaret, phoned. She had slipped quietly away in the night. I could see that Jack was upset. Elsie had been part of his life for over seventy years.

Dorothy was eight when Jack arrived. She too went to the clog works for a time until, like her sisters, she married and left home. Only now, when there is no one left to ask, do I realise that I know nothing about Dorothy. I believe she and her husband adopted a daughter. They lived in Nuneaton and Jack's older children remember visiting her once on the way to Cornwall. That is all I can say.

It was Ted, aged four, when his baby brother came on the scene, who was closest to him. For most of his life Ted was a foreman in the clog sole mill. He only went to a paper mill in Selby when the former closed down in the sixties. He always lived in Snaith. He married Dolly, and his children were Sandria and Nicky.

Home Quaint Home

"We lived in a quaint old shack."

Thus Jack often described his childhood home. Quaint it was. Shack it was not. The Puntons occupied a very old property at the western apex of the triangle of land beside the Pontefract Road known as Cross Hill. The structure was solid. It provided the family with secure comforts which many others in similar circumstances did not have.

"We paid the landlord," says Jack, "Squire Shearburn, half a crown or two shillings and sixpence a week for the privilege of living there and knew we were fortunate."

That is twelve-and-a-half pence in decimal currency and worth much, much more in real terms.

Cross Hill was poor and densely populated. Many of the houses have long been demolished. All that remains of Jack's house are a few grainy photographs showing two adjoining cottages of different heights which formed one five-roomed dwelling. Not obvious from the pictures is how the lower house on the right was neither square nor rectangular but of a trapezium shape. The two properties met at regular right angles, but the gable end of the low building slanted out obliquely.

A short passage and pantry separated the two ground floor rooms. On the right was the kitchen where the family lived while the other made a bedroom for Ada and one of the girls. From here a narrow staircase bent sharply and steeply to the chamber above where the two other girls slept. Both rooms were just big enough to hold a double bed and some small piece of furniture.

To move into the upstairs part of the lower odd-shaped house you went from the top of the stairs through a tiny door whose top, following the slope of the roof, was higher at one side than the other. At its highest this opening was four feet six inches. At the wall side it was a mere two feet six inches high. The space beyond was partitioned to make two minuscule bedrooms separated by another similarly proportioned door. The second room, being at the gable end, not only shared the same unusual shape as the house but also had the only window of the two. The ceiling slanted to a brave five feet six inches at the roof ridge. You really need a diagram to explain the peculiarities of this area under the eaves for that was not all. Two massive wooden supporting beams ran from wall to wall, each only three feet six inches above floor level. To enter either cubbyhole, for they were little more than that, you had to negotiate the funny doors whilst at the same time ducking yet deeper to avoid the balks, as they called them.

I feel claustrophobic even as I describe it and especially when I tell you that these were the sleeping quarters for the three boys. As they all grew to be six-footers, many a cracked skull resulted. The floor space in each room allowed one double bed, one upright chair, and nothing else. The bed heads fitted neatly under the balks which ensured that the lads soon learned to get up carefully. With no furniture the balks also made shelves for the night candles and other bits and pieces. The whole set up was a serious fire risk.

In the floor of the gable end bedroom was a trapdoor through which all items of furniture had to be passed up for both houses. The stairs were too narrow and angled for anything bigger than an upright chair. I know the old iron bedsteads came apart. I still wonder how they got them through the trapdoor.

Jack loved his home where he spent the first twenty-two years of his life. It was only after his brothers and sisters all married and left home that Jack and his mother moved to number 8 Selby Road. At last life was easier for Ada, and she could afford something bigger and better. Amongst other luxuries the new house had gas lights and, for what it was worth, a double-seated privy. What she gained in convenience she lost in character. I have never heard Jack enthuse about the new residence whereas he constantly talked with real affection about his first home, that "quaint old shack."

Some Good Old Days and Ways

In those distant so-called good old days, there was no electricity although Snaith was fortunate. It had its own coal-fired gas works. There were gas lights in the streets and a few well-to-do houses. Otherwise most homes depended on coal fires for heating and candles and oil wick lamps for lighting. These latter had to be regularly cleaned, trimmed, and filled. Many families had a kitchen range for cooking—a sturdy iron stove which was the forerunner of the Agas and Raeburns of today. Very poor people might only have a fireplace which heated an oven alongside it. I'm not sure what facilities Ada had, but

I think she had a range. Cooking was still a practised art, for there were no convenience foods or gadgets, not even fridges. You could only keep food fresh for a short time in the pantry which was a little room with stone shelves and floors positioned in the coolest part of the house.

If the Puntons were poor in material things they were rich in love. If they had few luxuries they were always well fed on plain, wholesome food. Jack used to say, "When I think about my mother's baking days I can still smell the yeast and loaves and cakes in tins on the hearth in front of the fire to rise. A man called Frank Kirby came round selling his wares and shouting, 'Kippers and bloaters. Kippers and bloaters.' We ate tripe and chicklings, and I remember so well my mother sending me to the butcher for a sheep's head and pluck." Chicklings, I am told, are from a pig's small intestine. Pluck was a mixture of heart, lungs, and liver. According to Jack it made, along with the sheep's head, of course, a delicious broth. With Ada's home-baked bread it was wonderful.

Occasionally Ada could afford some stewing meat or, as a special treat, a piece of belly pork. There were three butchers in Snaith, and they all made potted meat. This was another favourite, especially that made by one particular butcher which seemed to have more meat in it. Jack always chuckled as he described an old man telling another butcher. "Thy potted meat's nowt but pig's lugs and whiskers."

As a matter of interest, butchers in those days killed their animals behind their own shops. This was a spectacle not to be missed by the local boys. One day a young gentleman named William Ramsey sat astride the high wall surrounding the yard to watch. When the butcher had finished he looked up at Bill and said to his assistant, "We'll have that young lad next."

Needless to say, "that young lad" disappeared hastily, but he will reappear on several passing occasions later in this story. Although Bill was some ten years younger than Jack, the two men were friendly all their lives both as local preachers and members of Snaith Methodist Chapel. When you meet Mr Bill Ramsey again, you will know who he is without further introduction.

Immediately behind the school was Old Hall Farm and Granny Golton from whom Ada bought fresh butter, milk, seasonal vegetables, and eggs. Jacky revelled in the farm. He spent many happy hours there looking for eggs which the free range hens deposited in the strangest places. He even went into the stalls where the big shire horses stood. He crawled beneath their massive legs and pushed their feathered fetlocks aside so as to reach the corners where some hens habitually laid. The huge animals good-temperedly heeded the will of the small boy and whickered their affection. The only horse you could not be sure of was Prince, a young stallion. You avoided his stall if he was in it. Often, Granny Golton gave Jacky something to take home.

"Sometimes," said Jack, "the farmer let us, boys, ride the horses to their work in the fields. We were experts. We rode bareback with only a frayed rope halter for control. We could manage them. We said 'gee up' and 'whoa' to start and stop them. A sing-song 'gee back' meant go right and a falling, drawn out 'aa-av' turned them left."

I imagine it was the intonation rather than the words that the animals recognised. They were magnificent, powerful beasts and yet so gentle with children.

Apart from their normal diet, the children picked berries and nuts in the countryside and nibbled the leaves of wild plants such as sorrel and other unknown species. Meanwhile, back on the farm there was a further source of sustenance.

"I thought the world of the cowman, Mr Thornham," Jack relates. "I liked nothing better than turning the handle of the machine that cut the linseed and molasses cow cake into pieces. I then carried them in a hamper to the feeding trough in the fold. That cow cake was good, and I often ate a piece."

Packed with vitamin B and other nutrients recommended by today's health addicts, I feel sure it did him more good than harm and like all lads of that age, he had a good digestion and was always hungry. Fortunately there were plenty of perks.

"Granny Golton often let me take milk in an enamelled can to some old ladies in Beast Fair (a street near the centre of Snaith). One lady, Mrs Stacey, used to put a piece of cake in the empty can for me to have. At weekends I used to take the 'drinkings' to the men in the harvest field. It was a bucket of tea with a lid on and some mugs and a bag of sandwiches with thick slices of bread and a hunk of cheese. The men would give me a piece of bread and cheese."

As far as clothes went, everything in Ada's family was handed down and mended until it was beyond repair. She taught all her children, boys as well as girls, to mend, darn, and sew on buttons. Jack further admits, "I didn't have a pair of pyjamas until I grew up. I slept in an old shirt. We had no money for lots of new clothes. If we did need something, we went to Mr Edgerton Wood, the draper. I shopped a lot for my mother whenever she needed stockings, a reel of cotton, or buttons. The draper's shop fascinated me with all the stands of dresses and coats and shelves filled with a host of things a draper stocks. Little did I ever dream that those premises would one day be mine."

Mr Edgerton Wood was a dapper gentleman with a waxed moustache of which he was extremely proud. It so happened that he had a rival. This was a door-to-door salesman who came round with a suitcase full of ladies' underwear. They called him "the knicker man." Naturally this made the boys laugh.

Changing the subject from food and clothes, there is one more important thing to mention about Jacky's life in the good old days. Six yards from the back door stood the privy and ashpit.

"Well," said Jack, "every household had a privy, and it was always outside and as far from the house as possible for obvious reasons. We had no flushing water or proper sewerage. It was a lean-to hut. Inside was a wooden box with a hole on top, and there you sat. Below the seat was the cavity we called the ashpit. All the ash from our fires went there. It covered and absorbed things and helped keep the smell down. A local man came once a month with his horse and cart to empty it. There was a hinged flap behind the privy so he could shovel the contents out into a barrow and wheel them to the cart. What a stink! Nobody stayed around when he was at work."

So much for the good old days and ways!

School Days

Jacky started school at two and a half as a favour to his mother to free her for work in the clog mill during the day. His first memory was of messing his pants and sister Dorothy taking him home to clean him up. Did she, I wonder, hold him under the tap in the kitchen yard? After that initial misfortune, Jacky soon learned to enjoy school.

There were only three classrooms—one for the infants, one for the intermediates, and one for standard four and five, the big children. There were few textbooks, and the pupils did their written work on slates. Education was basic, the three Rs—reading, writing, and arithmetic. They did grammar and spelling and learned their tables by rote. They studied simple history and geography and had a regular singing lesson. Jack particularly enjoyed drill and sport, especially when a new headmaster, Mr Longdon, got a football team going which played in competition with Goole schools.

Jack does not recall many children from Snaith passing the scholarship exam and going on to grammar school in Goole. One must not thereby conclude that Snaith had no bright pupils. It rather indicates that few parents could afford the costs involved in fares, uniforms, books, sports equipment, and so on. Moreover, they needed their children to leave school at fourteen and start working. Despite all this, the abler ones had a firm foundation for self-education in later life.

One girl from Jack's class whose parents could afford to send her to school in Goole was called Mary Mitchell. Mary qualified as a teacher and taught Jack's own children who remember her as being very strict. Often when Jack took Sally for a walk, he would come home saying, "I just popped in to see Mary on the way back."

Mary herself once told me, "We always asked him to bring Sally into the house as she and the cat liked each other. I'd give him a cup of tea, and he'd sit back and doze. We'd laugh about it. We were very old friends."

"Mr Sandoe," Jack told me, "was the headmaster, the 'Gaffer' or 'Old Charlie' we used to call him—a very strict man who used the cane when we misbehaved. Most of us, boys, came in for a few strokes on our hands. I can't remember him ever caning a girl. After he retired we were all sorry to see him go. We had a great respect for him."

Jack showed me Mr Sandoe's grave one day. Whenever he passed it, and as an undertaker it was often, he would give the edging stones an affectionate prod and say, "That's for all the times you caned me." The score has long been evened.

One day Old Charlie, a kindly man at heart, announced to the older boys,

"You can go and watch the Badsworth Hunt gathering this morning."

What excitement! Out of school they dashed and raced the short distance down the Pontefract Road to the back of the Downe Arms where the hunt traditionally met. Jack grinned.

"Three of us took advantage of the privilege and followed the hounds and riders. On we went, down lanes, across fields, over hedges. A titled lady fell at a fence. We all cheered. The titled lady swore but remounted. We had the time of our lives. We spent the afternoon playing on the Willow Garth, a swampy copse where there were water hens and coots. I don't remember any fox. I do remember creeping into school next morning. The Gaffer was furious. He caned us all very hard."

"Did you ever mind getting the stick?" I was thinking about modern views on corporal punishment.

"Never! We knew the rules, and they were reasonable. If we broke them, we took the consequences. Old Charlie could give a good whack, but he was never brutal. And he was always fair. It did us more good than harm."

On his own admission Jack was a slow learner although he tried hard. At the same time he loved reading. He always did. I seldom knew him without a couple of books on the go. He tended to read slowly and for short spells but retentively. Coral Island was a childhood favourite, and later he enjoyed biography and some of the devotional Christian classics. Encyclopaedic works fascinated him, from which he would pass on to me items of strange and possibly useless information. I once watched him peruse a dictionary for an hour and wondered if his spelling might improve as a consequence.

The person who reads widely educates himself. I saw this in Jack all the time. He did not have the trained mind of the academic, and his thought processes tended to be slow but astute and sure. Although I have university qualifications I never felt in any way intellectually superior to my wonderful husband. We were well able to discuss all manner of issues together, and I quickly learned to value his judgement above my own.

Fun and Games

Outside of school hours the Cross Hill lads played football and cricket on the main road. They used their jackets as goal posts and improvised stumps from bits of wood. With scarcely one car an hour, and that's travelling at only twenty miles an hour, the road made a safe playground. As often as not the vehicle in question belonged to the doctor who was the only person in Snaith to own a car. That same Pontefract Road is crossed with great care today. In the warm evenings of summer, as dusk fell, the bats came out. The boys threw their caps in the air and tried to catch them. Do you know the kind of caps I mean? They were really men's caps, only a size smaller, not schoolboy ones. Needless to say the bats were too elusive ever to be caught.

Football was Jack's passion. One year, and the memory remained vivid, he received a very special present. In his own words I record his reaction.

"My first real football. Wow! Oh boy! How I remember it. Santa Claus must have got it cheaply as it was a bit out of shape, but to me it was wonderful. My very own football. I used to think there was no team anywhere as good as Snaith Amateurs until I heard about Aston Villa and how they won the cup scoring a goal in the last minute of the match. I read that they began from a Methodist Sunday school. That impressed me, and they have been my favourite team ever since."

Even in his eighties Jack unfailingly turned the Saturday afternoon sports news on to see how Villa had done. He was always disappointed when they lost a game.

The boys roamed far and wide. They knew the ponds where they caught tadpoles and tiddlers. They found birds' nests in the hedgerows and climbed trees in the woods. Jack, at least, always treated any notice saying "Trespassers will be prosecuted" with respect. He thought it meant you would have your head chopped off.

The squire, Mr Shearburn of Snaith Hall, allowed the children to play in his park across the road and once let the Scouts camp there for a week. Although they were only a few hundred yards from their own homes the boys were thrilled with the novel experience of sleeping under canvas. Squire

Shearburn was a fair man and a good landlord to his tenants, of whom Ada was one. He never minded what the youngsters did provided they left his trees alone. He once caught Jack and a boy known as Golly (George) Beevers up one of his trees. He paced around purposefully below.

"There was no escape," admitted the culprit. "He waited until we came down then belted us with his cloth cap. If people could still deal out that kind of rough justice, we'd have less mischief makers around. He didn't hurt us, but we knew he meant business."

Snaith Hall is now a nursing home, its regency lines hidden by a useful but ugly filling station. Many of its trees have gone, and a new housing estate occupies one end of the park. Only a small part remains as a playing field for a primary school. Changes come, and yet still a few of the people who remember those distant days remain. For instance, when Jack took me out in my wheelchair we often met an active octogenarian called Arthur Walker riding his bike about town. He was in Jack's class at school. Arthur had a brother, Albert, who hurt his leg as a child. As a result he developed a TB hip which confined him to one of those old-fashioned spinal carriages where a person lay propped up with outstretched legs. The local boys were unusually kind to Albert as Jack describes, "We pushed him on walks down stony lanes. We hung a board with nails in it low on the privy door so he could play hoopla with us. We got him to hold a bat at the side of his chair. He hit a cricket ball pretty well so long as the bowler delivered straight. One of us ran for him."

"Did he die young?" I wondered.

"No! When he grew up he read an article which encouraged him to seek help. Although his leg muscles were very wasted he improved so much after treatment that he was able to walk with crutches. He took an interest in local affairs and got elected to the town council. He lived into his sixties."

Pranks and Peccadilloes

As we sat talking together about those distant days the doorbell rang loud and long. We waited a few seconds. Sure enough we heard running feet and laughter. Our front door opens directly onto the High Street, and we knew the children were up to their tricks again. How many times had Jacky and his friends run along the same pavement knocking on the self-same doors or jangling their bell pulls? There were no electric bells then, of course. We could afford to be tolerant with our present pranksters. As Jack said, "We weren't angels, far from it. We often did foolish and mischievous things, but we were not malicious. And we were not hooligans. I suppose we were high-spirited rather than bad."

"Tell me what you got up to."

"Well, take the paper shop down the street. It was owned by Ms Whittaker, a fussy elderly lady. She felt the cold and always told her customers to 'shut the door.' We would deliberately leave it unlatched just to hear her say in her high-pitched voice, 'Shut the door, shut the door.'"

"Then there was a large shop and house where the fire station is now, owned by a person called Earl. I liked this shop and spent my Saturday halfpenny there or penny when I had one. They always had lots of spice (sweets) on the counter. The only time I was ever tempted to steal was when I went in one day to buy my spice. It seemed ages before anybody came to serve me. I couldn't resist nicking three boiled sweets and putting them under my jersey. When I came out with the sweets I had bought, the ones I had nicked fell on the floor. The lady who served me ticked me off and said she would tell my sister, Mary. I don't think she did. Mary never said anything. I felt very guilty, and I've never stolen anything since."

Opposite Squire Shearburn's Hall stands the Brewers Arms, a Georgian building with an elegant facade. At one time this was the Lodge, home of a Mrs Eadon. One day Mrs Eadon went away leaving her gardener in charge. The gardener's son assured his cronies, in good faith we believe, that they could go into the hot houses and help themselves to some of the produce. Stifling any qualms, the boys climbed over the wall. In Jack's words, "We stuffed ourselves until we were almost sick. It was the first time in our lives we had ever seen, never mind tasted, such exotic fruits."

The depredations were too extensive to go unnoticed. A policeman came to school and the culprits were cautioned. It was enough. The incident was not repeated.

West of Snaith beyond the new cemetery lies Dor Lane, a country track cutting north between fields to the railway line and the Gowdall Road. Jack once pushed me there in the wheelchair. As we walked he told me about the fire.

"A crowd of us came here one Sunday afternoon. Someone had a box of matches, so we decided to light a fire. It was summer, and we didn't realise how dry the grass was. The fire spread so fast we couldn't stop it, so we ran away and left it. It burned a whole corner of Dor Lane including a tree and a large pile of wicks (long creeping grass roots that had to be removed from the ground whatever) that had been left by the farmer."

"Did you get into trouble?"

"No, I don't think anyone ever knew who had done it, but they might have guessed. A lot of men gathered and got it under control. We never let on."

Seventy years later the only two of those involved who were still around were not so reticent, one being my Jack and the other a gentleman named Gordon Miller.

Pleasures and Pastimes

Once a year the feast came to Rawcliffe. It still does. With its rides and amusements it attracted visitors from all round. Ada too took her family and, like many others, they walked there. She had little money to spend, but it was fun mingling and watching everything. And she somehow managed to give each child a treat.

At one time some strolling players brought their act to town for a week. They presented melodramatic mysteries and romances and were so well received they stayed for three weeks. There were other treats as Jack recalls.

"Circuses and menageries used to come for a couple of nights. It was fun watching the men erect the tent. 'Big Top' it was called. The clowns sometimes invited us onto the ring. I once rode round the ring on a horse with a belt around my waist attached to a rope on a pole which swivelled and held you up if you fell. There were sideshows with a tiny, little dwarf and a very fat lady. A man used to shout 'Come and see the fat lady. When she walks she wobbles.' We giggled and gaped in wonder."

Then there was Christmas when children from poor families went round carol singing and reciting a traditional jingle.

I wish you a merry Christmas and a happy new year,
A pocket full of money and a cellar full of beer,
A big fat pig to feed you all the year,
Mr and Mrs, how do you do,
Please can you give me a Christmas box,
If you haven't a penny, a ha'penny will do,
If you haven't a ha'penny, God bless you.

Being the baby of the family with some of his brothers and sisters already working, Jack always had a good selection of Christmas presents. He was so pleased one year with a meccano set and a clockwork engine on a circular track that Lizzie had been given for him from Dr Walker's son, John. Nevertheless, a few pennies collected by carol singing meant a lot, and young Jackie liked to decide for himself how to spend them.

Something else that Jack enjoyed was a boys' paper which, amongst other attractions, serialised the stories of murderers of the century. He listed them off for me: Jack the Ripper, Sweeny Todd: The Demon Barber of Fleet

Street, Charley Pearce who, if I remember rightly, was the Sheffield Strangler. Did I also hear mention of Crippen, or was he later? Poisoners, stranglers, throat slitters—Jack gloried in the details and proudly claimed to know every gruesome one. He was, I suppose, a typical boy.

When Jacky was seven he joined the Scouts where his brother Billy was a patrol leader. Imagine the excitement when they heard that Baden Powell was coming to Goole. At that time the railway line through Snaith was busy with goods and passengers. The Scouts therefore arranged to travel to Goole on an express train which, for this noteworthy occasion, stopped to pick them up as a favour. It was Jack's first time on a train.

"I was amazed how quickly houses and fields rushed by. In Goole we marched to the Victoria Pleasure Grounds where Scouts from all over had assembled. I felt very small and lost because I was younger than most of them, and I was the only one without a uniform. My mother couldn't afford it."

Perhaps that was why the great man noticed him and went across to pat him on the head. Back home his mother asked, "Did you see Baden Powell, Jacky?"

"No!"

"Of course you did," countered Billy, "he patted you on the head."

"Oh! Yes, I saw that *man*."

It was always a puzzle to Ada and Billy to know what Jacky had thought Baden Powell was.

"I just didn't know," explained Jack in later life. "I certainly didn't think it was a man. It might have been a monkey for all I could tell."

Look Back Down the Years

During our engagement I accompanied my fiancé to a Pensioners' Lunch Club Christmas Dinner. I went prepared to observe the formalities, as I understood them, of such an occasion. I was soon surprised at the way things went.

Here were all these people, I thought, with nobody bothering to make sustained conversation or draw out the reticent on what was, after all, a special event. Then it dawned. These men and women had no need to make polite small talk or consider formal etiquette. They were comfortable with each other. As I soon discovered, then and later, half those present had grown up together. Some had even shared the same desk at school.

I cannot talk about all those sitting down that long table that day, but a few merit mention. The first is Kath (nee) North who married Arnold Miller, son of one of Snaith's three butchers and cousin of the aforementioned Gordon

Miller who reputedly started the Dor Lane fire. Kath was in Jack's class at school and was his first date. When the Scouts had their Christmas party they each invited a young lady along. Very shyly Jacky went round to knock at Kath's door. Equally shyly she accepted. Shortly before he died Jack met Kath on the street. She had a bad leg. With the unselfconscious familiarity of an old friend, she lifted her skirt to show him the swollen knee. I only mention the incident to illustrate the relaxed familiarity between all the people at that dinner party.

Kath's father was the whistling postman. He delivered mail to villages as far as seven miles away, all on a push-bike, whatever the weather and with many a rough farm track en route. You heard him coming long before he arrived for the sound of his cheery whistling carried far. What a mercy he did not have to handle the junk mail of today. He would have needed a horse and cart.

Opposite and to the left sat Norwood Howard. At first I was not sure I liked the way he kept staring at me until I realised that he was extremely curious about the woman Jack was to marry. For good reason! He and Jack went to different schools but became friends in the Scouts. In fact, they grew up to become two young men about town together as Norwood himself later told me.

"We both joined the Rawcliffe Musical Society. The bus fare for our weekly practices cost threepence in predecimal money, but we preferred to cycle so we could afford fish and chips before we set off for home. We also went to the pictures in Goole on Saturdays. That cost us one and three each, sixpence for the train, sixpence for the cinema, and three pence for sweets. We walked around a bit looking at the girls although we were much too shy to talk to them. When Jack married I visited his home a lot. Margaret, his wife, always welcomed me and was very kind."

One day in the supermarket Jack introduced me to yet another of his old companions. This gentleman was the son of the man who had owned the Rawcliffe chip shop patronised by Jack and Norwood over sixty years before.

Norwood inherited his father's coal business and worked hard all his life. The coal came in bulk by train to Snaith. It was tipped onto the sidings and had to be shovelled into sacks for delivery to customers by horse and cart. I have come to admire Norwood. From childhood he has struggled with severe deafness and not everyone has shown understanding. Perhaps this is one of the reasons why he stayed a bachelor. Despite the difficulties, he has faced life positively throughout.

Accompanying Norwood was his sister, Margaret Marsden. She was an attractive (and I use the word deliberately) nonagenarian, smartly dressed, and with the figure of a slim young woman. In her youth Margaret worked in Snaith post office which was then the sorting office and telephone exchange for a wide area. After the postmaster lost his wife he married Margaret. This always interested me as the age gap between them was similar to that between me and Jack. Mr Marsden was Jack's scoutmaster and a good one at that.

On our side of the table sat Alice Eastam, another spry little lady. Jack first knew her as Alice Forkingham. It was her father who emptied the ashpits. He did other jobs with his horse and cart too such as helping Norwood's father with the coal and, as a matter of interest, his horse was white. Apparently he could often also be seen cycling to Selby market with a couple of hens in a box for sale.

Yes, those around that table were old friends with no need to observe social niceties. They could sit like a family in easy silence and then pick up a conversational thread from a few minutes back or, with equal ease, from seventy years ago.

Few, if any of these people, will be with us by the time you read about them. Some mentioned in this chapter have even passed away while I have been writing this book. When their generation has gone there will be no one left with firsthand memory of those distant days and ways. Meanwhile I can only say that it has been my great privilege to meet some of them and to look back down the years through the window that they and Jack himself opened so widely for me.

A Sun that always Shines

As I close this chapter and its joyous record of Jack's boyhood memories, I ask myself some obvious questions. Did the sun always shine on those childhood escapades? Did we produce more colourful characters then than we do now? Were the olden days really the good old days?

Of course the clouds lowered and the rain fell but memory, especially that of happy beginnings, nearly always recalls the past in a rosy glow. In retrospect, even the sting of the cane on the palm becomes something to laugh at, not to cry about. As for more colourful characters, I do often wonder if the moulds of mass advertising and television turn out more uniformity of personality today than of old. Who knows? Certain it is that the good old days had their downside with no welfare state to cushion calamity and no clever conveniences to lighten workloads. By contrast most of the less helpful pressures of modern living were nonexistent and that, surely, was no bad thing.

One thing remains constant, irrespective of place or century, human nature does not change. In Snaith, as in any other community, Jack came across meanness, violence, dishonesty, quarrelsomeness, cruelty, and scandal. I give only one example. He had a little friend who often slipped into the classroom at seven in the morning when Ada was lighting the fire. He came to get away from a drunken father with a vicious temper and to receive some desperately needed mothering from Ada. No, Snaith was no more a heaven on earth when Jack was a boy than it is now.

Having said all this, it is not my intention anywhere in this book to deal with the sad and the sordid. If we want such things, we can turn elsewhere and find them in plenty. Jack was a man who saw the best in people and made the best of situations. Jack's world, from his boyhood to his dying day, was a good world. To complain, be a talebearer, or indulge in criticism was not his way; and I rarely heard him do so.

It therefore follows that for the purposes of this book, the sun shines, the birds sing, and Snaith, though no Utopia, is still a good place to live. The people you will meet, if not exactly saints, are no great sinners either. It must be so because this is Jack's story, and this is how he perceived his world. He was not unrealistic as I hope you will agree when you read on. He was simply a man who focussed on the best and the beautiful in life. Any story about him must do likewise.

Jack's early home. The odd ended shape is hardly discernible here.

A debonair young man.

Jack with Ada his mother, her lovely nature and strong character evidenced in every line of her face.

CHAPTER 3

JACK AND THE BEANSTALK
or
HOW JACK BEGINS TO MAKE HIS WAY IN LIFE

To Be a Farmer's Boy

On a dark winter evening I enjoy tackling a jigsaw. Jack watched with interest as one particular scene built up. On the right a shiny green steam engine was at work, fly wheel whirring and smoke puffing upwards over the trees. A system of belts and pulleys linked across to a threshing machine with men balanced aloft forking bundles of wheat into its jaws. Nearby a man hefted bulging sacks into a cart drawn by a shire horse. Further beyond more men were building hayricks and hauling other sacks along the picture. A terrier chased rats and scattered hens in the foreground.

"It's just how I remember it," Jack enthused. "We had three threshing engines in Snaith. At harvest they went round all the farms in turn, and everyone helped each other. Those sacks in the cart are full of grain. The man on the far side is filling a sack with chaff."

Now I would never have known that—about the chaff, I mean. The whole process was out of my experience, but I had got my husband going.

"There were always lots of rats around. We sharpened sticks to a point and tried to impale them on the end."

I did not want to know about that and was relieved to hear that they rarely caught any. At a later age Jack's views about the value of all life were to determine, at personal cost, the course which his own life would take. As a boy his opinions were still unformed. Like most lads he was unimaginative enough to enjoy the sport of rat sticking.

Soon after, Jack took me to a farm that specialised in demonstrating old farm machinery and working animals. We chose a threshing day, and he was so excited to see it all again. Even the mice obliged and scurried round at our feet. There were no rats.

Now all this is by way of saying that when Jack left school at fourteen and began to climb the beanstalk of life, he would happily have gone onto a farm as a farmer's boy. He understood what the work involved and liked the animals, especially cows and horses. He was not so keen on the pigs. They could be vicious.

The Statute Hirings

Agricultural labour was traditionally taken on by the farmers at Martinmas in November during the statute hirings. The hirings lasted for two days, and Jack called this period Plewstots. It was a time for jollification as well as business. Schools had a half day, and the Morris Dancers performed. This, I gather, is where the term Plewstots comes in.

Plewstots, apparently, was a Morris Dance which enacted scenes and traditions from the ploughing season which happened at this time of year. Doubtless, some of the customs portrayed had pagan origins although they have long been overlaid by Christian rituals, such as services for the blessing of the plough. This ceremony still takes place in our area despite the fact that ploughing is now such a mechanised affair.

The word *plew* obviously means a plough while a *stot* is a young ox. An old friend of Jack's, Thomas Laycock, was a gentleman who won and judged ploughing competitions all over Britain. Although oxen are traditionally associated with this activity he never used them and did not remember them ever being used in these parts. They were too slow. Be all this as it may, Jack's vague recall of background facts was vivid enough for the event.

"Young men dressed up and painted their faces. They danced in the streets then collected money from the bystanders."

I hope my husband was not maligning some innocent revellers when he went on to add,

"I never knew what they collected the money for. I suspect a lot of it ended up in the local pubs that same evening. It was a holiday, and everyone had fun."

And now, after all the build up, comes the anticlimax. I have to tell you that Jack was not destined for farming life. The twenty-four-year-old Billy felt responsible for his younger brother and decided that he would learn a trade. He arranged to apprentice him to one of his own older friends, a joiner and undertaker named Fred Robinson. Jack accepted that Billy knew best.

The Saw Not the Scythe

Fred's workshop was an old chapel in West Cowick about half a mile away just outside Snaith. Jack describes some of his experiences.

"I was really proud when I first went to work in a boiler suit with a two-foot (folding) ruler in my pocket. I had to walk to work for eight o'clock each morning. We couldn't afford a bike. I used to walk home at twelve noon for my lunch and walk back for one o'clock. I didn't have much time."

The new apprentice soon found out what a good tradesman his boss was and set about learning all he could from him. Often he worked with Edgar, Fred's brother, who was only eight years older than Jack. Then there was Mr Twybill, Fred's grandfather, who occasionally helped out and took Jack with him on jobs. Jack continues, "We always had to walk pushing a handcart with the materials, timber, etc., and our tool bags on it. We sometimes walked as far as Carlton and Gowdall to do repair work at houses and farms. I remember well painting all the buildings at Old Hall Farm. I often had more paint on my clothes than on the doors. It showed. We used red oxide paint."

One of Jack's first jobs with Fred was nearly his last and almost put him in one of Fred's own coffins.

"This day we went to demolish a windmill in West Cowick, not far from our workshop. After we had dropped the sails the next thing was to get the roof off—that dome covering at the very top. It was held by wooden spars all round. We loosened these then the men sent me up to fix a rope to the roof so that they could pull it down."

I knew that Jack hated heights all his life although he never let his fear get the better of him. Even then, evidence of his refusal to be daunted by circumstances showed. Up he went without a protest despite much inner stomach churning.

"I'd barely tied the rope when, with no warning, the roof tipped, taking me with it. I flailed out for something to grip. Nothing! Then my body jerked, and

I found myself dangling in midair. A loose spar had hooked into the back of my jacket. It held me. At the same time the roof jammed and steadied. It felt a lifetime before the men got me back to safety."

For Whom Tolls the Bell?

As far as the undertaking side of the business went, the young apprentice mostly helped behind the scenes, learning how to make the coffins to measure and watching as the older men laid the bodies out. The first person Jack himself laid out was his own brother, Billy, many years later.

Fred transported coffins and their contents in the same way as his tools and timber, on the handcart, albeit respectfully draped with a black cloth. There were no chapels of rest. People lay in their own homes until the undertaker wheeled them through the streets to the churchyard gate. From there family bearers carried the coffin into the building. After the funeral, they bore it out to its last resting place in the churchyard.

While all this took place, the church bells tolled their unmistakable message. Everyone understood their language. Jack's recollections, like those of his elderly contemporaries, are selective; but this, I believe, is what happened. As the cortege trundled through the town, the "calling in" bell alerted the inhabitants to listen for what was to follow. After a pause came the measured tones of the deep "death bell."

For whom was that solemn knell sounding as the coffin made its humble approach to the churchyard gate? Man? Woman? Child? Count the strokes! Only three? The sick child had failed to make it. It was so sad, but infant mortality was high and an accepted part of life. Six? That would be for the old lady who enjoyed ill health all her life and had at last succumbed to nothing more malignant than old age. Nine strokes? Here was tragedy, a young father taken in his prime by the dread consumption. There was no immunisation against tuberculosis. It was rife, and it killed.

Again there was a pause. How old was that child? Once more the bass bell delivers its melancholy tidings. Only two strokes sever the still air, over as quickly as the little one's short life, and then eternal silence. How old was the ancient crone? On and on booms the bell until the listeners lose count. Perhaps the bell ringer does too. Eighty-nine, ninety, ninety-one—one year more or less, what does it matter at that age? And the father? Thirty times the death bell tolls while the young widow, with her three little ones clinging to her skirts, weeps and wonders why it should have happened to her.

The Clog Sole Mill

At eighteen Jack broke his apprenticeship and left Mr Robinson. He felt that he had learned all he could; he had no prospects, and the pay was poor. He was never ambitious for position or money, but it was always his nature to press forward to things better and beyond. To you and me the clog mill may not seem like a big step up. It was for him. The wages were better, and he was more of his own man. He stayed there until he was twenty-four.

A lot of working men in those days wore clogs—not the Dutch style fashioned from one block of wood but the kind that had a separate wooden sole nailed to the uppers. As the name implies, our mill specialised in making these soles. There were only two such places in England—one here in Snaith and the other in Lancashire.

The wood came up the river Aire, not cut into planks but as whole tree trunks. I believe they grew in Scandinavia and were shipped up the Humber estuary into the port of Goole. At that time, rivers and canals provided the most common form of freight transport along with the railways. Lorry traffic was only just developing in the early decades of the twentieth century, and the roads were still inadequate. On the other hand, almost every little village in our part of Yorkshire lay alongside a river and had its own landing stage. True, the rivers in their lower reaches were tidal and dangerously unpredictable, but trade had plied their channels for centuries.

For example, a vessel could sail down the Ouse from York then divert to the Aire, where it enters the Ouse, and go back inland to Leeds. It could join the Don, another tributary of the Ouse, to end up in Doncaster, or it might meet the Trent yet further downstream and find its way to Nottingham. Such journeys took weeks, but the pace of life was slow and the routes, though tricky, were tried and ancient. When the more efficient canals and railways were built, river trade began to decline. The arrival of road transport and a proper road network finished it off completely.

All this gives a background to the clog mill story and explains something that used to puzzle me.

"Why," I once asked Jack, "are there so many pubs around with nautical names, like the Sloop or the Ship Inn, in places so far from the sea?" Here was my answer. Each little hamlet and settlement had once been a tiny port, linked to the world beyond by its river. Evidence of Snaith's old landing stage on the Aire can still be seen if one knows where to look.

The mill worked efficiently and wasted nothing. I assumed that the great saws used to cut and shape the wood were powered by coal-fed boilers.

"Not at all," I was told. "We fuelled the boiler almost entirely with the by-products of the work—sawdust and wood chippings. At night we banked it down with wet sawdust which created lots of steam. The steam was directed into steam rooms where the wood was laid out. The hot moisture dealt with the sap more quickly than seasoning the wood in the open air. When they opened the vents in the morning there was a great whoosh and clouds of vapour rose into the sky. We then stoked up the boiler and got a head of power going for the day."

Even when electricity became a regular source of power, the mill continued to generate its own supply, still from its own surplus sawdust and chippings. When the demand for clog soles decreased the mill diversified into chisel handles. It also sold sawdust and chippings to farmers who strewed it on the floors of barns and animal stalls.

At twenty-four Jack left the clog sole mill to take up work as a joiner in the building trade. It was 1937, and the eventful developments in this phase of his life fit more appropriately into the next chapter. For the time being there are other things to discuss.

Four Lives Gone

It was in the clog mill that Jack's life almost ended for the second time.

"I was alone in the workshop one lunchtime and had turned off the machinery to repair a belt. Someone came in and switched it on again. He hadn't seen me. Without warning the belt began to move, and I found myself caught. As it twisted tighter and tighter round my arm it also drew me towards the saw blades. I screamed. The man realised what was happening and stopped the machinery in time. It took over an hour to cut me free, and I was off work for three weeks."

"Have you had trouble with that arm since?"

"No! I made a complete recovery. I was lucky."

You were that, I thought. *You could have lost the arm or been killed.* That mill was a dangerous place. There were no proper machine guards or safety regulations in those days, and there were plenty of folk walking round Snaith at that time with missing fingers and worse.

I often think that Jack had as many lives as the proverbial cat, and he had lost four of them before he was thirty. Take the time he nearly bled to death! He had only had a troublesome wisdom tooth extracted, but it refused to stop bleeding.

"I was spitting blood, and lots of it, all evening. Eventually I went to bed. A few hours later I woke up. The pillow was soaking, and I felt really groggy. I got up to get my mother. The next I remember was lying at the bottom of the stairs and my mother sending for the doctor. After he plugged the socket he said, 'It's a good job you called me now. If you'd waited until morning I couldn't have saved you.'"

One weekend Jack and Ted decided to have a day out on their bikes. They would go to the coast which included the novelty of crossing the new swing bridge at Airmyn over the Ouse between Goole and Howden. It had just been opened in 1929 and, like the Carlton Bridge just outside Snaith, was designed to handle the increasing road traffic of those times.

"When we approached the bridge a lorry came up behind. The road was narrow, and as it passed it somehow clipped me on the shoulder and sent me spinning to the ground. My bike went under the wheels and was crushed. I lay stunned and bruised but alive. Ted thought the wheels were going to go over my head."

What followed then Jack barely remembers. He rather thought that the driver stopped and that eventually he recovered enough for him and Ted to walk the seven miles back home. He was tough, even when I knew him in his eighties, so what he was like in his twenties can be imagined.

"When I got home," he went on, "and began to clean myself up, great clumps of hair covered in blood came out in my hands. The lorry wheels had actually grazed my scalp, so close had they been to crushing my skull."

Excuse the pun! It was a close shave.

Music While You Work

My life with Jack was full of song. He sang as he washed up or made the bed. He sang nonsense songs to amuse me, once giggling like a schoolboy as he imitated the falsetto tones of a counter tenor we had just heard on the radio. After the American World Cup and the Three Tenors' Concert the strains of "Nessun Dorma" took over, complete with a white handkerchief (slightly less than white to be honest) to add authenticity to the performance. I called him Jack Pavarotti.

Al Jolson, Kathleen Ferrier, Elijah, the Mikado, grand opera, country and western—he loved it all. The last record he ever played, on the day before he died, was Tosca. He sat there, quietly absorbing every note sung by diva Maria Callas. Dare I say it? To me it sounded a bit shrill. I prefer instrumental music. To Jack the human voice was the perfect musical instrument.

"I love Tosca," he said. "It's my favourite opera. I tingle all over when I hear that aria. It makes me want to cry."

How moved he was at that moment.

For a man with such a rich baritone voice himself it is surprising to learn that he showed so little talent in his early years that they sent him off to read during singing lessons at school. It was Ada who recognised some musical aptitude and who paid from her meagre earnings, for the nine-year-old Jacky to have piano lessons. It was also Ada who made sure that her slightly recalcitrant son practised for an hour each day.

"How I hated having to stay in. I could hear the boys playing football outside, but my mother was adamant. I quickly discovered that the less I grumbled and the more I worked, the sooner my mother let me out."

It paid off in other ways. Not only did Jack start to enjoy his lessons, he did well. His teacher was a Mrs Field who lived in St Laurence House in Market Place. She soon had him and a girl from Cowick playing piano duets at local concerts. There he learned to bow and acknowledge audience applause. Mrs Field entered him for the Royal Academy of Music exams. The first one was held in the Railway Hotel in Goole.

"I was terribly nervous," Jack confessed, "and failed it. What made it worse was Ronnie Coldwell just managed to pass. I burst into tears when they told me I had failed. Anyway, over the next few years I passed three exams with honours. These were held in Doncaster. I didn't take any more because we couldn't afford the expense. In the end I never kept up with the piano seriously although what ability I had often came in useful. I'm always glad my mum started me off."

Even in his eighties Jack liked nothing better than to accompany himself on the piano as he sang his old favourites. There was one about a senorita being serenaded by a donkey and another about a young chap who contemplated joining the foreign legion in order to show the girls who ignored him what a dashing fellow he really was. I preferred the sergeant major on parade, all dapper with his Sam Browne belt, gleaming boots, and buttons brightly polished, of course, by his batman. The man had the ladies admiring and new recruits quailing and yet, for those who dared to look, a twinkle might be detected in his eye. I am afraid the accompaniment was vamped and far from accurate, but what it lacked in polish it made up in vigour. His family laughed at their dad, as families do, and fondly took pleasure in his wholehearted enjoyment of his own performance.

Returning to the early days, it was only when his voice broke that anyone, Jack included, realised what a fine voice he had. As he began singing in choirs and groups his reputation as a singer spread despite the fact that he was entirely untrained. When he was twenty-four a Dr Chappell from Pontefract asked to see him. Now Dr Chappell was a well-known and highly qualified voice teacher. He had heard about Jack and wanted to hear him sing. He was impressed and offered to give him singing lessons at a reduced rate. Jack took only one term then gave it up. Regretfully he explained, "I didn't have much money, and the bus fares and fees were more than I could afford. Also Dr Chappell didn't want me to sing with the music society I belonged to. He wanted to control my singing programme."

Almost certainly the doctor had Jack's interests in mind and saw the possibilities of a professional future ahead. It was not to be. Even so, that brief, early training was never lost. It showed whether he was only singing hymns in church or ditties in the shower.

All Work and No Play

According to the dictum all the former and none of the latter makes Jack a dull boy. If our Jack worked hard he also played hard, and he was never a dull boy. His musical talent became both his challenge and his relaxation. When he was eighteen he and three friends started a dance band.

"I played the piano, Billy Hodgeson and Bob Haigh played fiddles, and Herbert Steele was our drummer. We called ourselves the Sunny Bank Dance Band because Herbert lived in a house of that name in George Street, and we did our practising there. We spent a few years playing mostly at whist drives and dances. The whist finished at ten when we took over for the dancing until two o'clock in the morning."

Realising that none of the four had a car I wondered how they managed on further afield gigs.

"Oh, we biked it, carrying our instruments." (Not the piano, I hasten to add, but Jack helped with the drums.) "Occasionally we could save a couple of miles by taking a shortcut across fields. In that case we left our bikes behind a hedge and walked. They were always there when we got back in the early hours."

He sighed with nostalgia.

"Ah well! We were young, and they were happy times. We got ten shillings (50p) for a night's work."

I wish I could remember if it was ten shillings each or between them—probably the latter if you recall that ten shillings would have paid Ada's rent for four weeks. It does not matter. They enjoyed themselves so much that Jack, at least, would have done it for nothing.

One year Bassett's circus set up in Snaith for a week. For some reason they had no musicians with their show. Who stepped into the breach?

"Someone sent them to me and Russ Whitehead, who played the violin. We played every night for their different acts. One of them involved a pony and a clown doing tricks. I also helped them out when they moved on to Goole."

To the very end of his life Jack had incredible energy and none more so than in his youth. Along with everything else he did, he learned to play the tenor horn, for Snaith boasted an excellent brass band. I was shown the inevitable photograph, and very smart the bandsmen were in their uniforms and peaked caps. To my surprise Jack was not amongst them. Apparently he joined them for a while and even rendered a short tenor horn solo at Snaith Show one year. In the end he was too busy with other things to commit himself and left. However, he always had a soft spot for Codge (George) Clayton, the conductor.

"Oh, Codge was a great character," he explained, "and he was a first-class musician. He conducted that band with one hand, blowing away on his cornet with his eyes closed. He went through piece after piece and never looked at a single note of music. Mind you, he got results. That band had a reputation. He used to play the 'Last Post' in church on Remembrance Day."

"Tell me more about Codge."

"Well, he had twenty-four children. There were no twins, and they all survived. They lived in an ordinary house in George Street, and he worked in the clog mill. I could never imagine how they managed but Mrs Clayton always had them well turned out and happy."

There is one more thing to add. When my mother took ill during our first year in Snaith, we had to have help in the house. The lady who came to us was called Jessie, and she cared so gently for my mother towards the end. Ernie, her husband, looked after our garden. Ernie was Codge's youngest son.

Hidden Talent

In the end Jack chose to concentrate his efforts on his singing. When he was twenty-two he joined the Rawcliffe Musical Society which had a reputation for putting on excellent productions, mostly of Gilbert and Sullivan operettas or romantic musicals. In his first year Jack sang with the chorus and did two walk-on parts. He had no aspiration for greater things. The producer thought differently, especially when he found himself looking for a replacement for his male lead who had to retire.

"To my amazement," said Jack, "he asked me to take the main role for the next show. I was petrified and said no. I could sing a little, but I had never acted seriously, let alone attempt a principal part."

The producer was persuasive.

"Just take this home and look it over," he coaxed as he handed over the script for a scene and music for a couple of songs. "We'll go through it next week and see how you feel then."

When next week arrived, Jack felt no better, yet somehow h
refuse. Give him a challenge, he had to face it. All his life it was so

"As the weeks passed," the reluctant Jack told me, "soon I beg
myself and gain confidence. Although I never felt I was good enough, everyone
kept encouraging me. Then on the big week I started a nasty cold. I had to
force my voice which did it no good, and I felt anxious."

To Jack's surprise, when he sang his main song, "Queen of My Heart," the
audience kept applauding. He tried to continue with his lines, but the clapping
was insistent.

"Sing it again," whispered the conductor. It was unheard of in the middle
of a scene, but he did. Later the producer ticked him off.

"You'll have no voice left for tomorrow night." He did, and he managed.

Thus it was that in subsequent years an always nervous Jack delighted
his fans. Invariably and with minor variations on the theme, he played the
penniless but handsome hero who falls in love with the rich heroine, even
though she may or may not eventually marry the dull but worthy count chosen
for her by her father. There, to prove his thespian triumphs are the numerous
curling photographs of all the casts. Prominent centre front is usually a smiling
Jack with his arm around the leading lady's waist. These arms about pretty
girls' waists caused much later amusement to Jack's family.

The last production they ever staged was *A Country Girl*.

Says Jack, "Phyllis Greenwood, a local lady, was given the leading part.
She was lovely to work with and did a super job. Well, the following year the
war came. A number of members were called away for war duties. The society
disbanded and never regrouped. It was a pity. It had brought a lot of pleasure
over many, many years."

The week before my husband died he visited a Phyllis (I think nee
Greenwood) in Rawcliffe. In a matter of weeks Phyllis herself also passed
away.

Bachelor Boy

There is no question but that our Jack was an eligible bachelor by this
time and also a very well-known one. Apart from the dance band and the
musical society, he was also a keen sportsman. He played, for a time, for Snaith
Amateurs' football team although bad varicose veins in both legs restricted his
prowess. Of his cricket exploits he has this to say.

"I played first for Cowick. Snaith had a very strong team, and I couldn't
get a game. I became captain of Cowick, and the highlight was when we beat
Snaith in the evening knockout competition. I scored thirty-nine not out.

Later I transferred to the Snaith team and captained them for three years before the war started."

In fact, this gifted, popular young man was everything a young lady could want. He was tall and handsome with a strong physique. A work out in today's gym is no substitute for the manual labour which developed Jack's muscles. His hair was fair, his eyes hazel, and his complexion tanned from outdoor pursuits. In the then current fashion he wore his hair short and sleeked back with Brylcreem. This accentuated his one poor feature, prominent ears. Later, longer hairstyles without the Brylcreem hid this. In every picture of him, he smiles.

What is surprising, given his high-profile lifestyle, is to discover that he was actually a shy person and quiet, who always said how lacking in self-confidence he felt. He might be, and often was, at the centre of the action. Nevertheless, the observant bystander would note that while others fussed and chattered around him, he himself seldom had much to say. Better still, he was entirely unassuming and unspoilt by his successes. He gave himself no airs, which is probably why everyone liked him.

Did he never meet a girl he wanted to marry? There were plenty who would have had him. Yet Jack was elusive. That information comes, not from the man himself but from more than one ageing lady to whom my husband has introduced me. Tongues, freed from the sensitivities of youth, have loosened to confide early female crushes, their own or someone else's, on this presentable young man.

I often wonder if the circumstances of his birth held Jack back from any serious relationship for fear of rejection. A starry-eyed girl would have had him with never a question. A Victorian father, of whom there were plenty in those days, might well have opposed the match. Jack was too realistic not to know this and too sensitive to risk such a snub. Deep down he was easily hurt. At the same time, it does appear from what he has told me that he never met anyone whom he seriously wanted to marry at that stage of his life.

The happy days of the dance band, the musicals, sport, and light-hearted flirtations were soon to end. They did not last long. The sound of military jackboots on the march drew ever closer as the war years approached. Meanwhile, there are other things to talk about in this chapter.

The Best Place in the World

"I just love Snaith."

Merely to read these words can never convey the feeling with which they were uttered. Jack had recently completed a twenty-two-mile walk to York to raise funds for a new sports centre being opened near the school. It was an achievement as it was his first full day's walk since the heart problem that had put him into hospital the year my mother died. He had also been asked to serve on the committee for the sports centre representing the town's older citizens. He declined the offer though it gave him satisfaction to be asked. Lastly, he had been given the honour of opening a new playground in one of our small housing estates. Such things gave him untold pleasure for, as far as he was concerned, there was no place in all the world so dear as Snaith. Every landmark evoked a memory and had entwined itself into the emotional fibre of his being.

Of that spreading tree at Cross Hill whose foliage shades the wooden seat surrounding its trunk, Jack could say, "I saw it planted, a tiny sapling, outside our front door. It grew as I grew."

Of that new playground where he cut the opening ribbon, he could say, "I too once played here when there was nothing but fields and hedges and Squire Shearburn's precious trees."

Of that modern electrical goods' shop across the road from his own DIY business, he could say, "I first knew those premises as the British Legion where we, lads, spent many a fun hour on the snooker and billiard tables."

Not, therefore, to tell you more about Snaith at this juncture is tantamount to omitting to describe a very formative influence in Jack's life. Besides, our town has many unusual historical and geographical features which I would like to tell you about.

A River Girt Island

The name Snaith derives from the Norse "sneyde" meaning a detached or cutoff piece of land. It refers to the geographical phenomenon whereby the rivers Aire and Went, together with the pre-seventeenth-century course of the Don, so surround the region that they virtually make it into an island, impossible to enter or exit without the aid of ferries or bridges. Do note, however, that this virtual island covers a large area incorporating a number of villages. It does not refer to the town of Snaith alone.

Because the highest point of our river girt enclave is only some twenty-five to thirty feet above sea level, Snaith and its environs were always prone to flooding. Way back in the mid-sixteen hundreds a Dutchman named Vermuyden drained some of the marshes and diverted the lower course of the Don into a channel known as the Dutch river. As a matter of interest he also helped drain the fens in East Anglia. The work on the Don thereafter prevented excessive inundations but not always. In the harsh winter of 1947 the rivers could not cope with all the melting snow. Flood waters rose to the eaves of the garage near Carlton Bridge, covered the railway crossing and lapped to the foot of George Street. According to Jack they were the worst floods of the century in our parts. I can add that the autumn of the year 2000 also saw severe flooding. River defences protected Snaith itself but Gowdall, two miles upstream, was flooded up to the eaves of many of its houses and suffered badly.

Bridges and ferries were important. Snaith and Carlton are less than two miles apart. Between them lies the River Aire, which waterway in days gone by was a formidable barrier. Looking at the sluggish, silted stream today between its steep banks is deceptive. Though so far inland, the river is tidal and may still rise on occasion to overflow on to the adjacent fields. Shoals and variable water levels made shipping on the river a risky business whilst the ancient but essential ferry crossing was perilous due to unpredictable currents. Burials from Carlton all used to be in Snaith churchyard. Records relate how many a coffin, complete with body, ended up in the river when the ferry capsized. Other cargo sometimes went the same way, and plenty of people were drowned too.

It heralded great progress when, in 1777, a toll bridge was built. It was a swing bridge whose wooden centre section lifted to allow the passage of masted ships. This piece of local history still stands, though now defunct and with its centre part removed. The two toll houses at either side of the Carlton bank approach continue to guard the crossing. They look like and, even at close quarters, appear only marginally bigger than two sentry boxes. One was the toll keeper's dwelling and the other his box office.

In 1927 the powers that be opened a meccano-style metal bridge. It was needed to take the increasing flow of road traffic which was fast replacing the horse, cart, and carriage era. It is, of course, the main route between Snaith and Selby and even York. Naturally Jack's memories bring it all to life.

"I was fourteen when they opened the iron bridge, but I well remember the last toll keeper on the old bridge before it closed. He was in his seventies when he finished. As pedestrians we paid a ha'penny to cross his bridge, there and back. Carts and animals cost more. In winter Carlton fishponds regularly froze over, and we all went skating. They always held the Yorkshire ice skating championships there, and we crossed over to see them."

The trusty toll bridge did come into its own again recently. The iron bridge had become so corroded that it was dangerous. While it was being repaired, some temporary refurbishment allowed light traffic once again to cross the toll bridge. Heavy lorries and buses had to make a long diversion. The iron bridge soon reopened, and the old one again was relegated to a disused but important piece of local history.

Probably the main reason why Snaith is administratively closer to Goole than Selby and comes under the East Riding of Yorkshire County Council is because of its topographical position. The distance between Goole and Selby is the same, and rivers are no longer a barrier but old partitions persist long after their raison d'être has gone.

Market Town

In Jack's youth the estimated population of Snaith and Cowick was somewhat in excess of sixteen hundred. Today the parish magazine is distributed to around three thousand households. Although it must be noted that the parish also includes a few small villages round about, we are still probably talking of a fivefold growth in the town's population over the century. Also in Jack's youth there were eight public houses in Snaith alone. The fact that Snaith was the market town for all the surrounding countryside doubtless explains the high proportion of pub to person. The right to hold a market and certain fairs goes back to 1223. Over the centuries the market day changed, but the wares traded remained much the same—agricultural products, grain, leather, meat, animals, butter, cloth and flax, or "line" as they called it, to name but a few. We still have streets called Market Place, Beast Fair, and Butter Market.

When Jack began to prosper in life, he once bought a small stone structure abutting the east wall of the churchyard. This was the actual butter market where butter had been sold by weight and "the yard" at least since the mid-sixteenth century. Having decided that it was not much use to him, he let the property go again. He always regretted it for it was later demolished. A unique part of the town's heritage had gone forever.

By the end of the nineteenth century Snaith market was no longer held. Notwithstanding, the charter giving the right to hold markets was publicly read each year. A town dignitary stood behind the churchyard wall, just above the butter market site and proclaimed the charter to a small crowd of people below. Traditionally anyone who heard the charter read was eligible afterwards for a free pint of beer in one of the local pubs. Jack recalled the custom of reading the charter well. It ceased in the 1930s and was never revived after the war. Of course the right to have a market was never revoked, which leads to an interesting speculation. I am given to understand that if, on a Thursday, someone set up a stall in Market Place, he would legally be within his rights. I wonder? It would certainly disrupt the traffic. Nobody has tried it.

Amongst the market officials whose tasks were to oversee prices, weights and measures, and the standard of goods were certain gentlemen known as ale tasters. They checked the quality of ale on offer. Imagine the results! Which brings us to the municipal lockup. The lockup is an eighteenth century building which adjoined the former butter market. It now stands alone against the churchyard wall—a single-storey, three-roomed structure which is officially listed with grade-two status. Various suggestions are made about its use, the most likely being that it was a short-term prison for those visitors to the market who had imbibed too freely of the aforementioned ale. It seems to have been a poor deterrent to further excess. Apparently fellow carousers continued to pass liquid comfort through the windows to the miscreants inside. The iron grilles which were subsequently installed were no bar to ingenuity. People brought the long-stemmed clay pipes known as churchwardens' pipes. They placed the bowl in the beer, passed the stem through the grille, and the prisoner sucked it up as through a straw.

There are similar lockups elsewhere in the country, but ours is considered to be unique in both its situation and appearance. However, it is in its ecclesiastical history that Snaith lays greatest claim to distinction.

The Peculiar of Great Snaith

Snaith has a long history, possibly going back to Roman times if the unearthing of a skeleton and Roman coins is any evidence. The story of its church is especially fascinating.

The church of St Laurence (note the spelling) is named after a martyr of that name who met his end in Rome in AD 258. Soon after his death some of his relics, a finger I believe, were brought to the north of England. It is, therefore, a reasonable conjecture that our church was founded not too long after the demise of its patron saint. Obviously the present building is Norman, but this does not negate the existence of an earlier building. What we are sure of is that religious life flourished here in Anglo-Saxon times and for three reasons.

To begin with, the church is known to have links with St Ethelreda who founded Ely Abbey in 673. Her sister, Hilda, founded Whitby monastery in 657. Pilgrims to Whitby and other religious centres in the north may even have visited Snaith en route.

Second, inside the present building is a niche, now empty, where once a statue stood. The inscription attests the name St Scytha. She is thought to have been an Anglo-Saxon princess.

The third and most telling piece of evidence comes from 1275 when the archbishop of York's treasurer visited Snaith chapel. He found there a large number of copies of a handwritten Anglo-Saxon service book. It was noteworthy that the place not only had these books at all but also had them in quantity.

By 1066 and the Norman Conquest, the area covered by the parish of Snaith stretched some twenty miles from Whitley to Whitgift and

Adlingfleet. It also had special status as a royal estate which meant three things. It belonged to the crown, its wealth must have been impressive, and that wealth helped to support the crown and its affairs. The kind of wealth we are talking about mostly was the income from taxes, tithes, and various ecclesiastical levies.

Snaith is not listed in the 1086 Domesday Book as is often erroneously stated. This document is a census of English landowners and their property drawn up to give the Norman conquerors of the country some idea of what their new assets were worth. There was no need to specify the royal estates for their valuation was already known. Where Snaith is mentioned, and that three times, is in the survey from which the Domesday Book was compiled. However, sometimes this survey is also called the Domesday Book.

In 1100 Henry I bequeathed the rectory of Snaith to the archbishop of York. He in turn gave it to the newly founded monastery or abbey in Selby. It was no mean gift as was indicated by the fact that the new owners at once appointed two monks to take up residence in Snaith in order to oversee the affairs of the parish. Later three priests joined them to form a priory of five persons. The church is often called the Priory to this day.

The church was also a "Peculiar," which means that it had the right to hold its own ecclesiastical courts instead of having to submit to the higher jurisdiction of York. The court dealt with such things as wills and intestacy matters. It licensed schoolmasters and midwives, ruled in all offences to do with church affairs, and determined questions of church upkeep. The consistory courtroom is still there, at the west end of the north aisle of the church. It is the only unconsecrated part of the building.

The parish is always known as the parish of great Snaith, meaning the parish of greater Snaith, yet in a very real sense it was a great and important setup—busy, wealthy, and quite magnificent. The grandeur ended with the English reformation and the dissolution of the monasteries in 1539. The priory and priests went as did the ritual. Thankfully the religious life of the parish was self-perpetuating and continued robustly, albeit with diminished pomp. The parish boundary has contracted to make way for new parishes with their own new churches. Burials are permitted elsewhere and not only in Snaith churchyard. Times have moved on, but still we remain the great parish of Great Snaith.

Time Is Short

Jack, though proud of his hometown's past, was no historian. It was the tangible church of the present that lived for him. With its tower—squat, square, solid and strong, and built over eight hundred years ago—it epitomised stability and security.

Did I say security? You know how Jack hated heights. Unfortunately visiting friends often requested a trip up the tower. The view is superb but the parapet is low, barely above knee height and no protection against vertigo. He last went up when he was eighty-two with a young great-nephew from Canada. "Never again!" he vowed. Thereafter he called upon his son John to do such honours. John does not like heights either.

The church clock always had a place in Jack's affections. Its lozenge-shaped surround, now blue, used to be black. An inscription round the edge has proclaimed for many a year that "time is short." Now everybody knows this, but not one person I have talked to other than Jack is aware of the play on these words which used to be subtly illustrated on the clock dial itself. On most timepieces each five-minute span has four dots dividing it into its five separate minutes. As Jack recalled it, the section between one and two had only three dots, giving the illusion of only a four-minute interval. Time was indeed short. One day the clock was renovated. With regrettable lack of imagination and humour, the restorers returned the missing minute to its place.

The Realm of the Spiritual

Although we like to think ourselves grown-up by the time we are twenty, the truth is that for most of us our twenties continue to be a significantly, formative period in our lives. This was true for Jack in one very important area, the realm of the spiritual. Each week Ada sent her children to Sunday school in the parish church. Sometime in his early teens Jack was confirmed under Canon Moxley, rector of the parish.

"What did your confirmation mean to you?" I wondered.

"It was important but . . ." He struggled for words. "Somehow impersonal."

If I had asked who was confirmed with him or for a description of the ceremony he would have had no difficulty in recalling names and describing the event with all the verve of the born storyteller. To articulate the inner, abstract experience never came easily for Jack. The deeper the emotion, the less he could express it. Not, apparently, that his confirmation had evoked any great soul stirring. It had not. Therein lay his problem for he felt that it ought to have been a momentous, life-changing step.

As he said, "It was never in my nature to be hypocritical, and when I made my confirmation vows I was sincere. I used to enjoy going to the evening service and listening to Canon Moxley. I also loved the church bells and was in the church choir. I understood the basic doctrines of Christianity, more or less, and believed them and I tried to put Christian standards of behaviour into practice in my everyday life. In the end I still had the uncomfortable feeling that it was all a bit theoretical and that something was lacking deep inside me."

One day, when Jack was eighteen, he was cycling home from work with one of his mates whom I shall call Will because I do not know his proper name.

"What are you doing on Sunday?"

The question came from Will who was an older man, known to be a staunch Methodist and a bit of a character. Incidentally, he was also known to be a man whose life matched up to the faith he proclaimed.

"Nothing very much," responded Jack.

"Then come along to chapel with me."

"I'll think about it," responded a rather surprised Jack.

"Aye! Do that, lad."

Having felt the fish nibble, the wily Will reeled out a little more bait.

"We need a good voice like yours in the choir."

Sunday came and found Jack doing other things, not important things but somehow they were preferable to making the effort of putting on his suit and going to chapel. For a few weeks Will persisted whilst Jack proffered flimsy excuses. Then one Sunday there came a knock on the door.

"I've come to take you to chapel," stated the importunate caller in tones that tolerated no refusal. Jack quickly donned his one and only best suit and set off with his mentor.

"You know," he told me a lifetime later, "it just shows the importance of persevering with people in our Christian witness. If Will had given up on me my whole life might have been very different. Many people today would think he was too pushy, but I'm glad he was."

As a result, there in Snaith Methodist Chapel Jack found Jesus. It did not happen immediately in that first service but in the weeks that followed as, for the first time in his life, he heard the message of a personal salvation. Gradually all the theory of Christianity learned in Sunday school, all the Christian standards taught by Ada in the home, fell into place in the person of Jesus. They ceased to be abstractions. They suddenly became intimate realities. Jesus, a man, was the key.

Faith of a Lifetime

After Jack died I found a file of some of his old sermons for he eventually became a local preacher. Most date from the sixties and seventies although he was preaching long before then. I did not need them to explain the essence of his religious experience to me but the extracts I quote show how, even in later life, he never lost the reality of this experience and the thrill of what his faith was all about. Jack's thinking was usually deceptively simple, but as this illustration from one of his sermons shows, never simplistic.

To him the humanity of Jesus was always important as shown in an illustration from a sermon on the topic of "The Word Became Flesh and Lived Among us."

> *A little girl was alone in her bedroom one night. The wind was blowing, making the windows rattle and the curtains move. She got frightened and called out, "Mummy, come quickly and stay with me." Her mother came and tucked her up and tried to comfort her. "You don't need to be afraid. Everything is all right because God is with you every moment." To which the little girl replied, "But, Mummy, I need a God with skin on."*

This story encapsulates the profound theological truth that changed Jack's life. In Jesus he found "a God with a skin on." He went on to say,

> *If we really seek to see the kind of person Jesus is, we can discover what God is like.*

Later he added,

> *We look at Jesus, and we see the kind of person we can become. In him we see what God intends us to be.*

Jack was a man who had heroes, people like Gandhi who lived out their convictions and thereby changed society. From the moment when he first found his "God with skin on," Jesus became Jack's greatest hero, and he tried to emulate him—both in his relationships with people and in his attitudes towards things and circumstances.

Commendable as this was, Christianity for Jack was far more than mere copycat hero worship. All through his life the cross was central to his faith. In a sermon entitled "The Lifting up of the Son of Man" he wrote,

> *The cross of Jesus brings home to us our sin. We can see what pride, selfishness, and mean ambition are because when they have their way they crucify the son of God . . . . I am convinced that the cross of Jesus is the only thing that can defeat sin and make us clean. There is nothing and there never has been anything in this world that has revealed love*

more than the cross of Calvary . . . . Well, it may be easy to stand and look
at the cross and say that love won a victory, but it's another thing to keep
that conviction so that it becomes the main principle of our life.

Jack meant these words. Something of the suffering of Jesus on the cross
seared his own soul. He responded to such love with a wholehearted repentance
for all that was sinful and unworthy in his own life. He made a full committal
of himself to the one who had been willing to die, to give his all, for him.

The faith my husband found in those early years remained precious for the
rest of his life. Referring back to it many years later in yet another sermon, he
testified how such an experience

lifts you out of the uncertainty of things and gives you a feeling of security
and assurance and confidence which will stay with you forever . . . . You
have a feeling that you never forget as long as you live . . . . Everything
we possess, treasure most must take second place [i.e., to following and
loving Jesus].

There was something else. One night Jack went to bed. Now when Jack
went to bed, Jack went to sleep, speedily and soundly, as anyone who knew him
well, either then or now, would testify. On this night he suddenly awoke. The
room was filled with light and the wonder of the presence of God. It was not
a brightness perceived by the physical senses, yet it was very real. God was in
that room. There was nothing supernatural about the experience. Indeed, it felt
at the time like the most natural thing in the world.

If, in Jesus, Jack found a "God with skin on" whom he could emulate, then
in the glory he found a God of wonder whom he could adore.

The Cowick windmill that Jack helped demolish but that nearly demolished him in turn.

Leading man in a Rawcliffe operatic performance. Note arm around leading lady

Fifty years on and still acting around—"Sound of Music".

Brigadoon also with Goole Amateur Operatic and Dramatic Society.

CHAPTER 4

JACKBOOTS ON THE MARCH
or
HOW JACK SPENT THE WAR

Methodist Mayhem

It is India in the 1930s. A missionary doctor sits in his dispensary, a simple room, one wall of which is lined with shelves holding medicines. A ragged man enters leaning heavily on a stick. He is obviously ill. The doctor rises and moves forward to greet the sick man. With expansive gesture he pulls forward a chair and as he does so his outstretched arm catches the shelves, whereupon the whole flimsy structure overturns scattering pills and potions everywhere.

For one ageless moment the doctor and his patient gaze aghast at the mess then suddenly convulse into embarrassed mirth. Within seconds their bemused audience follows suit. The circuit play for the Methodist Foreign Missions' Week is underway. Eventually order is restored, and the scene gets off to a second start.

If religion, for Jack, was a serious business, it was at the same time fun and even hilarious, for Jack by the way, was the patient in the sketch. Occasionally it could also be hair raising as the next story illustrates.

It all began when a new minister, the Reverend Ernest Smith, formed the group performing these missionary plays and invited Jack to join. As Foreign Missions' Week falls in late October or November, the would-be thespians found themselves travelling all over the circuit on dark nights during the foggy season. Fortunately some of them had cars. For Jack, who was used to cycling everywhere, this should have been a luxury.

"But it had its drawbacks," he explained. "We often got caught in thick fog coming home. I well remember Mr Morris's car running off the road with four of us in it and landing up in a hedge. When visibility was almost nil Wilf Richardson and I would get out and walk on either side of the road waving our handkerchiefs for them to follow. The roads were so narrow and winding and there were no lines or cat's-eyes. If one of us disappeared the driver knew where the ditch was."

On a more serious note, Jack also joined the choir. He described the choirmaster, Mr Smithson, as "a very strong-willed, severe man who knew a great deal about music and singing." He taught Jack a lot about both and for this the young choir member was grateful. The choir tackled some challenges such as "The Messiah" and Stainer's "Crucifiction." Jack felt very proud as well as nervous when Mr Smithson gave him his first big part, a bass solo in "From Olivet to Calvary."

Before long Jack began to go out with ministers and local preachers. Maybe he gave his testimony or read a lesson but he always sang. He made his first solo debut in Camblesforth (halfway between Snaith and Selby) Primitive Methodist Chapel when he was nineteen, with two well-known hymns, "The Old Rugged Cross" and "Rock of Ages." Though young, nervous, and untrained he was quickly in demand for special occasions, both sacred and secular. Under Mr Smithson's tutelage his singing career started and took off.

One day a new minister came who was much Jack's age. The two young men shared instant rapport and the Reverend Reg Walker soon had him helping with the youth work. A newspaper cutting describes, in the pedantic prose of the day, one of Jack's more ambitious projects by which his children in Sunshine corner attempted to raise funds for the Methodist National Children's Homes. It was a lighthouse demonstration, complete with model and appropriate spiritual lessons. Once again, it was a happy time for all.

In those days every village and hamlet had its Methodist chapel, invariably well attended and with two Sunday meetings and a Sunday school. I always felt sad when Jack drove me out to see how many are now closed. Some are private dwellings, warehouses, or workshops. Others have been pulled down, and all that remains to indicate a former site is a road of new houses predictably called Chapel Row or suchlike.

In happier vein, everywhere we went Jack would point out other places.

"Do you see that farm down the lane?" I did.

"The old farmer was one of the chapel stalwarts—it's his grandson who farms there now. Well, when we took the Sunday services, that's where we went for our dinner and tea. What a cook his wife was! She gave us plates piled high with roast beef and Yorkshire pud and then thick slices of apple pie with their own fresh cream."

Jack would be almost drooling. All these farmers' wives could cook. I gather too that my husband often walked off his hefty repast in the afternoon, down country lanes, accompanied by the pretty daughters of our hospitable farmers. However insistently elusive the young bachelor had remained, he still recalled past female attentions and recounted them sixty years later to his new wife with glee.

Maturing Convictions

If Jack's Christianity was evidenced in his outer life, it influenced his inner life no less. Snaith Methodist Chapel was still in what is called its heyday. People who were already becoming important names, not only in Methodism but in world Christian circles, occasionally preached in Snaith. There was William Sangster, then in Scarborough, Leslie Wetherhead in Leeds, and Donald Soper in London. Jack heard them and others and felt the impact of their teachings, diverse though their styles were.

The man whose views struck a harmonising chord in his own heart was Dr Donald Soper. By now some of Jack's own convictions were clarifying. Dr Soper's Christian socialism with its acted-out concern for all human beings, but especially for the working-class man and the downtrodden, appealed to him. Soper was also a pacifist, and Jack was fast reaching his own conclusions about that too.

On a wider canvas there was Gandhi with his passive resistance to and policy of peaceful noncooperation with the British Empire in India. That story, of course, was still unfolding; but the world was watching and already knew that Gandhi's methods were unstoppable by military might. Gandhi too believed in the worth and equality of human beings irrespective of sex, caste, race, or religion. He spent his life practising the creed he preached and thereby changed a continent and swayed the world. It mattered nothing that Gandhi was a Hindu. Everything he stood for embodied the essence of what Jesus taught. Gandhi was one of Jack's heroes. He kept a black-and-white print of him amongst his papers. He learned two things from him above all. It was important to have convictions, and convictions stood for nothing if you did not stand by them.

Simultaneously with these external influences, Jack was also reading his Bible seriously and learning more about his faith. Slowly, everything came together as he began to formulate what he felt were the most important guiding principles for his own life. His thinking starts with a quote from one of his sermons.

> *When God made man He put something of Himself in him and it is still there. He made him in His own image and it is still there . . . .*
> *Because of sin men have forgotten what the real essence of their being is.*

This basic doctrine, that God made us in his own image, was central for Jack. I cannot quote all that he wrote, but he drew a threefold conclusion from it. First, we must try to see our fellow men through the eyes of Jesus and focus on their potential rather than their faults. Second, we should direct our own actions towards helping them to fulfil their potential by knowing God's presence within their lives and by realising the power of Jesus to uplift and transform. His third conclusion he expressed as follows:

> *I shall always seek to bless others no matter who they are or how far short they fall of God's image within their lives.*

This notion of "blessing others" became one of Jack's guiding ideals for life, and it was for life, as all who knew him would testify. How, then, did it work out in practice in those heady days of his young manhood? It was soon to be tested.

Want and War

There were two overriding concerns in the thirties, work (or lack of it) and war. As Jack once said,

"We had just gone through the great depression which brought unemployment and so much suffering to working-class people all over Britain but especially in the north of England. It didn't touch me or my family greatly, but we knew people who were affected. We were still struggling with all that as a country and then we were faced with the possibility of war."

These two major issues presented themselves to Jack's generation in little over a decade. If, as Jack believed, human beings were to be cherished, what could he do, however insignificant, to help combat such evils? He thought long and deeply until his own way became clear. He knew that he could not change society or deflect the course of history, but he could appease his own conscience. He could vote, and he would refuse to fight.

The Labour party was founded in 1900 and had already become a political force to reckon with. Jack believed with conviction that it offered the working man the best deal and the best hope. Therefore he began to vote Labour and he did so for the rest of his life. He never went so far as a future Labour MP friend of his who created a furore when he allegedly stated, "No Conservative can be a real Christian." (Or was it vice versa?) He did often say to me, "I don't know how a Christian can vote anything but Labour."

As for fighting, in the thirties pacifism was a popular creed and not only amongst Christians. Naturally, however popular pacifism may be in peacetime, it loses its appeal when war threatens. In the years immediately preceding the outbreak of war there were two good reasons why this should happen. A rearmament drive in 1937 and 1938 suddenly brought work to the longtime unemployed. War might be regrettable but it had an upside. Also, events in Europe at this time persuaded some people that this would be a just fight against a dangerous dictator. For many sincere, would-be pacifists, expediency prevailed over principle.

This was not so with Jack. When the heart searching was over and done with, it was all very simple in the end. He could not handle weapons to take life. He openly declared himself to be a conscientious objector. Within Methodism there were sufficient numbers of conscientious objectors for Conference to advise its ministers to offer them every support. The Reverend Reg Walker was a rock of strength to Jack in the difficult days ahead. He listened, advised, and accompanied him to his two tribunals when that time came.

There were those in Snaith who commended Jack for his ideals but at the last, apart from Reg, he stood alone. He was not aware of anyone else in the district who followed principles of nonviolence through to the end. Even those who praised him to his face were less ardent behind his back, and some people were openly hostile. I am only telling you what he told me, and even after all those years I sensed that it still hurt. Apart from Reg, he felt that he stood alone.

Build up to Hostilities

"So," I wanted to know one evening when we were sitting quietly together. "What happened to you when war was finally declared?"

The curtains were closed. I was doing a tapestry, and Jack had just drawn a pencil sketch of Sally the dog asleep on a chair. He liked drawing and his efforts, though untutored, were quite good.

"Not a lot to begin with," he replied. "I had left the clog mill in 1937 and was working as a joiner for a local builder. It was a reserve occupation which meant that I did not need to be called up." He looked across at me with an enigmatic expression and concluded, "I was sitting pretty."

I was beginning to know my Jack. There had to be more to it than that. There was, but first we must hear how the war came to Snaith.

For some time it made almost no difference. The initial arena of activity was far away, in the realms of crackling wireless broadcasts, yesterday's newspapers, and two-week-old news films in a Goole cinema. Yet change was all around. Jack's memories began to come, jumbled but clear.

"My mother and I were in Selby Road by then. We had gas lighting, but even so we stocked up on candles. I helped her hang thick curtains at the windows for the blackout. I think we used an old blanket somewhere. It was like Hodges in 'Dad's Army.' The air raid warden patrolled the streets and pounced if even a chink of light showed. It didn't seem all that important. We heard the enemy planes in the distance, but they rarely flew overhead. The church bells stopped ringing, and the clog mill siren no longer sounded for the shifts. It only blew if hostile aircraft were around. We were more put out when evening activities in public places had to be cancelled because the venue could not be properly blacked out, and the clog mill hooter was the town's main timepiece. And we missed it."

"They removed station names and signposts and village names to confuse the enemy, only we saw no sign of an enemy to confuse. Local men began getting their call up papers and one by one disappeared. One young fellow lost his. We suspect that his mother burned them. It didn't matter. I forget what he did, but he was probably in a reserve occupation anyway. Girls who were in service went into the land army. The whole social setup of being in service never came back."

"Then there were the ration cards and the rationing of food. That must have been hard for people in the cities, especially later on when goods were scarcer. In the country you could at least keep a few hens in the back garden and grow some vegetables. They also issued us with gas masks—" Here I interrupted.

"Clumsy, ugly things!" I said. "I must have been very young, but I can still see my father putting his gas mask on. And I was so frightened, I howled. They had a small one for me, but I screamed and kicked when they tried to make me wear it."

Gradually a picture materialised. I was just old enough to visualise some of the things Jack was telling me from my own dimly recalled experiences of these times—about the air raid shelters, for instance. My grandfather in Leeds had one in his garden. It was a corrugated iron affair, about the size of a small garden shed, sunk down into a deep hole in the earth. The roof protruded above the ground and was covered with grass sods to camouflage it. You went down some rickety steps to get inside. Granny had a few things down there for an emergency, but it was dark and damp. And I did not like it.

Jack confirmed my description. This was the Anderson shelter, and apparently it was a standard structure used all over the country. People without gardens prepared safe places in their homes in cellars or junk cupboards under the stairs, neither of which appears terribly secure to me if a bomb happens to land on your house.

Although I was only born in 1939 and spent most of the war years in the Shetland Isles, we did visit relatives in Bridlington once during that time. I woke up frightened as enemy planes flew low overhead. After a sortie inland they dropped a last bomb on the east coast towns as was their custom, as they returned home. My father comforted me. There were some hits that night, but we stayed upstairs in bed. My relatives all huddled under the dining room table. That was the best that they and countless others could do. It seems pathetic now.

The initial period of quiet could not last considering the strategic importance of the area surrounding Snaith. Over a millennium ago Vikings and Danes had invaded our shores by way of the Humber estuary and the confluence of rivers flowing into it. The land was still open to invasion even in the twentieth century. Hull and Goole were strategic ports. Hull, in particular, suffered badly in the bombing, for it was an obvious target for destruction. Many Hull evacuees were sent inland to places like Snaith.

The flat fertile Yorkshire hinterland behind the estuary and down into Lincolnshire was vital for agriculture and keeping the nation fed. There were also the coalfields and large industrial towns of the north east, so crucial to the war effort. In the centre of all this sat Snaith, not a target in itself but unavoidably aware, nonetheless, of all the comings and goings of military activity.

It was not long, therefore, before the soldiers arrived. Cowick Hall, a seventeenth century mansion a mile east of Snaith, was requisitioned as a military barracks while a camp sprang up at Pollington, two miles to the west. The men paraded (compulsorily) in church on Sundays and frequented (voluntarily) Snaith's numerous pubs on weekdays. They were, for the most part, decent chaps. Some were little more than boys, inexperienced and bewildered. Others were family men, worried about loved ones left behind. Most were homesick and, though they hid it with bravado, pretty frightened about the future.

Soon a military airfield took shape at the Pollington camp. Once operational they flew nightly bombing raids across to Germany and tried to intercept the German planes flying inland to attack us. A nearby ordnance factory helped to feed the insatiable demands for bombs. Jack reminisced,

"It was funny, you know, there was no proper security for such big projects. I suppose they were in too much of a hurry to get things up and working. We could cycle past the Pollington airfield and look over the hedges to see what was going on and even chat to the soldiers inside. One place where they did have a guard on duty was Carlton Bridge. I came home from Carlton late one night with a girl. When the sentry challenged she went first. Everyone knew that the sentries were nice to the girls. It worked. I followed, and he let us across, no bother."

By now the tread of military jackboots sounded all around. It only served to reinforce Jack's own convictions. He would not handle weapons to take life.

Deciding Days

We were just engaged. I was working round the house, and Jack had made some coffee for us both.

"I would fight for you, Anne."

Now what prompted that? The sentiment was straightforward enough though a mite unexpected. It was the almost reluctance with which he spoke that puzzled me, and he was not keen to elucidate. I did not then understand his views on violence. Only later did I realise that he could never have said those words easily. I still do not know exactly what he meant. I am quite sure that he was not denying the proven principles of a lifetime.

Back in 1939 the hostilities were of a different degree. Everyone had to register at the Labour Exchange in Goole for war service. As previously stated, Jack, as a builder's joiner, was in a reserve occupation and exempt from call up. He could keep his convictions intact without making a public issue of them. Not Jack! Such was not his way. Though not without much trepidation, he openly registered as a conscientious objector. In due course he was summoned to a military tribunal. The judge was not pleased.

"Young man," he declared, "you're wasting my time. You're in a reserve occupation already. Get out of here and go home."

As you know, Jack was a popular gentleman but having declared his stance so openly some of his workmates became restive. The boss had a problem for he too was a Christian and not unsympathetic to Jack's case. His son told Jack one day,

"You know my dad's taking a lot of stick because of you."

To give him credit, the boss tried to support Jack as long as he could, but one day he came to him.

"Jack, I'm having to lay off men. I'm sorry, I'll have to ask you to go."

Jack understood. After years of unemployment the war effort had brought work in plenty to the area. It was better to get another job than work with men who were hostile, and his boss would soon find another joiner, which he did a week later. Jack had known there would be a cost to pay, and he was ready.

"I just wish," he said wistfully, "that the real reason for my dismissal had been stated openly." He paused before continuing,

"I went back to the Labour Exchange. They offered me work as a joiner at the army training camp in Pollington. I refused. They then came up with a labouring job building air raid shelters. I felt able to accept this, but it was only temporary and not a reserve occupation. Before long I moved to a tile works. It was a case of filling in time before going to another tribunal, and naturally I had to work for my living. There were undercurrents of antagonism wherever I went, even in places where I might have expected more understanding."

Support, of a kind, came from an unlooked for source. A certain Mr Willie Hinsley, a joiner and undertaker from Carlton, met him one day.

"I hear you're having a hard time. You can have a job with me if you want."

The sympathy meant as much as the work, and Jack found himself back in a reserve occupation. Understandably, the powers that be were in no mood to mess about. The second military tribunal was already fixed for August 2, 1940. Jack attended. The Reverend Reg Walker again accompanied him.

At the Tribunal

At the tribunal, held in Leeds, the chairman, Judge Stewart, allowed Jack to state his case before examining him on a few pertinent issues. Though inwardly quaking, Jack was not prepared to be intimidated.

"So you won't fight, not even in self-defence or for your country?"

"No, sir!"

"What would you do if someone attacked your mother?"

Too late Jack saw the trap. He had no time to think and answered on impulse.

"I'd go to her rescue. I'd probably kill him."

The judge had his victim where he wanted and pressed home his advantage.

"So much for your principles then. You'd kill for your mother but not for your country. What's the difference?"

"With respect, sir, there is a difference. This war is real. The case about my mother is imaginary. I've had time to consider my attitude to war, and you know my views. If my mother was attacked, my reaction would be instinctive. There'd be no time for thought. I wouldn't mean to kill anyone, but I just might if I hit him hard enough. I'm pretty strong."

The judge looked at the man before him. Even in his Sunday suit the powerful physique showed. Indeed he appeared to have grown in stature as his fervour increased while he spoke. Jack continued, "I agree that it is inconsistent, sir, but instinctive reactions often are."

Jack stopped. What a mess he had made of it. The judge, whose job was to probe and assess, was sufficiently experienced to appreciate the complexities of human behaviour. He appeared satisfied and changed direction.

"If you persist in your views, I can send you to prison, you know."

Jack knew. Judge Stewart paused to let this sink in.

"Or," he went on, "you could serve in a noncombatant unit."

"What would that mean, sir?"

"You'd do jobs to do with defence and keeping civilian life going. You wouldn't have to carry weapons or work with armaments, but you would have to wear a uniform and," he added, "you'd always be a private."

"I'd be prepared to do that, sir."

The judge pounced once more.

"You're inconsistent again. Everything you do will in some way help the war along, and wearing uniform identifies you with the army. No doubt you'd prefer that to prison?"

"I look at it this way, sir. We're at war whether we like it or not. Even if I go to prison, I cannot opt out of the system completely. I'll do my bit for my country in the best way I can. I'll wear uniform in the Non-Combatant Corps. I'll even go to the front in a medical corps if they'll have me. Either way I'd be more use than sitting in prison."

Apparently his cross-examiner agreed.

In one of Jack's scrapbooks, a four-inch column of tiny newsprint summarises the business of Jack's tribunal. Judge Stewart was very scathing of a certain Mr Leaver, a Jehovah's Witness. There were, of course, plenty of Jehovah's Witnesses who were every bit as genuine as Jack. There were obviously others, and it was the tribunal's task to sort them out. Mr Leaver claimed exemption as "an ordained minister of Jehovah God." Here are the judge's remarks as reported.

> *But you have been a cabinet maker and a grocer's assistant until a couple of months ago. Your case is about as thin as anything we have had . . . . This society supports cases in which a man has joined about five minutes before registering, claiming exemption on the same footing as ministers who go through long courses and are ordained with formality into different churches.*

Mr Leaver got short shrift. The tribunal rejected three appeals, one man was to continue his work as a teacher, five were to be registered for work on the land and eight, including Jack, were to be registered for noncombatant duties only. They came from all over Yorkshire, the nearest to Jack being a Quaker from Pontefract.

Report for Duty

Jack duly reported for duty with the Non-Combatant Corps (NCC) on January 2, 1941. He went to Liverpool to an intake and training camp, not knowing what to expect. When he had first made his stand he had thought that he must be one of the few people in the country to do so. After the tribunal he realised that there were others like him around but still not many. He felt terribly alone. Suddenly he found himself with some two or three hundred other men, all of whom had felt the same. The relief for everyone was enormous. Spirits rose. They understood each other without having to explain or be on the defensive. They shared instant camaraderie.

Early on each man was interviewed in order to decide what best to do with him. One of the officers was unfriendly, and some of the men were upset. It was like a tribunal all over again but more hostile. Jack was forewarned as he entered the interview room. After a few minutes of grilling he said, "I'm sorry, sir, I refuse to answer any more questions. You are only going over things that I made clear at the tribunal and which should be in my records. You have no right to do this."

Jack was a mild man and not quickly riled, but he was annoyed. And it showed. The officer backed down.

The new recruits all had to have medicals. One particular man, who was not Jack, went to the MO (medical officer) who firmly sounded and pummelled him. Satisfied with his findings the MO then handed him a jam jar and indicated a door.

"Go in there and fill that with water for me."

He went. After a few minutes the doctor shouted, "Don't take all day about it. What's keeping you, man?"

A worried face appeared at the door.

"I'm sorry, sir. I can't find the tap."

"Just piss in it, man, piss in it," came the exasperated reply.

Later on the newcomers were lined up for blood samples and injections. As the MO came round with the syringe the men began to fall and long before their turns arrived. According to Jack, the same needle was used for every victim.

In Liverpool the new members of the NCC had their initiation into the parade ground. On the first morning they stood to attention whilst each person called out his name.

"Baker, Thomas! Punton, Jack! Hargreaves, Joe!"

A titter went round the ranks, quickly quelled. Already everyone knew that private Hargreaves was actually a very self-conscious Cecil. He won the day, however, and Joe he remained thereafter.

They were not long in Liverpool. From there they were divided up and sent to join smaller units all over the country but not before lasting friendships were already being made. When Jack died in 1999 I had a letter from a famous organist in South Africa, a Mr Gerald Horner. I quote.

> *My association with Jack goes back to 1941 when we were training together at Liverpool .... Another memory I have of Jack is that whilst at Liverpool we adopted a little stray kitten which Jack christened Tinkerbell. When we were given orders to transfer to Codford someone said, "You're not taking the kitten with you, are you?" Jack's reply was "Certainly!" However, on arrival at Codford our new CO ordered Jack to get rid of Tinkerbell, and we found a good home for her in the village.*

I knew all about Tinkerbell. She travelled to Codford tucked up inside Jack's great coat which he was wearing.

There was another organist destined for world fame whom Jack met in Liverpool, a Mr Arnold Loxam. In this case the link was brief as they soon transferred to different units. Fifty plus years later they met up again at an organ recital in Snaith chapel. He continued playing for many years until he died in his eighties.

Life in the NCC

I cannot take you through a chronological record of Jack's five years in the NCC. It might be boring if I did. I simply do not know the details of all their movements and ploys. Nor can I present a historian's record of what life in the NCC was like. I can only tell you what it was like for Jack.

To begin with, he moved around and saw places. He slept, for instance, in the stables at Newmarket. He narrowly escaped injury in a country mansion at Minehead when a large bow window shattered during a bombing raid. He had been sleeping on a straw palliasse in the curve of the window when one night he suddenly had the feeling that he ought to move. He did. It probably saved his life. They slept in tents in the snow in the middle of winter whilst they built their own camp which, even when it was finished, was only a series of bleak nissan huts. Mostly they remained in Wiltshire, Oxfordshire, and Somerset with settled spells in Codford near Salisbury and Didcot near Oxford.

It was, however, the people he met who made Jack's years in the NCC so special. Labourers, shopkeepers, and tradesmen shared barrack space with university dons, businessmen, professional actors, and musicians. Communists square bashed alongside Christians. Jehovah's Witnesses peeled spuds with Baptists. If the social, religious and educational backgrounds of the men varied so too did their philosophies. Many were Christians but of denominations as far apart in their theological ethos as Quakers, Pentecostalists, Plymouth Brethren, and Anglicans. Some eschewed any religious ethic at all and called themselves atheists and humanists. A few were Communists and one or two, but only one or two were rebels against society and the establishment in general.

During the First World War the soldiers sang a satirical chorus,

> We are Fred Karno's army
> Fred Karno's infantry.

Fred Karno was a famous impresario of the day whose name was a humorous byword for chaos and confusion. The men of the NCC produced their own version.

> We are Fred Karno's army
> We are the NCC.

It went on to list the "Christians, cranks, and Commies" found in their ranks, but unfortunately I do not recall the exact words. I say unfortunately. Perhaps it is just as well. They were clever and funny, but they were not overly complimentary about king and country nor of Mr Churchill and the war. In a totalitarian state they would have been deemed highly seditious and anyone caught singing them would expect to be taken out and shot at dawn. Thank God for the British sense of humour!

Like Meets Like

As you might expect, the Christians in the unit soon sought each other out and wherever they were stationed made links with the local churches. Jack and a Baptist friend, Jack Ash, did a lot together. In fact, Mr Ash's daughter wrote to me when my Jack died and his widow passed away shortly afterwards. They helped in the Sunday school in a church in Didcot and occasionally gave their testimonies. My Jack sang solos and joined the choir. They even got permission from their CO to be involved regularly with some week night youth work.

In return, church members opened their homes to the soldiers. This welcome hospitality resulted in a funny incident. Jack was invited out to tea one Sunday and arrived in his uniform and heavy army boots.

"Why don't you take your boots off?" suggested his hostess, "You'll be more comfortable." She assessed her guest's large feet, "I'm sure my son's slippers will fit you."

Jack demurred and reddened.

"No, thank you! You're very kind but I'm OK."

The lady persevered until a shamefaced Jack complied. The holes in his socks were too huge to hide.

"The silly thing was," he told me half a century later, "I could darn very neatly. My mother taught me when I was a boy, and I used to teach the lads in the unit who didn't have a clue."

Jack's contribution to the Methodist church in Didcot was such that even after he had moved to Bridgewater in Somerset, they included him in their 1944 Christmas gift list. Nor did they fail to wish him "a happy future in the event you soon hope to celebrate," which event you must wait to hear about in the next chapter.

Gerry Horner, whose letter I have already quoted from, was another of Jack's Christian comrades and, as you will gather, a lifelong friend. Here are more extracts from two of his letters.

We were transferred to Codford near Salisbury. I had been befriended by a couple who were society stewards at a Salisbury Methodist church and so I played the organ there on many occasions. If my memory serves me correctly (although it often lets me down nowadays as I shall soon be seventy nine) Jack sang a solo in that church more than once . . . .

Yes, as you say, we did have lots of fun in those far-off days, and met a lot of interesting people. One of these was the Precentor of Salisbury Cathedral . . . .

The precentor was instrumental in persuading the cathedral organist, Sir Walter Alcock, to let me play the magnificent cathedral organ whenever I was in Salisbury, as long as it was not inconvenient to the authorities.

Incidentally, the precentor, whose name was W H Ferguson, was the composer of the tune "Wolvercote" used in the hymn "O Jesus I have promised."

Although Gerry's memories are not Jack's, I include them here because they are relevant. It was in Salisbury Cathedral at this time that Jack heard a superb rendering of "Elijah" which he considered to be a highlight of his life ever since. For myself, I am interested to learn about the tune "Wolvercote." "O Jesus I have promised to serve thee to the end" is one of the hymns I want sung at my funeral because it sums up the spiritual struggles and aspirations of my life, but I prefer the tune "Day of Rest."

Getting Down to Business

Jack always said that the NCC did not properly know what to do with its men. I think he was right and for two reasons.

First, and as we have already seen, it took some time after the outbreak of war to sift through the genuine conscientious objectors. It was 1941 before Jack went to Liverpool and was finally moved south in a smaller unit. Even then they had no proper place to go and lived in tents whilst they built their own camps. The truth is that the NCC was establishing itself and developing its own infrastructure and modus operandi as it went.

Second, and it sounds snobbish to say it, some of the men were socially, intellectually and educationally in a different class from their officers. On that level there were those on both sides who did not quite know how to relate to each other. Workwise there were things to do whilst military drill and discipline took no respect of persons. In other areas there were problems.

Take the compulsory lecture and cultural evening which, apart from the church parades, was the other big social event of the week. The usual army talks on the danger of VD in the forces and what to do if you thought someone might be a German spy were drawn on. Some stock subjects, however, were not quite so acceptable in a noncombatant company. Then somebody obviously had a bright idea. Half the men were intellectual types, so why not give them something cultural? The person with the bright idea had poetry in mind. He even knew someone who might come and give a lecture on Keats.

On the night in question the company gathered, laughing and chattering as they waited for proceedings to start. The noise grew. Adults are seldom quieter than children at such times. The sergeant major entered, irately anxious to restore decorum before the CO arrived with the guest speaker.

"Quiet!" he bawled. "I've never heard such a racket in all my life."

In the sudden stillness someone sniggered at the back of the room.

"Silence!" he yelled again. "You're an ignorant lot. Some of you chaps wouldn't even know a keat if you saw one."

After a while it was possible to determine the skills and aptitudes of the individuals and to allocate them to tasks commensurate with their abilities. Our old friend, Mr Gerald Horner, is an example; and once more I quote.

> *I was sent to London on a course of office administration to equip me for work in the Orderly Room of a POW camp. After successfully passing the test at the end of the course I was posted to No.53 POW camp at Brayton (or was it Gateforth?) near Selby.*

This was in 1943, and it could well have been Brayton, only about six miles from Snaith. Meanwhile there was work for men like Jack to do as well.

Daily Duties

As far as barrack life went, the sergeant major had his new recruits out on the parade ground, drilled and disciplined to perfection. They were not allowed to be sloppy. They all had their fatigue duties round camp, and everything functioned with military precision.

Outside of the camp their jobs were varied. They loaded and unloaded lorries and trains. They built Nissen huts and other innocuous army installations, which was when Jack's life was nearly cut short for the fifth time. Someone accidentally dropped a sledgehammer from a roof. It landed on his head and felled him to the ground, semiconscious. There was blood everywhere. They sent him back to camp, and no great harm ensued. He was tough, but it might have been serious.

Another time a small group was sent to work in a quarry. Now Jack was not only used to manual labour, he always loved it. The lads used to feel his arm muscles with envy. They were acquired in a hard school. He and a pal therefore set to work with vigour. Some of the others who were neither so fit nor so keen held back a little. At midday break the officer in charge called Jack and his friend over.

"I've been watching you two. That lot over there are shirkers. You've done more between you this morning than all of them put together. You're dismissed for the rest of the day. Let's see how they manage without you."

One job that nobody liked was boiler room duty. You had to be up soon after 4:00 a. m. to get the furnace, which had been damped down for the night, stoked and blazing, and hot water and porridge ready for breakfast. Certainly you were off duty after dinner and free for the rest of the afternoon, but you had to be back again late evening to damp down the fire for the night. The hours were unsociable, and it was dirty work, shovelling coal and so on. Jack saw it differently.

"I liked it. No one else did, so I volunteered to do it all the time and was accepted. The boiler room was always warm and I could have a cup of tea whenever I wanted. I had peace to read my Bible quietly or to write a letter, and I could sing as loudly as I wanted without disturbing anybody. I had a nap in the afternoon, and the rest of the day was mine."

Jack also liked sentry duty at night.

"Nothing ever happened, but it was a formality that had to be observed. If anyone was out late we had to check their identity before we let them in. There was this sergeant major. He could shout with the best on parade ground, but I'm sure he was a softie at heart. He often came to me late in the evening. I don't think he came when the others were on duty. We had a little room beside the gates with a stove and a couple of chairs and a table. I would give him biscuits and cocoa, and we'd talk. He was interested in religion, and he wanted to know about my faith."

"I sometimes wondered if he was lonely. He moved before long but he came specially to say good-bye and to tell me how much he had appreciated our late-night chats. I still wish I knew what became of him."

"What were your officers like?" I asked.

"All right mostly. They came and went a lot. I used to think that some of them were with the NCC for some respite after a hard spell at the front or while still convalescing from war wounds. In that case they could hardly have felt very sympathetic towards us."

Perhaps it was not so for Jack felt that they were friendly enough. Overall the group dynamic of the whole company was good.

Off-Duty Amusements

In their spare time the men played cricket and football. Despite the varicose veins in both legs which caused problems, Jack refused to give up his football. He played with his legs in crepe bandages. Soon he was made captain of his unit's official team.

"We were playing once," he told me, "when this officer joined our side. I immediately deferred to him as I was only a private. He was having none of it. I was the captain. It was only a game, and he would take his orders from me."

"The MO then decided that my veins were so bad it was dangerous for me to play. He arranged for me to have them seen to. In no time at all, there I was in a military hospital, all warm and cosy for Christmas while the rest of my company shivered in tents in the snow. It was all done free of charge. We had no health service in those days, and I could never have afforded to pay for treatment myself."

In the military hospital Jack found himself with a lot of war wounded who, not surprisingly, felt very hostile towards a conscientious objector in their midst. He understood and made every effort to explain his position and be friendly. Because his operation was delayed and he was still mobile, he tried to help those who were bedridden in any way he could. They appreciated his attempts. In the end, however, the surgeon decided to transfer him to a civilian hospital to ease the tension. When the time came to leave one of the patients who had been most antagonistic called him over.

"I just want to say good-bye. I don't agree with you and you're wrong, but I can see that you mean well. You're a decent chap, and I wish you all the best."

One memorable Christmas the men put on their very own pantomime, a version of Cinderella. It was a lavish affair. Wives and mothers apparently helped supply gowns and makeup, otherwise the men had to improvise costumes with army sheets and safety pins. Somehow they managed to produce blonde, curly hair, and big bouncing bosoms. Jack was Mr D. King, the Demon King, obviously chosen for the power of his vocal chords. He could sound very ferocious if he tried. At one point he had to bound on stage declaring in full voice that whenever he appeared,

"Locks, bolts, and bars
All burst asunder."

In the subsequent group photo of the happy cast, Cinderella looks very fetching while the smiling Mr D. King, despite his horned helmet and blackened eyebrows, appears most benign.

Many years on, Jack was working at the back of his shop when a smart stranger and his wife entered. It was John who went forward to serve.

"I'm looking for someone called Jack Punton. I think I've got the right place. Is he around?"

"I'm his son and yes, he's out at the back. I'll get him for you. What name shall I give?"

"Just tell him an old friend wants to see him."

Jack came in, curious but unable to recognise his visitor. The visitor now takes up the story in one of his letters.

> *I am always glad that on our brief visit to England in 1990 I made a point of going to see him. At first he couldn't quite place me, bearing in mind that it was getting on for fifty years since we had last seen each other, but when I said, "Jack, . . . locks, bolts, and bars," he said, "Gerry Horner! I never thought I'd see you again," and tears ran down his cheeks as he threw his arms around me. It was a very moving moment for both of us.*

At times No.9 Company produced very high brow efforts with nothing amateurish about them. They had enough talent to put together their own orchestra. Some now tattered, hand-typed programmes indicate the works they tackled, ranging through the classical composers to their own times. Jack's solo repertoire from these occasions included such contrasting pieces as Handel's "The Trumpet Shall Sound," Moss's "Floral Dance," and Sterndale Bennett's "Leanin." A newspaper cutting of one of their concerts given in a local church and arranged by Gerry Horner, singles Jack out for special mention.

> *Private Jack Punton possesses a fine baritone voice and was heard with splendid effect in "Darkness Shall Cover the Earth" and "The People that Sat in Darkness" from the Messiah, and the solo, "Lord God of Abraham" from Mendelssohn's Elijah, accompanied by Private Horner on the organ.*

All about Pete

Overall the men were happy; they were treated well, and morale was high. But then there was Pete, a young man so disgruntled that he decided he had had enough and was getting out of it.

The men in Jack's hut got up that morning as usual and prepared their dormitory for the daily inspection. Pete rose too but left his bed unmade and his kit strewn around. When the sergeant major's step sounded he knelt before the fire at the end of the room and busied himself poking the meagre embers. His comrades stood to nervous attention at the foot of their beds. The sergeant major entered. He sensed the atmosphere before he even saw the less than spruce bed and heard the clattering fire irons in the hearth.

"What's going on here?"

The uncertainty of his glance around belied the fierceness of his voice.

"You there, what do you think you're doing?"

Pete placidly continued to poke his fire.

"You there, what's your name? Stand up and pay attention."

Pete placed his poker on the hearth with premeditated precision. He stood up slowly and turned to face the fuming officer. In the politest of tones he enquired,

"Are you by any chance talking to me, sir?"

The outcome of Pete's rebellion was that they sent him to a detention centre in Manchester. It was not a nice place. The inmates were military prisoners, mostly there for criminal offences and sentenced to hard labour. They were denied creature comforts, and they were humiliated by having their heads shaved and being treated as scum. For Pete, who was not a criminal, it was his way out of the army. After a few intolerable months, if he behaved himself he could expect to be discharged. He deemed it worth it.

An officer and a private were detailed to escort Pete to Manchester. It was a two-day job by rail in those days with an overnight stopover. The officer came from York and chose Jack to accompany him. Hopefully they could both spend the night at home. As it happened, by the time Jack reached York there was no way of getting to Snaith. He stayed with a cousin instead.

Before setting out with Pete, the officer handed Jack a set of handcuffs.

"What are these for, sir?"

"Well, the prisoner will be handcuffed to you during the journey in case he tries to escape."

"I'm sorry, sir, I'm not having anybody handcuffed to me. You'll have to take someone else with you."

The officer had not expected this. Jack went on, "That man won't try to escape, sir. He's getting exactly what he wants."

The officer was sensible enough to realise the truth of this. Nothing more was said or seen of the handcuffs, and Pete behaved perfectly throughout the journey.

A Broadening Experience

Whatever Pete felt about life in the NCC, for Jack and many provincial young men like him, it was a uniquely broadening experience. Although comfortable in his own local environment, he had little wisdom in the ways of the wider world and no great certainty about his standing in society in general. He returned home, still unassuming and a little shy but confident that he could hold his own with anybody and in any situation. Such quiet, self-assurance never left him. There was something else. He realised that he was capable of achieving things if he put his mind to it. He proved this many times in the NCC and especially in all that led up to it. An example that impressed me was when he gave up smoking.

I had come across a snapshot of some of the NCC lads relaxing and, to my surprise, there was Jack puffing away at a pipe. I could hardly believe it. The Jack I knew hated smoking, refused to let anyone smoke in his house, and had an official no smoking logo on the wall in his entrance hall. Was he, I wondered, just larking around with an old pipe?

"No, I really did smoke a pipe in those days. I started when I was quite young. I never liked cigarettes, but I found a pipe very satisfying."

"Why did you stop then?" I asked.

"For a number of reasons, I suppose. I had a bit of a conscience about it because smoking was frowned upon in many Christian circles. I have to admit that I soon realised it was an expensive and a dirty habit, and I never had much money to spare. If ever I were to have a family it would seem wrong to indulge my tastes and probably have to deprive them of little extras. I also knew that most people find it almost impossible to stop smoking, and I didn't like the thought that there was something in my life that I couldn't control."

"So how did you stop?"

"A few of us went one Christmas to a hospital to sing and entertain the patients. Afterwards the matron gave us tea in her sitting room. When one or two men began to light up I made up my mind there and then. No more smoking for me. Obviously I'd been thinking about it for some time, but that was the moment of decision."

"Was it hard?"

"For a few weeks it was dreadful, but I was not going to be beaten. There's no such word as 'can't.' Then suddenly the worst was over. I've never smoked since."

How often had I heard Jack say this sentence, "There's no such word as can't"? Many times. Suddenly his eyes would begin to shine and a boyish smile would spread across his face. From experience of the signs I knew exactly what was coming as he would begin to declaim,

> *Somebody said it couldn't be done,*
> *But he with a twinkle replied*
> *That maybe it couldn't, but he'd not be one*
> *To say so until he had tried.*
> *So he buckled right in with a will and a grin,*
> *At times if he worried he hid it,*
> *And he tackled the thing that everyone said*
> *It couldn't be done—and he did it.*

I am not sure that my strong-willed husband came across this rhyme as far back as his NCC days. The sentiment, however, was undoubtedly part of his creed from his young manhood. I could, of course, have quoted it in the second last chapter on "Jack's Philosophy of Life." Somehow I feel it fits more appropriately here. It also sets a background for reading on and seeing the things that Jack attempted in order to make a living and provide for his family.

And so, in ways great and small, Jack was the first to acknowledge that the NCC years were a formative period in his life. I never heard him talk about that time negatively. It may seem out of place to some who hold different convictions, but I would even say that he looked back to the NCC with much pleasure and pride. In growth of self-confidence and character development, he was the one who benefited. As someone who served alongside him, let Gerry Horner have the last word as he wrote in his letter of condolence when my dearest Jack passed away.

> *We must rejoice that he has now met the Lord whom he served so faithfully all his life and whom we firmly believe has even now accepted him into the place reserved for them who truly love Him . . . . I would like to add that he was a true Christian gentleman and that his own faith must have rubbed off on many others . . . . I shall always remember Jack as a "man's man."*

Gerry was in a position to speak. His witness to Jack's character all those years ago is precious to me now.

Time out for music. Jerry Horner takes the baton, but which one is Jack?

Jack in the Non Combatant Corps (NCC) during World War II.

The man who later had a No Smoking sign in his lobby, really did smoke a pipe then.

CHAPTER 5

JACK OF HEARTS
or
HOW JACK FINDS ROMANCE

A Meeting in the Bushes

As Jack entered the barracks one chilly March evening in 1944, his pal, Jack Ash, greeted him, "You're late tonight. A long-winded speaker then?"

Our Jack had just been to the midweek fellowship meeting in the Didcot Methodist church.

"No! I've been rescuing a damsel in distress." The line was guaranteed to raise interest.

"You know how dark it is outside the chapel. Well, as I went down the path after the meeting I heard a rustling in the bushes and someone calling out. It was a funny place for anyone to be so I stopped and looked around. There was this girl. I'd seen her in the church, and she said she'd got confused coming out of the light into the blackout. She said she'd missed the path and wandered into the bushes. I helped her out then I took her home. She's a nanny in the Day Nurseries in Aylesbury."

It was later that same week that private Ash sought out private Punton.

"You know those tickets for the show on Saturday? I've just got leave to go home for the weekend. Can you find someone else to take my place?"

Before private Punton had time to think private Ash went on, "What about that girl you met the other day?"

"Do you think she'll be interested?"

"Ask her and see."

Thus it was that the following afternoon a hesitant, though not unwilling young man in uniform found himself knocking at the door of a certain establishment in Aylesbury. The matron herself answered and graciously allowed Ms Ward to speak to her caller, even though it was within working hours.

In such fashion Margaret and Jack embarked on their first date. The show was a production of "Wild Violets." Somehow everything fell into place from the start. Jack was seated next to a harassed mother with a fretful little boy who was disturbing everyone around. After a while he took the child on his knee where he remained, contentedly quiet, for the rest of the evening. Margaret, who understood children, was impressed. She did not then know that the man beside her also loved children and had a reputation for being able to pacify a crying child just by holding it.

Within three months the young couple were engaged and planning to have six children of their own. They were married on January 1, 1945. They had one week on honeymoon in Blackpool before Jack returned to his unit and Margaret to the nursery. He was a month short of thirty-two and she was twenty-four.

There are three "incidentallies" to add to this story. For the first, Jack maintained all his life that Margaret deliberately wandered into those bushes and could see well enough to call out when he was passing. She would neither deny nor admit it and kept him guessing to the end. In the second incidentally, Jack and I both felt how fortuitous a coincidence it was that the first show he took me to see was also a production of "Wild Violets" being staged in Goole. The third incidentally was added when Jack Ash's widow died in January 2000, and their daughter wrote to let me know. The two Jacks had never lost touch.

An Engagement is Announced

When Jack announced his engagement his mother wrote and told him about his birth. Her letter recalled him to what he felt were his obligations. He had to tell Margaret. It might make a difference, if not to her then to her parents, especially her father whose views were forceful. With more heart searching than we shall ever know, Jack confided his secret to the girl he loved. Her response was almost an anticlimax.

"What does it matter? It makes no difference to me."

By this time Jack was actually weeping.

"You mean to say you'll still marry me?"

"Yes!"

Margaret had no doubts, and Jack was comforted. Already attitudes towards illegitimacy were subtly changing and were to do so even more rapidly in the postwar years. Margaret was a modern young lady. She had left home to earn her own living and to live her own life. She, like her father, had a mind of her own. Although happy for the man of her choice to observe convention and ask the father's permission to marry his daughter, she was not likely to acquiesce meekly were permission to be refused. Nor, for that matter was Jack.

There was no problem. Stephen Ward approved of his prospective son-in-law even before he met him. Perhaps in the less conventional society emerging during the war years the father sometimes worried about what kind of man his independent daughter would eventually choose. His fears were relieved when Jack introduced himself to his future mother and father-in-law by letter. It is worth quoting from Stephen's reply, dated June 25, 1944. Despite the circumlocutory style, his remarks are welcoming, but he deals with the issues closest to his own heart first.

> *It is always a matter of great interest for me to make the acquaintance of one who in any measure resists the government order to destroy human life . . .*

> *I rejoice that you, in this crisis, should have . . . refused the compulsion to do so. These events in our lives compel us to face up to certain issues, and happy is he who refuses to compromise his allegiance.*

These words were not platitudes. Stephen too was a conscientious objector and had gone to prison for his beliefs during the First World War. He was also a Christian and a good Methodist. He continues,

> *I fully endorse the tenor of your letter and emphasise that the best in life is to be found along the road where a knowledge of God, "the only true God and Jesus Christ whom He has sent," is made the controlling feature.*

Without doubt Jack was accepted as a man after Stephen's own heart.

> *Your announcement in the* [Methodist] *Recorder calls also for my pleasure, notwithstanding the fact that my information is still incomplete, but I have confidence that as my knowledge increases, my pleasure will not be lessened . . . . May be sooner than we think, we shall meet on more intimate terms when you shall discover my severity.*

Stephen's confidence was not misplaced. He liked and respected Jack. Although privately Jack confessed to being always a little scared of his stern father-in-law he met him on equal terms and refused to let it show. That too would be a mark in his favour. To this day nobody really knows what Stephen meant by his "severity."

A Word about the Wards

The Ward family hailed from a tiny scattered village on the north Cornwall coast called Crackington Haven. A narrow steep-sided valley cuts through the hills down to the sea, where it ends in a cliff embraced bay. The place is beautiful and isolated. Within the valley itself it remains almost as unspoilt today as it was all those years ago when Jack first saw it.

As teenagers, Margaret and her brothers, Raymond and Leonard, went to school in Bude. Though only eleven miles away, they stayed in digs during the week, such were the complications of travel in country districts before the family car became the norm. Margaret then trained as a children's nurse with the Methodist National Children's Homes before becoming a private nanny to the family of Major and Mrs Wigram. She moved about with them for a while until she went to the Aylesbury day nurseries near Didcot where Jack was stationed.

From childhood Margaret grew up to have a Christian faith of her own and while still in her teens became a Sunday school teacher. On one occasion she went to a conference for Sunday school teachers and left a diary of the proceedings. It was a spiritual highlight in her young life. As we also know, it was through her continued involvement in church life, even although she had left home, that she met Jack. In the difficult days before she died, the faith that she and Jack shared helped them both.

Margaret's upbringing was, as far as I know, happy but strict—too strict in her opinion. Being adventurous and freedom loving, she eagerly left home to experience what a wider world had to offer. The prospect of living in Yorkshire in those days—a long, expensive, and difficult journey from Crackington Haven—did not daunt her. She would have gone anywhere with Jack.

Stephen Ward was a clever man and an architect by profession. He also ran a small holding, mainly for poultry but with a few crops and livestock. Some people found him difficult and unapproachable. Jack's older children remember him as a distant old gentleman with whom you were on your best behaviour. I like Jack's story of how he once took his visiting father-in-law to see York Minster. Stephen's verdict, delivered with deep-voiced deliberation, was, "Jack, I am not impressed."

Returning to the "severity" issue—I wonder if Stephen was proud, and rightly so, of the strength of character which had put him into prison as a conscientious objector rather than deny his beliefs? It must have been a hard experience. Did this make him rather inflexible in later life? He certainly continued to express himself publicly, in talks and newspaper articles, about matters that concerned him, even if his views were considered unpopular. Perhaps what he had in mind in the allusion to his "severity" was this firm adherence to his principles and a refusal to be anything other than himself. I do not know and only form a judgement from the little I have heard about him, mainly from Jack, but also from a few things that he wrote which I have happened to see.

It also occurs to me that maybe, even in his own time, he was already a relic of a bygone era in an age which had moved on. If so, then sadly his values were no longer appreciated but were probably worth more than he was given credit for. What you must know is that Jack found him friendly and reasonable. Though he was somewhat in awe of him, he held him in esteem.

When Stephen died, his ashes were scattered to the sea from the Cornish cliffs. The gusting wind blew them back into the mourner's faces.

"Cussed to the last," was the comment of one of his sons. But then, sons can say such things.

Margaret's mother, Edie (Edith), was, according to photographs, a vivacious beauty in her youth. A history of the Oliver family with whom the Wards are connected records that she and her sister, Eva, were chatterboxes with bright, busy, outgoing natures. The match between Stephen and Edie was obviously an attraction of opposites. Sally, Edie's granddaughter, still possesses one of the love letters they sent each other in code. She did manage to decipher it, but it is not our business here to pry into its contents.

From her youth two of Edie's main interests were Sunday schoolwork and the church choir. As a Sunday school teacher she helped many of her pupils to gain distinctions in the scripture examinations of the Methodist circuit and district. She was also organist and leader of her church choir for many years and generally took an interest in community affairs. In addition, I believe that she acted as a correspondent on church matters for a local paper (or was it for the Methodist Recorder?) All in all she was an active lady with a great ability to cope and manage.

Jack held his mother-in-law in high affection. His impression was that she was an able lady of great warmth and some determination who managed her equally strong-minded husband with wifely skill. He always spoke of her with a smile, concluding simply,

"She was lovely."

In the final years of her life Edie's memory failed. They cared for her at home where she lived, increasingly unaware of people and her surroundings but apparently happy. Maybe she had a form of the then unheard of Alzheimer's Disease. It was sad. After a long illness she died at St Mary's Hospital, Launceston.

To conclude the word about the Wards, I must briefly mention Margaret's brothers. Both married and had families, providing a wide network of cousins for the Punton children.

Raymond worked for the post office most of his life and held a high position in his job. He spent some years in Nepal and in the Westward islands, helping them to set up an efficient postal system.

Leonard remained in Cornwall and continued for a long time to run his father's farm. Apart from being a first-class surfer, he had an encyclopaedic knowledge of local history and things Cornish and achieved the high honour of becoming a Bard of Cornwall.

A Wartime Wedding

War weddings were affairs of contrivance and ingenuity, chiefly because everything was in short supply and rationed. Everybody had two different-coloured ration books of specifically allocated coupons, one book for food and the other for clothes. You were allowed a tiny amount of butter, cheese, sugar, flour, jam, bacon, meat, bread, and other basic comestibles per week per person. The shopkeeper would carefully cut out the appropriate coupons—no perforated edges then—in exchange for goods. You could save your coupons and use them later, but once you had used them up nothing more was forthcoming.

Foods that we take for granted now were unavailable during and even after the war. For instance, I never saw an orange or a banana until I was seven. A fresh egg was a treat, unless you kept chickens. My mother mostly made do with dried egg powder. She reconstituted it with water, or milk if she could spare it, to make scrambled eggs. Pregnant and nursing mothers and young children had special allocations of things like powdered milk and concentrated orange juice.

I well visualise my mother mixing black tea into a Christmas cake starved of dried fruit and brown sugar to make it look darker. She also had a recipe for substitute marzipan using semolina and almond essence. Long after the war Jack's daughter Sally and her school friends gathered rose hips. They were collected from schools all over the country and processed to provide rose hip syrup, rich in vitamin C, for the health of the nation. The emphasis was not on luxuries but on maintaining health and survival.

To get ingredients for a wedding cake and to put on a simple reception meant hoarding the whole family's coupons for weeks beforehand as well as negotiating swaps with friends and relatives in exchange for something they might want. Our happy couple were married in Cornwall, and Margaret's parents arranged a family buffet at home. Having a farm, they probably managed better than most.

As for clothes, every article and length of material had its equivalent in coupons. A new suit or a wedding dress had to take up most of a year's allocation. You will understand, therefore, why one of Margaret's best friends, a Mrs Mary Law, wrote to me as follows when I asked her for some information about those days.

> *Margaret was my bridesmaid . . . as we were friends at school. Some months later the exigencies of rationing meant that Margaret wore my veil and headdress at her wedding and her bridesmaid wore the dress that Margaret herself had worn at mine.*

Neither Jack nor his bride-to-be had any money for an engagement ring, and the wedding ring was what was known as a utility one. The utility standard was imposed on all goods such as furniture, household equipment, and other common essentials. The standard was plain, serviceable, and uniform but by no means shoddy. It was not a question of whether you could afford something fancier or more luxurious but what was available in the shops, and the shops stocked utility items. A utility wedding ring was an unadorned band of metal containing a mixture of gold and a cheaper ore. Years later Jack wanted to buy his wife a better ring. She refused. The old one was precious. When she died he kept it amongst his treasures. He showed it to me with emotion one day. It was tarnished and movingly thin. How honoured I felt that he wanted me to see it.

Firstborn

After the honeymoon Margaret continued working, but Jack moved on from Didcot. However, they managed to see something of each other, though never enough. He once recounted an amusing incident from those days.

"Margaret was in lodgings with her friend and bridesmaid, Joyce. I went to see her and didn't notice how quickly the time passed with the result that I missed the last train back to camp. There was nowhere to stay so the two girls smuggled me into their room for the night where they shared a double bed. The three of us got in together, Margaret in the middle next to me, of course."

Joyce did not remember the occasion. Perhaps I am wrong and it involved someone else. Jack is not here to check with now.

Before long Margaret was pregnant and soon returned to Cornwall to await the birth of the baby. Whenever he had to leave Jack went to see her. He travelled to Bude with his bike in the guard's van, often arriving late on the last train. He still faced eleven miles to cycle along hilly, country roads in the cold and dark. He did not mind, especially after his daughter was born in February 1946.

The day before he died he was busy organising some hundreds of tiny, muddled up snapshots of all his children when young. I wheeled across and looked over his shoulder. He picked up the only professional print amongst them.

"What do you think of this, then? That's our first, my beautiful Sally. Isn't she lovely?"

I had seen the photo and heard the pride in his voice before. I recalled a recent occasion when Sally had accompanied him to a function which I was not well enough to attend. With the same note of pride he had said simply,

"I always love going out with Sally."

Indeed he loved going out and doing things with each one of his children for he thought the world of them all. He always claimed, and I am sure it was true, that he had no favourites. They were all different, and they were all precious in their own way. Yet surely there must be something unique about a firstborn which cannot be duplicated?

The pictures still lay on the table two days later, partly sorted. He never finished the task.

The Carlton Years

Round about June 1946 Jack went to Fulford Barracks in York to be demobbed. He had left Snaith five years earlier, a carefree bachelor. He returned home, a happy husband and proud father, though no longer entirely carefree for he possessed neither a house nor a job. These were his immediate priorities.

Unable to find accommodation in Snaith he eventually rented a cottage in neighbouring Carlton, two miles away. Workwise, Mr Hinsley who had employed him briefly before the war, took him on again as a jobbing carpenter. As the story of how Jack earned a living is told in the "Jack of All Trades" chapter, I need say little more on this subject at this stage. All you need to know is that he was poorly paid, and the job had no prospects. Dead end or not, it was a job, and it was a start.

The house had three small bedrooms, a sitting room and a decent-sized living room. There was also a small scullery where Margaret cooked and did the washing, by hand of course. As a matter of fact, the family washed themselves there too for they had no bathroom. They could boast only one tap for the whole house and nothing but cold water. Every drop of water for all purposes was boiled on the big range which though in the scullery also efficiently heated the family living room.

Within eight years there were five small children in the house. Imagine the problems! Disposable nappies, for instance, were unheard of. Mothers used white terry towelling squares and giant safety pins. Sometimes they added an inner square of soft muslin to be more gentle on tender bottoms.

They soaked the dirty nappies for a few hours before scrubbing and boiling them. They then hung them out to dry, preferably in the sun because of the bleaching powers of sunlight. It was a matter of pride and much labour for women to get their nappies pristine white. A mother with stained nappies on the line was considered to be a poor housewife and slovenly. For many a year the Punton household had its quota of buckets and daily full lines.

Once a week all the pans and kettles came into use. It was bath night. Jack carried the big zinc bath in from the outhouse and set it before the living room fire. I say "big." It was oval, with handles and only with some contortion could an average-sized adult sit in it, knees drawn up to the chin. A mere two or three inches of water lapped one's lower quarters, and the kettles were kept warm on the hobs for top-ups. Jack often told me about bath night in Carlton and how, when the children were finished and tucked up in bed, he and Margaret took their turn, washing each other's backs and enjoying the moments of intimacy before the warm fire.

Potties are now collectors' items and serve to display plants or flowers. In the days when few homes had a bathroom or indoor toilet, they were essential household utensils, hidden under every bed. During the day, of course, you visited the shed at the bottom of the garden. The old ashpit of Jack's childhood was mostly a thing of the past but the arrangements were only marginally more savoury. The wooden seat with the hole was still there but underneath fitted the "elsan" bucket. The "elsan" contained a quantity of strong-smelling disinfectant which only in part masked less unpleasant odours.

The sanitation men emptied the elsan once a week, by which time it was pretty full, especially as the family grew. They came around, not with the horse and cart of the ashpit days but a lorry covered in at the back. Either way it was not a pleasant job. If an overflow was imminent, Jack himself would have to dig a deep hole somewhere and bury the contents. Some houses had two buckets and two seats side by side, a chummy and practical convenience for the larger family.

In place of the exceedingly inabsorbent "san izal" toilet rolls of the day, poor households cut old newspapers into squares. You crinkled them up before you used them in a futile effort to make them softer. The print smudged blackly over your fingers and on to other parts of your anatomy. The most annoying thing was to read part of an article on one square and then go through all the others in vain, seeking the end of the story. Why was that snippet of news always so riveting? And how come you missed it when you read the newspaper intact?

Despite the fact that the arrangements now sound so primitive, they were commonplace then. The house was adequate for a young family which was just as well for, if you remember, Mr and Mrs Punton had set their sights on six children. Sally was followed by John in September 1947, then Jane in July 1949, Ruth in July 1951, and Simon in April 1954. Joyce, who arrived in September 1956, was not born in Carlton, and often regrets that she does not share some memory of those happy years. Neither does Simon. He was only two when they left.

Make Do and Mend

Jack constantly talked to me, and in detail, about his early life. Some things I visualise most clearly from my own distant experience as a child. In one house where we lived we had an elsan toilet in the garden and an old tin bath in front of the fire, a kitchen range and even water that Dad had to pump up every morning out of our own well. At the same time, I am greatly indebted to Jane, Jack's daughter, for many things in this and the following chapter. When I was asking the family for childhood memories, Jane wrote to me as follows:

> In 1985 I had to write an "Autobiography of Childhood" for a college class when I was thinking of becoming a social worker . . . . It was never meant for anyone but myself and the teacher . . . . Read it and use it in any way you like . . . .

Jane's record is intimate and reveals much about herself as well as the Punton family life. It immediately gave me a framework for the only two chapters of this book which I did not know how to tackle. I gladly accept her offer and quote extensively from her work as I try to bring together memories from all the family, including Jack, to make a unified account.

How the young parents managed is hard to say. Jack did odd jobs for people in his spare time, but money was tight and they struggled. The wartime trend of women going out to work continued, but there was no question of

Margaret doing this. She had plenty to do at home, and neither she nor Jack approved of a mother working while the children were little.

Fortunately Margaret was a great manager. In part this came naturally to her but in part she had learned the necessary skills of coping from Edie, her own mother. It is worth noting also that rationing was only phased out during the midfifties, which did not make life easy for anyone in the immediate postwar years, even if they had money. Jane says,

> *We had no money and we lacked nothing . . . . Mum cooked, did laundry and baked cakes and cookies* [Jane now lives in America where biscuits are called cookies]. *I loved to scrape the bowl when it was my turn. Next best was to lick the wooden spoon . . . . We fetched our milk from a local farm, sloshing it on the street as we carried it home, fresh and warm from the cow.*

> *We ate a lot of porridge (which I hate to this day) and a lot of bread and jam* [It is the syrup sandwiches that John drools over]. *Fish and chips, sausage, beans and mashed potatoes were other staples and on Sunday after chapel we always had a joint with roast potatoes and Yorkshire pudding and a vegetable. Nothing came in tins or packages in those days, at least not to our house.*

I imagine that if Margaret was like my own mother, even the fish and chips would be prepared at home. It was so much cheaper to bread or batter your own fish and cut and deep fry your own chips than buying from a shop. Not only did hungry mouths have to be filled. Growing bodies had to be covered. Jane continues.

> *Mum made all our clothes. She was the cleverest woman I ever met in the practical sense. All my life she conserved, made do, improvised and always with admirable success. She unravelled knitted garments with holes that could no longer be darned and knitted them into new and colourful sweaters. She removed buttons, snaps and zippers* [press studs and zips] *before condemning a garment to the rag bag, and made floor rugs with the rags or sewed them into patchwork.*

> *She made cushions and beautiful, lined curtains. She made basket work and caned chairs, covered couches with pleats and piping and every stitch perfect and invisible. I never remember a time when she sat with her hands lying idle. The most beautiful dresses I ever wore were her own creations, handworked with embroidery, smocking, tucks, pleats and trimmings.*

119

Jack was particularly proud of Margaret's smocking. His home was filled with furnishings she had made. They were a source of comfort in the long years after he lost her. I never wanted him to get rid of things which meant so much to him and the family—apart, that is, from some curtains which were full of holes and the odd disintegrating cushion.

Having noted Jane's praise of her mother's gifts I am left wondering what Jack thought privately of my efforts to knit him a fair isle waistcoat. I used to knit a lot, but for the first time I used a circular needle and the waistcoat went wrong. We have a photo of me standing in front of Jack and the garment round us both. We considered sending the waistcoat to Pavarotti.

As the eldest, Sally did occasionally get something new from a shop. Any such clothes had to be serviceable and large so they could pass down to Jane and even Ruth. The Harris Tweed coat was one unfortunate example. It was plain, long, and clumsy; and Sally had set her heart on something feminine, fashionable, and short. The treat was spoiled.

It is always sad to hear, as we often do, of mothers who cannot manage on the means they have. I feel that the problem is not really lack of money so much as lack of basic cooking and sewing skills. Be that as it may, Jane concludes,

> *I look at modern conveniences and kitchen appliances and I look back in utter astonishment that my mother could do a better job with nothing and eight children (two foster brothers joined the family later) than a modern housewife could do with everything and with only two children.*

Humour and Drama

The Carlton home, though poor in material matters, was happy and filled with fun and drama too.

"Where's Daddy?" asked the young Sally on one occasion, to which her mother replied,

"He's making a hen run for Dr McGranahan."

Now Dr McGranahan, who will be featured again in a later chapter, was the village doctor who lived down the road. Sally, of course, was still unable to pronounce his name properly, but Jack always recalls the shine in her eyes when he came in and she rushed up to him gleefully asking, "Daddy, did you make Dr McG—'s hen run very fast?"

Chickens, a cockerel to be exact, played a part in Jane's day once.

> *Our house was rented from Farmer Smith who kept hens and roosters on the property. There was a haystack and behind it a barn. I remember*

playing in there and sliding down the haystack. I have a vivid memory of when I was about three or four and the rooster flew from the fence on to my head. I screamed in terror and Mum came running out. She got the rooster off my head and shamed me for my panic.

Actually a fierce cock could be dangerous to a child. One of our cocks in Shetland began attacking my brother when he was little. I am afraid he finished up in the pot—the bird, that is. My brother is still around.

One day Jack was working on the roof and putting up a flag to mark the 1953 coronation. Whilst his back was momentarily turned, the two-year-old Ruth was up the ladder as high as the guttering. He hardly dared move or call lest he disturb her. Eventually, with Margaret standing below braced to catch, he carefully climbed up and brought his unconcerned toddler safely down. It is still Ruth who does the parachute and bungee jumps today.

Then there was the time when Uncle Raymond came to stay. Jack and Raymond were carrying baby John in his carry-cot. As they set him down, one of them released the handle too soon. Out rolled John, right into a puddle.

Another day three-year-old Jane disappeared. Her panicking parents searched the village until a neighbour met them and asked, "Is that your little girl with a doll's pram halfway to Snaith?"

It was. Always independent, she had set off to visit Granny Punton who was a favourite with her grandchildren.

Daisy, the donkey, is another cherished part of Carlton life. Older Snaithites still tell me of the cart Jack made and how he would come into town with Daisy pulling the children in the cart behind her.

Daisy was a character and confident of her place in the family affections. One day, as Margaret sat sewing by the window, Daisy saw her. In anticipation of a titbit, the delighted donkey bounded up to her mistress—and right through the casement. Despite glass everywhere, no one was hurt. Talking of titbits, sometimes the offerings proffered were less than palatable. John and Sally once fed her a series of pages from an old magazine. Daisy happily munched the lot and with no identifiable ill effects.

The memories go on, vivid and joyous, and yet the family roots are firmly elsewhere.

Time to Make a Move

By 1956 the sixth and last baby was on the way. It was time to move. Although Jack had already begun to branch out for himself in business, it was only with a financial struggle that he bought two cottages in the Snaith High Street. They had been the gardeners' cottages for the big house now known as the Brewer Arms, on the Pontefract Road. Mrs Eadon, who formerly owned the estate, including the glass houses where so long before Jack and his pals had gorged on forbidden fruits, had long gone. Today, even the orchards have disappeared, and an insignificant cul-de-sac of modern bungalows curves into the old grounds.

The Puntons moved in April 1956, hence the name for their new home, April Cottage. Jack was back, only a few hundred yards from his birthplace and now diagonally opposite the sturdy Priory Church of St Laurence. Official records list 15 High Street as a "middle to early eighteenth century property." Jack and I were told that it was probably once a single farmhouse and only converted into cottages later. One thing for sure, it has character, with its massive, centrally placed chimney breast, wooden beams supporting low ceilings, and timber baulks beneath the roof.

The front door opens straight on to the High Street pavement, which apparent drawback was capitalised upon by the Punton kids. Lying in wait upstairs behind open windows on "mischief" night, they tipped water on to their unsuspecting "trick or treat" callers below.

At the back stretches a narrow long garden. Towards the end of the garden was a well, a common feature in this low-lying landscape where the water table is close to the surface. For instance, the Brewers Arms' well which is actually inside the house, is floodlit to reveal the skeleton (plastic, we hope) at the bottom. Jack wanted no mishaps with his well. He immediately filled it in.

Joyce arrived in September, 1956. How did Margaret cope with five very lively youngsters, a baby shortly due, and a far-from-simple move? Fortunately she had straightforward pregnancies, and she was a fit lady, but it was no easy time as Jane tells us.

Dad knocked down walls, moved doors, took out stairs and chimneys, put in stairs, replaced concrete floors, and our two houses became one, four bedroomed house. For a long time we lived in dust and climbed over piles of bricks and rubble. The budgie died of dust inhalation and we never had another caged bird in the house after that.

I am told that for some time the only way upstairs was by ladder and a hole in the ceiling. Jack carried the little ones up and down for bed and, after Ruth's earlier escapade with a ladder, took what safety measures he could. There were no accidents.

The toilet was down the yard but it flushed. Later Dad made one of the wash houses (an extension adjoining the back of the house) into a bathroom and the toilet moved indoors at last.

One of the attics was unusable . . . but the other became a fifth bedroom. When Sally was in her teens the garden shed became her bedroom, one of the most coveted . . . in the house. [Jack insulated and decorated it then ran electricity across.] *It was necessary because we added two Nigerian boys to our family. They were Dapo and Bayo, aged seven and six, and they were our foster brothers.*

April Cottage became home from the moment they all entered the front door. The temporary inconvenience of the renovations was worth it. The hardworking parents eventually had the place as they wanted it—and not only in terms of bricks and mortar. Together they reared their brood in happiness and security. The house still exudes a joysome, wholesome feeling. Having lived in over seventeen houses I recognise atmosphere, good and bad. Knowing nothing about April Cottage or the Punton family, I sensed the pervading contentment from the moment Jack ushered me into his domain to partake of "afternoon tea."

What more should I tell you? Jack paved most of the back garden. It made a great play area, so much so that he was soon putting up wire meshing to protect his windows from misplaced balls. Simon told me of some of their games, circuses and fire engines which, for reasons best known to those playing, involved climbing up on to the new bathroom roof. Only in later years did Margaret manage to reclaim the garden for her own plants and flowers and a pretty pond.

Inside, a downstairs room became a play and get-together area. Jack fixed a green board to one wall. It practically covered the whole space. The younger children drew on it. The older members of the family chalked up messages and left reminders of homework assignments or household chores.

The Wade children next door were of a similar age to the Puntons. Soon the two families were on close terms. They still are and, thanks to e-mail, remain regularly in touch from places as far distant as America and Australia. One day Mummy Wade came to Margaret saying, "I have to tell you something. My little girl just told me that she did a wee in Mummy Punton's wardrobe."

Mummy Punton was not put out by the information. She had handled worse things in her time, and she knew children. Indeed, as their own little ones began to grow up both Jack and Margaret were thinking ahead. They had so much to offer, and they could not visualise life without children. And this brings me now to Dapo and Bayo.

Dapo and Bayo

The advert in the Methodist Recorder read,

Long term foster parents required for two attractive but deprived Nigerian boys who need a sympathetic home.

The outcome of the story was that the Selby *Gazette* and *Herald* for October 28, 1966, featured an article entitled "Dapo and Bayo Make It Family of Eight." The accompanying photograph shows Jack with two black boys on his knee, flanked by Margaret and their own three youngest children all holding guinea pigs. Already Sally and John were at college and Jane was obviously busy elsewhere. Jack, by the way, was just a teeny bit put out that the paper put his age as fifty-eight. Carefully he wrote beside the offending statement, "mistake, I am fifty-three."

It was no mistake that he and Margaret chose to foster Nigerian children. The colour problem was a topical issue at that time when we had a lot of immigration into our country from places like the West Indies. Those were the days when MP Enoch Powell was making his controversial speeches opposing such large-scale immigration. A lot of British people agreed with him and feared that the incomers were taking much needed jobs from our own citizens. The *Gazette* and *Herald* article therefore opens thus.

A Snaith lay preacher and his wife have become foster parents to two Nigerian children as a "small contribution to the fight against racial prejudice."

Later on Jack is reported as saying,

We are both colour blind in this respect. We have talked about this for quite a long time and in fact, when my family asked me what I wanted for Christmas, I said "two black babies"—so they bought me a black doll.

Dapo and Bayo were born in Lagos. Dapo was seven and Bayo six when they arrived in Snaith. Their mother, Kathryn, was only twenty-three and separated from her husband. Although she lived in London, Jack and Margaret gave her as much emotional support and parenting as they could, along with her sons.

The *Gazette* article, written some three weeks after the boys came to Snaith went on,

> *The day after they arrived they started . . . school and the day after that they were calling the Puntons "Mummy" and "Daddy."*
>
> *"They are settling in smashing," said forty-six-year-old Mrs Punton. "They are both getting to be very popular indeed. There is no hint of prejudice anywhere although this did worry us at first. People have been overwhelming in their kindness and both Dapo and Bayo love it here."*

I understand that one of the few references to colour ever made came simultaneously from both boys themselves.

"The Brownies are having a jumble sale," said Margaret. "Have you children any toys we can donate?"

"Brownies?" queried Dapo and Bayo in unison. "Do you mean like us?"

The only disadvantage of their dark skins was that if they got into mischief they were easy to spot. Otherwise there was no colour prejudice in Snaith. Even now, people who were at school with them still ask for news and with genuine affection.

Settling in and Beyond

Up to this time Simon and Joyce had shared a bedroom. Now Joyce moved out to make room for the newcomers. In one sense it was already necessary for she was ten and Simon twelve. She was also glad to do so because, as she explained,

"Simon could 'torture' them, not me. He used to try to put my legs behind my neck and it hurt."

In another sense the timing of her move out was perhaps not ideal. As the youngest, it suddenly gave her a feeling of insecurity and being usurped. She could not analyse her reactions, but at bedtime on that first night she burst into tears. Margaret understood all too well and reassured her. Joyce soon adapted. Simon recalls how at first she constantly wanted to touch her new brothers and their crinkly hair. She had never seen anything like it.

Under Margaret's wise guidance the family opened their arms and took Dapo and Bayo to their hearts. In the interview with the *Gazette* and *Herald* she had already stated her policy clearly.

This is a family adoption and not just a mother and father's adoption.

Everyone had a part to play in making the venture work, including the boys as well. As long as they were in the Punton menage, and that could be for years, even into adulthood, they would be treated exactly as their own flesh and blood.

The newcomers had barely settled in when Mr R—y from the Welfare Department knocked at the door. Mr R—y had come to check the facilities. Where, for instance, were the boys sleeping? Margaret showed him. Mr R—y disapproved.

"Foster children are not allowed to sleep in the same room as your own children. They must have their own room."

"But now they are here they are my children and will be treated as such."

Poor Mr R—y was not to know that Margaret loved (within reason) a scrap. This time, however, she was angry.

"These boys are part of my family, and I will not segregate them from my own children in any way."

Mr R—y could do nothing. The arrangement was totally private. He tried another line. This was not fostering, he maintained. It was undertaking care for reward. He implied that the Puntons might be in for trouble. He had no case. No money had changed hands and never did. If Jack and Margaret received the state children's allowance for their charges, and I have no idea if they did or did not, that was all. They paid for everything from their own resources. I might add that these resources were not as flush as some imagined. True, Jack's business was prospering but out of it he now had eight young people to support and the older ones to see through college. There was not much to spare.

As a matter of interest, it was not the first time Mr R—y had clashed with Margaret. Once, when a local lady became ill, Margaret took care of her twins. The welfare officer called and told her that he had already made other provisions for the twins and had come to take them away. She refused to let them go. She had promised their mother to look after them and as long as that was what the mother wanted she would keep her promise. Mr R—y was not pleased, and as a result it would appear that he used his influence to block Jack and Margaret from fostering other children and also prejudiced other local councils against them. Margaret wrote to the papers. But that is not really part of the present story. With Dapo and Bayo she had her own way.

There was another problem, not so easily handled. As a result of early experiences, the brothers were disturbed and especially Bayo. Dapo soon responded to cuddles and judicious handling. Bayo found it much harder either to give or receive affection, although he loved Lenny, the cat, with passion. On the surface he appeared happy and reasonably well integrated, but deep inside he was hurting, and it came across to those most closely involved with him. It showed at night in persistent bed-wetting.

Nowadays help and counselling are available. Then Margaret and Jack struggled alone, barely aware how deeply their little boy was scarred. Margaret tried everything, reasoning, ignoring, scolding, cajoling. Above all she never lost patience during the years it took for Bayo to grow out of the problem. At least, by this time she had a washing machine, purchased when Jack received a small legacy just sufficient for the cost.

When Kathryn reached her thirties, she felt that she would like to have her sons back. They were in their early teens, hardly the best age for another major change in their lives. Everybody was upset. Jack drove them down to London. Bayo sat in the back, apparently asleep with his head on Simon's chest. When he moved, Simon suddenly realised that his jumper was quite soaked through with his brother's tears.

Both Dapo and Bayo have done well in life. Most recently Dapo studied Japanese, got himself a Japanese girlfriend, and went out to work in Japan. Bayo went to Oxford University. He is now something big in the financial world of New York. Sadly, their links with Jack lessened over the years, but only latterly did they lose touch completely. He tried to trace them but to no avail. He never said much, it was not his way. I know he was hurt inside.

Somehow Jack often felt that he and Margaret had failed with the only children they were ever privileged to foster long term. They had planned to do so much for so many needy children. In the end it was not to be, and yet maybe they achieved more than they realised. Bayo once visited Jane in America. She found him a much softer, caring man. How glowingly he spoke to her of what Jack and Margaret had meant to him. Who knows where Dapo and Bayo would be today, or in what case, were it not for the loving security they received in April Cottage?

Treadmill of Toil and Routine

By the time of the move to April Cottage Jack's business ventures were starting to prosper. Nevertheless, it took all his energies to provide for family needs. Often he started work at seven in the morning and did not finish until late evening, especially if he had bookkeeping to do at home. A telling diary entry for New Year's Day 1957 reads,

> *It is the twelfth anniversary of our wedding day. It is not much different from any other day. Work, meals, work.*

There was little respite. Am I right in saying that in those days New Year was not an official holiday for anyone? He was not complaining. He rarely did. At the same time he got tired and Margaret too. Obviously it was one of those days that we all know too well, as a continuation of the diary extract indicates.

> *The day began and ended with rain. Not many sweet tempers about through lack of sleep. I guess we are all too tired to be at our best. Such is life!*

"Such is life." This was Jack's great expression of assent to the vagaries of existence. Always he tried cheerfully to accept what came, good or bad, and he expected his share of both.

On January 2, someone came to babysit. Jack writes,

> *Margaret and me at Norwood's* [the friend mentioned in chapter 3] *until eleven o'clock. Time seemed to go very quickly but it was nice to have an evening out together without the rebels.*

The week moved on.

> [Friday] *Sally went to the dentist at Goole . . . Margaret developing cold.* [Sunday] *Margaret and children went to chapel a.m. I cooked dinner etc. I went . . . in evening . . . .* [Monday] *Margaret cold worse . . . . Margaret in bed all day. Children looked after house while I attended to a few jobs.*

Does anything on the domestic scene really change? One thing was sure for this couple, whatever the ups and downs of daily life they supported each other. She did what she could to encourage him in his growing business. He helped in the home and would change a nappy or bath a child on request. For the record I did not need anyone to tell me that. On one occasion I reluctantly sought his help with dressing. As he bent over to put on my stockings I braced myself for a fumbled attempt, feeling it might be easier to struggle on alone. Not at all. His touch was sure. He washed my hair. His hands were experienced. Suddenly I saw him as a father, adroitly manipulating wriggling bodies with a practised skill which had never left him.

At the same time he was easygoing and in the home Margaret was boss. Mostly he left her to organise affairs and exert the discipline. Occasionally, very occasionally his spouse protested.

"Jacky," his weary wife implored one evening, "I wish that for once you'd tell these children to go to bed. I'm tired of shouting at them."

Her obliging better half immediately complied, meekly saying,

"Come on, you kids. You heard what your mother said. Go to bed now."

Poor Margaret! All she wanted was for Jack to sound fierce and grab the ring leader by the scruff of the neck and haul him (or her as the case may be) upstairs. She ground her teeth and battled on. Where had romance gone?

Both parents worked hard and often sacrificially to rear their brood. Sometimes they went without things, especially in the early days, to provide for their little ones. They did not mind. They managed, and they were well content for the most part.

Romance Lives On

"Do you still love me?"

The question was unexpected but it was serious.

Jack replied, "Of course I do. Why do you ask?"

"You never tell me that you love me these days."

Jack thought hard. Maybe it was true. They were both so busy and often hardly had leisure to eat properly. They were rarely alone together except at night and then they were both so weary they fell asleep at once. At least, he did. Finally he responded.

"You know I'm not one for saying a lot, but everything I do is for you and the children. I can't show my love in any greater way."

Margaret understood. She had never really doubted, but femalelike, she did enjoy being told. There and then they promised that, however busy they were, they would say how much they loved each other once a day.

Regarding the decorating and joinery side of Jack's business, work soon came in for he was well liked and known to be reliable and reasonably priced. One particular lady with a large house and comfortable means often employed him or his workmen. Twice she asked him for a lift to Goole when he had to go there for materials. Once he arrived to find her prancing round the house in a skimpy swimsuit. He did not know where to look. From what Jack told me I do not doubt that the lady, though married, was making a play for him. He, who was friendly with everyone and expected the best in people, had no idea what was happening until one day Margaret confronted him.

"Everyone says you're having an affair with Mrs—. Are you?"

Jack was totally taken aback. Yes, the lady in question was friendly. She had given him a lot of valuable work, and he was grateful for that. But an affair?

The idea had never entered his mind. He did not like the thought of such a rumour going round.

"Well," said his wife, "are you? People are saying that you are."

"And what do you think?" asked Jack at last. He felt hurt and sad.

"Do you believe it?"

"No!"

His heart lightened.

"But I don't trust that woman one little bit."

"I don't care whether you trust her or not. She doesn't matter. What does matter is whether you trust me. Do you?"

Margaret did and Jack was satisfied. Their marriage was good.

By temperament Jack was quiet, relaxed, and, to use a current expression, laid-back. Margaret was more vocal and tense. She loved an argument, and her quick mind coped well with the cut and thrust of opposing viewpoints. Jack's mental reflexes moved more slowly. He preferred to keep his ideas to himself lest he appear foolish. According to her husband, Margaret hated to be proved wrong or found at fault. By the same token and still according to Jack, she would easily flare if provoked. Actually, Jack was not someone you could argue or quarrel with. Even before our marriage he told me that he disliked both. Rather than be drawn into either, he would, he said, go quiet and get away quickly.

The children, as children in a happy home do, took their parents' characters and relationship for granted and were never disillusioned. True, their everyday world centred round their mother who was totally available, night or day. Only in adulthood did they fully realise how surely their father's dependable strength had undergirded their lives. Margaret always knew.

In this connection, a conversation I once had with Joyce is interesting. She was only twenty-one when her mother died at the early age of fifty-seven. Something which helped to console her in that tragedy was how she began to know her dad in new ways as she started to relate to him in a manner she had never done so before. Maybe others in the family understand what she means.

I close this chapter with a final diary quote from Jack for the date February 2, 1963.

> *Today I am fifty years old. I feel it is a day worth recording. The children think it's wonderful that their Dad is fifty years old. I think it is too. I feel so happy that I have such a wonderful family. Every one of them this morning gave me a birthday card and a little present. Little did I know what was in store for me later when they presented me with a projector and screen . . . .*

Apart from a few twinges now and again and a bit of stiffness about the joints I feel no different than I did twenty odd years ago. I guess I am one of the lucky ones, or is it luck? I think it is something more than luck. It is my faith in and my love for God that has given me all this. I used to pray often that I would one day meet a girl who I could love and marry and have a family. She seemed a long time coming but she came and now we are just what I dreamed about.

Romance still lived on!

Wedding group with Margaret's family, January 1, 1945.

Austerity wedding breakfast. How many food coupons did it take to make the cake?

Young Sally with David the donkey.

Setting up home in Carlton.

CHAPTER 6

JACK AND JILL
or
HOW JACK AND HIS JILL CLIMBED THE FAMILY HILL

A Christian Foundation

As real Christians, Jack and Margaret reared their offspring in the traditional ways of Sunday school, chapel attendance, Bible stories, and bedtime prayers. Once of age, of course, people make their own decisions. I feel it is true to say that all the Punton children have, to some extent, questioned conventional Christianity. Their attitudes now vary from a selective acceptance of basic tenets to a free thinking approach. Some continue to attend churches of various persuasions, and others go rarely. All maintain high ethical principles and a caring way of life.

However orthodox the parents' religious instruction may be, children get their own ideas of what it is all about, as we learn from Jane.

I'm not sure what death meant to me. I believed in God who was in heaven in the sky, with angels all around him. It was golden and bright but nothing was happening and it was boring—not a place to rush off to if you could stay with Mum and Dad. God could see everything, my

Dad told me, and he heard everything and even knew what we were thinking. I felt very uneasy, hiding under the bedclothes and knowing it didn't do any good because God could see right through my pyjamas.

Every night in unison Sally, John and I and later Ruth said our prayer.

> *"Gentle Jesus meek a mile,* *
> *Look upon a little child,*
> *Pity mice in Plicity,* *
> *Suffer me to come to thee."*
> [*and mild and my simplicity]

> *"God bless Mummy, Daddy,*
> *Sally, John, Jane, and Ruth and*
> *make us all good children,*
> *for Jesus' sake. Amen."*

Sunday was my least favourite day. We had to go to chapel at 10:30 (Methodist) and Sunday school in the afternoon. Then came the good part, when we went for a walk together in the woods and lanes, and the evening was mellow, we played mah-jong or one of our many board games.

On our drives into the country, Jack often pointed out to me some of their old walking routes. Sadly, we could not retrace them with a wheelchair. For him, Sunday was a welcome day of rest from weekly toil when he could enjoy his family. True, he had his preaching engagements, but they were a pleasure and a foil to his everyday routine. If he sometimes left Margaret and the children picnicking in the woods in order to take an evening service, he would be home to join the fun later.

Jane's memories of chapel and the cycle of the religious year continue, although Easter and Whitsun get chronologically transposed in her rush of recollection.

> *I liked the singing at chapel but the sermon seemed so long. It was fifteen minutes! We had Sunday school anniversary at Whitsun and we all had new "best" dresses made for the occasion. I liked the sad hymns of Palm Sunday, for the tunes more than the verse, and Easter was an event. We each had a big, hollow egg wrapped in colourful foil . . . . We saved, smoothed it out with a fingernail, and used it in our play.*

Harvest festival was a special occasion in September and the chapel was beautiful—decorated with all the good things of autumn and sheaves of wheat, and we sang our harvest hymns. In summer there were church bazaars and outings by chartered bus to the seaside.

Happy Christmas

Christmas was one of the best times of the year. Undoubtedly the Christian significance of the nativity story was important in this family, yet who would be surprised if the youngsters focused on presents and food and maybe a trip to the pantomime during the season?

One year, all the clan visited Lewis's department store in Leeds as a treat and to see Santa Claus. The place was crowded with happy shoppers whilst the background strains of familiar carols flooded the air. So delightful was the music that Jack made enquiries and bought the record *Bells of Christmas*. Every Christmas of our five years together, it came out, as it had done for so long; and he played it yet again. Each time he faithfully told me the story of their memorable Christmas outing.

We all probably feel that the preparations for such a festival and the anticipation are almost as special as the day itself. At least they last longer. Young hands hung decorations round the house. Special baking provided bowls and spoons aplenty to be scraped and licked. Sixpenny pieces went into the Christmas pudding to be eagerly looked for at the eating thereof. Cooking smells intermingled with the crinkle of wrapping paper and conspiratorial whispers or furtive movements concerning presents. How thrilling it all was! Says Jane,

We trimmed the tree a week before Christmas [Ruth thinks they only decorated it on Christmas Eve. What does it matter, so long as there was a tree at all?] *We saved up our pocket money for inexpensive, precious, little gifts for each family member and whichever old and lonely people we'd have to tolerate with an almost genuine goodwill on Christmas day.*

We hung our stockings (Dad's socks) on the mantelpiece and pinned our names and requests on them. The atmosphere was warm, bright, cosy, loving, and exciting and we went to bed dreaming of reindeer on the

roof and hoping the fire would be out before Father Christmas came down the chimney.

The first to wake up . . . would reach in the dark to the foot of the bed and grope for the fat, crinkly sock, then hold it and feel it, guessing its contents, thrilled to our bones because Santa had been. We tiptoed to Mum and Dad's room and stood in the dark. Mum was awake in an instant . . . . At 4:00 a.m., she'd say, "It's too soon. Go back to bed." At 5:00 a.m., "Sh! Climb in. We'll wait for the others."

One by one they'd appear until six of us (eight after Dapo and Bayo came) were in and on the bed or on the floor. Each little novelty gift was individually wrapped—annual treats like chocolate coins, tubes of plastic bubbles, and twisty balloons. Then cups of tea . . . the queen's Christmas broadcast turned up loud on the radio [or wireless in those days] *while John, the family clown, insisted we all stand and salute* [or was it Jack who suggested the salute? Again, what does it matter when everyone is happy?].

Morning carol service at the chapel led onto a turkey dinner along with all the trimmings with the once-a-year luxury of real orange juice to drink. Do not forget that the Puntons were still poor and many things that are commonplace now were still scarce and luxury items then. After, and only after the washing up was done, everyone gathered in the sitting room. It is worth digressing here to explain that in those days sitting rooms were hardly used except on Sundays or for special occasions and to entertain visitors. Most houses had large kitchens which people lived in for everyday purposes. It is the all-pervading cult of the TV which has brought the sitting room into use as the main family living room.

Beside the gaily decorated tree in the best room of April Cottage, the old zinc bath came into its own once more. I gather that John still has this family heirloom somewhere in a junk room behind his shop. This time it contained the main presents from each other and relatives. Each gift was opened one at a time amidst anxious looks from the giver, quickly dispelled by hugs and kisses from the recipient. This went on for about five hours. In modern terms, the presents were small—records, board games, books, jigsaws, a cuddly or mechanical toy, a box of paints, and a painting book. Happiness, however, was not measured in size and cost but in love and togetherness. Even had the items exchanged been smaller and fewer, contentment and security would have been undiminished.

Beside the Seaside

Six months later came the next great treat of the year, the summer holidays. Traditionally, Yorkshire folks went to Bridlington or Scarborough for their summer holidays. A lot still do. Not so the Puntons!

> *We drove three hundred and fifty miles to Mum's home in Cornwall and we camped in a field by a stream. It was at Crackington Haven, a part of the jagged Cornish coast with its coves and smugglers' caves, its pounding surf and windswept cliffs. It was in our blood and we loved it with a passion only the child can feel.*

Early visits were budget-stretched affairs in cramped, leaky tents with a primus stove for cooking. As finances improved, so did the camping equipment, eventually running to luxury bedroom tents with a kitchen area and sophisticated cooking facilities. At one time they also had a caravan. As numbers grew, Jack bought a minibus. That way there was even space for the dog, although nobody had reckoned on her giving birth to a litter of pups on the journey. As if eight of their own were not enough, they usually took a couple of holiday children in addition. These generally came from London. They met their guests at Plymouth or Exeter railway station and delivered them back at the end of the fortnight. Even the minibus got crowded. Jack once said, "When we arrived at a campsite late one evening, we caused such a stir that all the campers came out of their tents to see what was happening. I think they thought Billy Smart's circus had come." It was the same if the holiday funds managed to run to a Cornish cream tea in a cafe. "We could just about fill a small tea room on our own. We persuaded waitresses to let us put tables together, and we more or less took over, usually to the amusement of other clients."

The best part of Cornwall was being with Uncle Leonard and Auntie Evelyn and cousins Trish and Ivor. Leonard continued to run his father's farm. He offered his nephews and nieces sixpence for every chicken they plucked. Sixpence in the old currency then purchased a big bag of chips or bar of chocolate. Its present equivalent of two and a half pence can buy pretty well nothing. He also let them try their hand, not very successfully, at milking cows. Margaret took them all on long treks and to her favourite places. Jane records,

> *We picked mushrooms and blackberries and went long, rambling walks while Mum named every wild flower and grass, every shell, and every*

seaweed . . . . Auntie Evelyn made junket with nutmeg, served clotted cream and scones and milk straight from the cow . . . . We envied them for living there all year.

They played team games and camp games. Jack's favourite was "spinny plate." You spun a plate, preferably a tin one, and called on someone to catch it before it fell. They went trips to nearby places and sat round evening campfires. Above all, they bathed in the sea and gathered pretty shells and pebbles. No matter how cold or wet it was, Jack insisted on his daily dip. He could not swim, but his one pair of swimming trunks saw service every year. No one knows how long he had had them, but he showed them to me with happy nostalgia more than once. I found them amongst his things after he died. It seemed like a betrayal to let them go to a charity shop.

So wonderful were these carefree summer holidays that even the rainy experiences were replayed in a sunny haze and frustrating moments now evoke a laugh. I think, for instance, of Jack's description of a stormy night in the cheap tents.

The children were too young for the flapping canvas to waken them. Margaret and I spent half the night securing tent pegs. It was a vicious gale and we were cold and soaking wet.

Once I was ill driving down. There weren't the motorways in those days. We used to set off at five in the morning and arrive late evening and I was the only driver. Well, I had to stop and rest. A chemist gave me something to keep me going but I was almost collapsing by the time we reached Crackington. They got a doctor. He insisted I was not to camp out so Evelyn and Leonard put me up. I spent a week in bed while Margaret and the children struggled alone in awful weather with sodden tents and mud everywhere.

By this time, the floodgates of the past were open, and Jack talked on.

I'll never forget the time we were over an hour on our way home when somebody noticed we'd forgotten the dog.

Once we visited Raymond and Dulcie in Sussex. We'd been to Chelmsford for our John's wedding (July 1972) and were going on from there to Cornwall. Margaret and Dulcie went off shopping. During their jaunt out, they were held up by an ambulance in a hurry. Little did they know that I was inside in danger of bleeding to death. I had been working on the caravan and had put my hand on the back to exert leverage, not realising that my hand was pressing against a window. The glass broke and severed an artery in my arm.

My arm was encased in plaster and very fragile. There was no way I could drive, and all the older children were elsewhere that year. In the end I phoned Ruth who was planning to join us later. She'd not been driving for too long and had never towed a caravan but she came to our rescue and managed beautifully. When we reached Crackington she had difficulty disconnecting the caravan and stabilising it for parking and I could not help her. We asked a gentleman on the campsite to help us. He made no demur and had the job done in a trice. Imagine our mortification when we saw that he had a hook for one of his hands.

The stories go on but we cannot. Recently Sally and Kevin, her husband, bought a house in Crackington Haven where Edie's sister, Eva, used to live and which Stephen had designed. Evocatively it is called "Bide-a-Wee," Scottish for "stay a while." Sally and Kevin took early retirement from their garden centre near Hull and now live there.

Jack took me down once for a week. The views of valley and cove are marvellous. Badgers and foxes come right to the back door late each evening for food put out for them. On the higher hillside is the little Methodist chapel where Jack and Margaret were married. Opposite stretches the windswept cemetery where their ashes now lie. One day, I shall rest there with them. The adult Puntons and their now grown-up children continue to holiday in Cornwall. It is still a favourite place and eternally in their blood.

Back to School

School figures large in the life of every child. When the Puntons were young, the system was as follows: at age eleven, all pupils sat an examination to determine whether they were better suited to an academic education at a grammar school or to the more practical approach of a secondary modern school. All six Puntons eventually made their way to the grammar school in Goole, but not without some anxieties. Sally led the way. Each successive sibling felt an increasing pressure to succeed. Jane confesses,

How I prayed that John would fail his eleven plus exam because Sally was at grammar school and if John went, that meant I would be the first to let the family down (a concept I dreamed up). John is clever . . . and of course he went to grammar school. Now the onus was on me and I secretly, silently worried and dreaded being eleven. This is one of the dark spots in my memories of childhood.

When the names were called that last day of spring term, my name was not on the list. My heart was like lead. I couldn't face going home to their sympathy and love because I felt I had failed and I wanted the floor to swallow me up. My name was the last to be called. I was so relieved and so happy I wanted to cry.

Like all parents, Jack and Margaret delighted to see their offspring do well. Sensibly they tried never to exert undue pressure and always emphasised that it was better to be good than to pass exams. Jane, the one with the most introspective nature, asked the question,

Why was it so important that we do our best? I think it came from our pride in our family and wanting to please Mum and Dad who cared so much.

It was to Margaret that the young students went for help with their homework. Not only was she the parent who was always at home and available—a rare commodity nowadays—but she had a better education than Jack.

Mum played guard while we did our homework and checked it before we could go off to play. She struggled to understand my math's textbook night after night so she could help me learn what I failed to learn in class. She patiently worked the problems with me while I wet the page with tears of frustration and despair. English was a different story. I was consistently top of the class. Mum would correct every grammatical error in our everyday language. We chalked up a personal triumph if we ever caught each other in error. It was fun.

Margaret gave each of her children the same individual care as need arose. No wonder the family was close, and Jane could go on to write,

After school we played with our friends for a while then we came home and played with each other. In my teens I just came home. We all did—it was where we liked to be.

In many ways we were considered weird by our contemporaries. Ours was the only family in school (bar one) that did not have a TV . . . . We were constantly quizzed about it.

"You don't have a telly? What do you do?"

We read books, we played games, we sang, listened to the radio plays and comedy; we did jigsaws, played card games. I don't know what we did that substituted for watching TV but I could never figure out how people found time to watch it.

Jane and her brothers and sisters developed imagination through play. They learned through hobbies and reading and were stimulated by using their own initiative to amuse themselves and follow up interests. They did things with their parents and helped Jack in his shop. They learned in such a school and thereby discovered some of the lost (in today's terms) skills of living and relationships. It has made them well-balanced adults.

Behave Yourself or—!

However well adjusted the home life, questions of discipline will assuredly arise. Neither Jack nor Margaret cared for spanking and only resorted to it when they felt very provoked. Can you call a couple of slaps on an arm or leg spanking? That was the most they ever did and only under pressure. John remembers his dad swiping out at him occasionally. He would duck and run off; and his father, having made his point, left it at that. To administer deliberate punishment would have upset Jack immeasurably, and he never did. Even Margaret, who had a "shorter fuse" and might deal out the odd slap, could not be too severe. Generally a reprimand was sufficient to maintain order.

Sally recalls her mother shaking a sweeping brush at John and chasing him down the garden. His original misdemeanour is long forgotten, but his quick tongue and tendency to answer back were probably what provoked his parent. The trouble was his cheekiest remarks were often funny, and it was galling to want to laugh when you felt so mad. John escaped over the fence. Margaret returned to the house grinning as she admitted, "I don't know what I'd have done if I'd caught him—probably burst into laughter."

John, however, decided he had overstepped the mark and let a cooling-off time elapse before he showed his face again.

Overall, discipline was wise and kind, and the children knew the parameters of what was permitted. There was also humour, such as the toasting fork ritual. If there was too much noise in bed at night, Margaret would shout for them to go to sleep. When that failed, she slowly and loudly mounted the stairs. That was the cue for her boisterous brood to leap into bed and pull the bedclothes over their heads. In she would come, wielding her toasting fork, and battering each one in turn through the thickness of the blankets. If perchance someone left part of their anatomy poorly padded, they might get more than they bargained for. That was the risk of the game, and the kids loved it.

According to Jane, punishments for being naughty—like telling lies and getting caught—were,

> "I'll dock your pocket money (that was a bad one)," "Go to bed and don't come down (banished)," and loss of the privilege of going out to play. Rarely were any of us spanked. I think I remember every occasion when I was smacked, and I remember it with anger, humiliation, resentment, and rejection. I don't spank my child because I didn't learn it as a parental reprimand and because I remember my feeling when my mother gave in to frustration. I never learned to be "good" from any kind of violence. I'd just be outraged.

> My mother . . . was strict and could silence us with "the look" and we didn't defy her. She was the source of discipline . . . . We didn't take Dad seriously but we jumped to Mum's commands.

In point of fact, they all took their dad very seriously, Jane included. Ruth, who has no memory of ever being spanked, vividly calls to mind the impact it made on the few occasions when her dad ticked her off. Someone else confided to me, I forgot who, that if their mum said, "I'll tell your father," they knew they had really upset her and had gone too far. However easygoing Jack was, he remained the final authority, and they all knew it.

He had his own ways of dealing with errant behaviour, and they worked, as for instance, on the day Simon was playing up. It was mealtime, and everybody had their own place round the table in the kitchen. Simon's seat was beside his dad. Jack quietly grasped his recalcitrant son's arm and, without fuss, held it firmly behind his back until he calmed down.

I love the story of how Jane and her friend misbehaved at school. With sibling glee, one of the others came home and told their dad, "Jane's been naughty. She got into trouble with the teacher."

Soon Jane herself arrived, uncertain about her reception. Her father simply opened his arms and said, "I hear you've been having a bad day, my love. Come and tell me about it."

There was little chance of playing one parent off against the other, as children will try to do. With everyday concerns, Jack left his wife to make the decisions. If his young ones came seeking his sanction to this or that, he invariably responded, "Ask your mother." In more important matters, they agreed policy together. The system worked. The children knew where they stood. It was all part of their network of security.

Gems of Growing Up

One day, Jack came home to me with a lady.

"I want you to meet Eileen Tune," he said. "When Eileen was a little girl, she lived next door to Heppie."

I knew all about Heppie, Mrs Hepworth. Way back in Carlton days, she helped Margaret in the house, babysat from time to time, and became a beloved family friend. It was Eileen who wrote to me as follows when I lost Jack.

> *Jack and Margaret … "adopted" me some fifty years ago. I enjoyed seeing their children grow. They moulded my life and gave me my faith. For that Jack will always be special.*

Although it has nothing to do with this chapter, for my own satisfaction, I must add her next comment.

> *I know how much you meant to him. He was a young man again, delighting in your life together.*

The aforementioned Heppie was a worker. When fitted carpets were unknown and floors were covered with linoleum and loose rugs, she washed and polished the "lino" into a glossy gleam. You trod with care on any mat in sight, lest you go head over heels on the shiny floor. Heppie was also a disciplinarian, loved but respected. Joyce still remembers a ticking off when she and Simon jumped on their parents' bed.

Once, Heppie came to stay when Jack and Margaret were away for the weekend. Now Saturday was pocket money day, and Heppie had the money safely in her care with details of what each child should receive. Came Saturday, and Heppie, no doubt busy, forgot. Disaster! For the first of many occasions since in life, the family got together to discuss strategy. Who would remind Heppie? Nobody dared. They were not very old. Then someone had the "idea." In best handwriting and with their politest words, they wrote a note and left it on the kitchen table. The result was all they hoped for.

As the years passed, the older children became the babysitters; and John took on the role of big brother, not always to everybody's pleasure.

"Come on, Simon, it's your bedtime."

Perhaps it was, but Simon objected to John telling him so. Besides, he wanted to stay up to listen to *The Clitheroe Kid*, a popular radio comedy of the time. The brothers argued until, in frustration, Simon kicked out. I don't know whether he was aiming at John, but to his horror, his foot went right through a cupboard door. He was aghast.

"To this day," he says, "I remember the shoes I was wearing when it happened."

John did not always win on these occasions. Simon would go off to bed then creep downstairs to listen to his radio programme behind the door, until someone twigged and meanly turned the sound too low for him to hear. He also discovered that he could climb out of his bedroom window onto an outhouse roof and go off and talk to his friends and no one the wiser.

One of the drawbacks of a big family is that your brothers and sisters laugh at you when you get things wrong. According to Jack, this next incident concerned Joyce, although John assures me it was Ruth. Be that as it may, the mistake I am about to relate was so logical that whoever made it really deserves the last laugh. John was going on a nuclear disarmament march, a very popular cause at that time of almost mass hysteria over the fear of atomic warfare. He carefully prepared his placard for the big event, proclaiming in large letters BAN THE BOMB.

"Oh, John," said his young sister, "you've missed out the *G* on bang."

Then there were the driving incidents. One day, Jack and I were out in the car.

"Right here at this corner . . . ," he said as we rounded a wide-enough bend, "almost went off the road when I was teaching him or her to drive."

Jack taught all his children to drive, and I honestly do not remember which one nearly landed him in the ditch. More than likely, they all did at one time or another. Whatever the traumas of learning, they all passed their tests the first time. Here again the youngest agonised over her ability behind the wheel, lest she be the only one to fail. Oh the relief when she too made it the first time round. It was still on L-plates that Joyce, on a driving lesson with her dad, once approached Selby Toll Bridge—no longer a toll bridge now.

"Slow down!" ordered Jack, as he handed her the four pennies' fee for crossing. "Take it easy, and give these to the toll keeper as you pass. You don't need to stop completely."

Joyce reduced speed, but not enough. She almost took the toll keeper's hand off, as she thrust the coins at him. He jumped back in alarm, and pennies rolled everywhere, as Joyce sped on and away.

On an earlier occasion, it was I believe the firstborn who set her placid father's nerves on edge, and for nothing more eventful than the fact that she had just passed her driving test.

"Dad," requested Sally, "can I borrow the car tonight?"

"What for?" The father suddenly felt wary.

"I want to meet some friends in Goole."

Quite unexpectedly, Jack felt strange deep inside. It would be the first time his precious daughter had ever driven alone. Scenes of crash and collision filled his mind. His chick was anxious to test her wings, and like all good parents, he knew he had to let her go. With hidden reluctance, he agreed. With no qualms at all, his offspring set off, revelling in her independence at last. Little did she know that a short distance behind, her father was following in his work van. Levelheaded Jack soon regained his poise. After all, Sally was now beginning to do exactly what he and Margaret had brought her up to do—namely, handle her own life. Margaret too had to let her fledglings fly. Ruth took an evening job, which meant getting home very late.

"Don't stay awake for me, Mum. I'll be all right," assured Ruth with all the confidence of the teenager savouring life.

Margaret was not given to foolish fears, but there was no way she would sleep soundly until she knew her daughter was safely home. In the end mother and daughter made a game of it. Ruth would creep in, silent as silent. *I've made it*, she thought in triumph each time she passed her parents' bedroom door with no response. She never did. As she tiptoed into her own room, she always heard her mother whisper, "Good night, Ruth."

One by one the fledglings tested their wings. They left home for college or other professional training. Jack, and usually Margaret with him, drove them for interviews and backwards and forwards between term times and holidays. They were proud to see their growing maturity; but always, like an eagle ready to support its wearying young in midflight, they were there in the background providing security.

Punton Pets

All youngsters should understand animals, and what better way to do so than to have pets? These the Puntons had in plenty. You have already met Daisy, the donkey. Also from Carlton days was Topsy Lou (from *Uncle Tom's Cabin*), a Pekinese that Jack bought as a puppy and loved dearly. Indeed, everyone loved her. Sadly, her death was one of the hardest experiences of Jane's young life.

> *When Topsy was old and sick she was taken to the vet and "put to sleep." It was explained to me that she was given a delicious meal that had poison in it and that after she had enjoyed her food she lay down to sleep and didn't wake up. Her painless demise was supposed to be reassuring to me but I was plagued with waking nightmares that terrified me and prevented easy sleep for several weeks. I can still conjure up the image that haunted me then—of Topsy lying dead beside a bowl of food, and it was dark all around.*

Is it possible to multiply anything by two and get twenty-seven? Yes, if you are talking about guinea pigs. When the Punton pair began to breed, I am told they did just that. Jack built a roomy run for them in the garden.

What happened next I have no idea. Once, Jack brought home an abandoned puppy when the local policeman told him they would have to put it down if they could not find a home for it. An injured duck was carefully tended in the garden. When recovered, it flew back to the wild, but not before it had eaten most of Margaret's beloved plants.

On Sundays, Jack loved to take an early morning walk before breakfast. In this way, he came across Vicky, a fox cub whose mother had been killed on the road. He took her home. She was weak and mangy, but injections from the vet and good feeding quickly had her in shape. The cub soon went everywhere with Jack, even sitting in the front seat of his car. Oncoming drivers almost swerved off the road, as they tried to decide whether they really had seen what they thought they had seen. Vicky remained nervous. She escaped a few times and was eventually killed by a car. It was as well. She had no future as a domestic pet.

Tommy was a tortoise and one of Jack's favourites. He had the freedom of the garden and rarely strayed. If you called, "Tommy! Tommy!" and waited for a moment, there would be a stirring in the undergrowth; and out would lumber Tommy hoping for food and affection. If he got cold, he would seek entrance to warmer climes by levering himself up sideways and tapping his shell against the back door. Object achieved, his goal was the hearth beside the fire and the bliss of warmth. Tommy drowned in the garden pond. It was a sad day; and Jack, himself alone by then, wept. He had lost a companion.

When I first visited Jack's home, I had to see his twenty canaries in their aviary at the bottom of the garden. Later they were stolen, and the four remaining birds soon died. He also introduced me to the three cats bestowed on him by Joyce when she went to live in America. One of these was Billy, a big, round-headed tabby, and a cat of decided character. Having concluded that my Sally, though a dog, meant no harm, he gave her a velvet clawed pat of approval on the nose, as cats will do with a dog that is not a threat when they make up their minds to accept it. In Billy's case, the pat was more of a whack, but Sally understood. She has always preferred cats to her own kind.

Billy loved being inside when visitors came. On this occasion, Jack wanted him out; and he firmly shut the door on him. Moments later, there was Billy, tail up, weaving round our legs, and purring pleasure. Then Jack bethought him of the attic where he was replacing a dormer window. We put puss out once more, and we followed him to watch. He topped a six-foot fence in one bound. A couple of feet higher, and he was on the flat bathroom roof which extended out from the house. Then came the feat which had us gasping. Up the side of the house, he leapt. There was no claw purchase in the bricks, and the eaves above overhung the wall. Effortlessly, he gained the roof. A few easy steps up, the tiles took him to the gaping window. When we entered the house, Billy was happily on the ground floor to greet us.

When the builder dug the foundations for our back extension to April Cottage, he kept unearthing old plastic bags. He was puzzled. He was finding the remains of family pets long gone. I say "long" gone. When did plastic first begin to enter our lives? No matter! The pets received a worthy disposal.

Caring and Sharing

If there was love to lavish on animals, how much more was there to offer to people? The principle that happiness had to be shared by caring for others was taught almost from infancy. Once more Jane talks of her experiences.

My doll was called Joanna and I loved her dearly . . . When I was five Mum told me that Nina Shelton hadn't any dolls at all and since I had two maybe I could let Nina be mother to one of them. She suggested I let Joanna go. I wasn't enthusiastic but together Mum and I cleaned her clothes, combed her hair, and Mum promised I could still be her Aunty Jane and visit her. Then I personally gave her to Nina. Nina and I became best friends.

One Christmas we were told by Mum and Dad that there were some children who wouldn't be having presents because their father had hung himself. We each chose which of our gifts we would give away, and Mum made up a food basket with some of the goodies we were enjoying that day. Then we made our visit. It was Christmas day.

The stories go on. "I don't remember a time," states Jane, "when we didn't collect people."

We collected waifs and strays, tramps, kids, lonely old people, lonely young people—anyone who needed a friend. Mum gave a meal to a tramp who asked her to fill his thermos, and the good food made him ill.

I had already heard about "Uncle George" from Jack who came home one evening to find this shabby gentleman sitting in his kitchen. I use the title deliberately. Uncle George was without doubt a "gentleman of the road." He may or may not have been a gentleman in the general sense of that word; but to Jack, every human being had value and was to be cherished. Margaret agreed with him; and together, they lived out this conviction in their daily dealings with people. They treated everyone with courtesy, including the Uncle Georges of this world. Jack, I know, proffered the sad gentleman in his kitchen no less respect than he showed to Princess Margaret when he met her some thirty years later.

The man looked ill probably because he was undernourished. Jack invited him to stay for the evening meal and suggested he take off his old army great coat which hung almost to his ankles. He declined. The kitchen warmed up with people and cooking. Eventually George was persuaded. Even today, my eyes mist a little, and I can hear the compassion in Jack's voice as he said, "Poor man! His trousers were in tatters from top to bottom."

Everyone pretended not to notice; but after the meal, Jack offered him a bath and bed which he gladly accepted. Jack found some of his own trousers which Margaret hastily shortened. They fixed him up in the garden shed which was not as callous as it sounds, since it had already been made very comfortable for Sally. George stayed for three weeks, slowly regaining strength. Sometimes he disappeared for the day, but always he returned at night. Jack gave him a few light jobs in the shop until one day he left, pushing his meagre belongings in a pram that Margaret gave him. There were others, but Uncle George stayed the longest.

At one time they befriended Jock. Jock, obviously, was a Scot. Things went wrong for him; and when his wife left him, he took to the road. Being an educated man, he appreciated an intelligent conversation and frequented public libraries to read the newspapers and keep up with current affairs. One day in Goole, he went into the Oxfam shop looking for a sleeping bag. By this time, Margaret was managing the shop. They had no sleeping bags in stock; but she suddenly thought about family camping holidays and all those sleeping bags at home, now no longer needed, as the family was growing up fast and leaving the nest.

"Go through to Snaith," she instructed her customer, "and give this note to my husband in his DIY shop. He'll find you a sleeping bag."

And this was how the Puntons got to know Jock. He came and went for a year or two and sent the occasional postcard proclaiming his whereabouts.

Then came the card from a hospital in Guildford. That weekend Jack and Margaret looked at each other. They had no need to explain.

"It's a long way."

"Yes, but if we leave early, we could do it in the day."

"We have to go. We're all he's got."

They visited Jock twice. He left the hospital. They had a few more postcards; then abruptly they stopped, and they never saw him again. They did know that he was afraid of letting emotional ties grow too strong, and it was possible that he deliberately severed the contact. Jack did not believe it. Jock was not well, and he felt sure that he had died.

Jane has other stories.

> We collected old people and got used to them just sitting there while we got on with family life. Miss Elwiss was a permanent feature . . . for many years until she died. She was uneducated, senile, childlike, and pathetic. When Mum found her she was ill, uncared for, and hadn't a single person who cared about her. It would take a book to describe the changes made in her life by my parents, and though we (the kids) often tired of her presence we were fond of her too.

Hanging on a hook from one of the roof beams in our house was a pair of perfectly handcrafted leather boots, so small they would almost fit a doll. They were worn by Ms Elwiss as a toddler and were made by her father who was a shoemaker and cobbler. He did not show much affection for his daughter; but she gave them, the only cherished memento of her past, to Jack and Margaret. They valued the tiny boots for her sake. They would undoubtedly grace a museum as a beautiful example of the Victorian shoemaker's craft.

To the children's delight, after visiting the toilet, Ms Elwiss habitually returned announcing informatively, "I ain't been moved. Nowt but wind and watter."

Naturally, and despite parental chiding, the children encouraged her.

"How did you get on, Ms Elwiss?"

Ms Elwiss obligingly played up to their expectations.

"I ain't been moved," and so on and so forth it went.

Even Ms Elwiss got into trouble when Margaret discovered that she was using a flannel instead of toilet paper.

Mrs Merritt was a large old lady who, when wedged into an easy chair, found it difficult to rise. In effort, she would rock back and forth, grunting and showing an expanse of fat knee and elasticated knicker leg. The young Puntons watched in covert fascination. It was surely too much to expect them not to react. Even Jack in later life, when his knees stiffened after exertion, would deliberately follow the same rising procedure—without the knicker leg you understand—and laughingly mimic his one-time guest.

Once, the children removed the springs from under Mrs Merritt's chair. When she sat down, she went through to the floor, luckily only a few inches below. Also, when Mum and Dad were not around to scold, they sometimes made their mild protest at these invasions of family space. They would never dare be rude, and they did it jokingly, but there was an edge to it.

"Would you mind fetching me a glass of water?" Mrs Merritt asked John.

"Yes, I do mind," was his response. In one sense he did, and in another he did not, but Mrs Merritt received her water.

"Would you mind letting me sit there?" the lady requested of Simon when she arrived one day to find him curled up reading in her usual seat. Simon did mind and said so while adding, "But I suppose I'll have to."

It was understandable, and I think the guests mostly saw the funny side of such remarks and ignored the underlying touch of resentment.

If Margaret gave these people home comforts, Jack handled business matters for them. Despite apparent poverty, some of them had property and money. He battled for his protégés in an attempt to improve their lot—dealing with bank managers, solicitors, and social services on their behalf. His great dislike of solicitors stems from these days when he took up the cause of another apparently impoverished lady who, I may add, is not one of those mentioned in this chapter.

"That man," he declared, and I had never heard such scorn or anger in his voice. "That man, I have no room for him. He knew the poor soul was a destitute, and he was sitting on her money. He did nothing about it, and when I tried to help, he was deliberately obstructive."

I think I am right in saying that, with the backing of the bank manager concerned, Jack received a power of attorney on the lady's behalf and was able to ease her lot. It was no thanks to the solicitor in the case.

I still have a couple of business letters in connection with people Jack tried to help over the years. They say nothing of importance, but they show something of how he involved himself in their affairs. Jane sums it all up for herself, and I am sure her words apply to her brothers and sisters as well.

> *What I am left with is the inability to look the other way. I have had to fight the need to save the whole world . . . . I am never good enough. I can never do enough. I can never give enough because I feel guilty with what I keep for myself. We had little and we gave away what we had to anyone who had less.*

Jane's final words are not insignificant. In discussing this chapter with different members of Jack's family, I have heard the same fact variously expressed.

"Because Dad had a shop, people thought we were well off."

"All my friends envied me because they thought we were rich."

"Nobody believed that we were poor and had to do without things and that Mum and Dad struggled to make ends meet."

Well, the Puntons were not rich; and if Jack's business was prospering, he had built it up from nothing and with nothing. Moreover, as was already pointed out in the previous chapter, it took all his profits to provide for his family, foster children included, and keep the business viable. He had nothing to spare. He occasionally had nothing to pay his employees' wages with at the end of the week and often depended on an overdraft with the bank. Sometimes they had more, often they had less; but all the family would concur with Jane, what little they had, they never hesitated to share with others.

Rawcliffe Hall

Rawcliffe Hall no longer exists. It was demolished round about the time Jack and I married. All that remains is a mile of high red brick wall fronting a new housing estate alongside the Goole road. It used to be a country mansion—home of the Creyke family, one of whose eccentric nineteenth-century members once rode bareback to London on a bull. For much of the twentieth century, it was what used to be called a mental hospital. In its place, a select new housing estate is arising.

I suppose there were some genuine psychiatric cases within its walls. However, many of the patients were only physically handicapped, or in the terminology of the day, a bit simple. Some had been there from infancy because they were illegitimate. A few girls were put there by their families because they had got pregnant. It was all rather sad, for by the time Jack and Margaret got to know them, they were totally institutionalised.

One day, the matron gave Margaret a list of those who had no visitors. For a number of years thereafter, Jack and Margaret and some of the children spent their Sunday afternoons singing, playing games, and exploring the grounds with twenty people who had no one else to care. Jack had a special feeling for one little lady whose bright nature belied a bent and twisted body. He pushed her in her wheelchair round the grounds and took time to talk to her. When he teased her, they laughed together; and she would turn her head, hunched into her shoulders, to look into his face and with twinkling eyes declare, "You bugger, you."

I doubt if she properly realised what she was saying. As far as she was concerned, she was expressing affection and pleasure, which is why I feel at liberty to write the word in full. Jack was probably one of the few men in her life, if not the only one, to treat her as an attractive woman, for he truly did see beyond her physical frailties to something beautiful beneath. When talking to me about her, he always said, "She was lovely."

Under government legislation of the eighties, places like Rawcliffe Hall closed. Provision, often inadequate and inappropriate, was made for most of the patients to live in the community. Sometimes this worked well, sometimes not. For three of the ladies the Puntons visited, the policy was a success. Emma, Marjorie, and Mary now share a flat in Goole. Emma is blind but bossy and tells everyone what to do. Marjorie does it while Mary happily says nothing and smiles her approval at everything. They are still in touch with Sally and

Ruth and buy and expect Christmas presents each year. One season, Sally called with their gifts.

"What a lot of cards you have," she said, looking round in some amazement.

"Yes, we saved last year's and put them up too."

When Simon left school, he worked for his dad for three years with no clear idea as to what he should do for a career. Then he tried a job as a porter at Rawcliffe Hall. That decided him. In 1976, he moved into nursing, specialised in psychiatric care, and has since progressed to the top of his profession.

Unfulfilled Dreams

As their own family grew older and began to leave home, Jack and Margaret still felt youthful, fit, and with a lot to give. They could not imagine an empty house and a life without children. Jack told me, "We enquired about fostering or adoption. The child care people made difficulties. They thought we were too old. Margaret was only in her forties, but they didn't seem to consider how highly trained and experienced she was. I heard Gladys Aylward speak in Leeds and appeal for people to adopt her orphans. We wrote to her and she replied, but nothing came of it."

Time passed. Jane started nursing in London. While there, she decided to visit two of their former holiday girls. She was shocked.

I tried to help the mother out of her hopelessness. She was an English woman, the common-law wife of an East African man, and they had ten children . . . in a basement apartment. She hinted that without the baby, a six-month-old girl, she would cope much better. I relayed the message to Mum and soon Georgina was two hundred and fifty miles away in Yorkshire . . . . Three months later Georgie was unrecognisable. She was healthy, strong, bright, laughing, sitting up, and playing. At six months she'd had no smile, no muscle tone, and was fat and pimply from malnutrition . . . .

When Paula (a sister) came to visit she was astonished and thrilled . . . The mother was happy and relieved. The father was jealous and proud . . . . He insisted Georgie be brought back. Dad drove her to London. Mum,

who had loved Georgie as her own daughter . . . was heartbroken. I have
never witnessed such grief . . . . As my reports . . . became more depressing
Mum stopped talking about her and asking. Her pain was intense and
she internalised it and carried on as if there had been no Georgie. A year
later she developed breast cancer.

We are told that there may be a link between stress and cancer, but we are not saying that this was necessarily so in this case. It could be, but we simply do not know. As for carrying on, as though there had been no Georgie, neither Jack nor Margaret were given to making a fuss; and they both knew that life had to go on in a normal way. They were both distressed, and they both immersed themselves in the work of the moment. Jack often wondered how Georgie fared. She is over thirty now.

This was not the only disappointment. Having told Mrs Punton that she was too old to foster or adopt at forty, the social services suddenly backtracked. They had a coloured baby up for adoption, borne to a twelve-year-old. Colour, they knew, was not a problem but, they said, "You probably won't want this one."

Jack and Margaret wondered why not. It turned out that the baby was born of incest. Nobody was prepared to take such a child. Mr and Mrs Punton were the last hope.

"Of course we want it."

They had no hesitation. If anything, they wanted it even more once they knew the background. With loving anticipation, they made all the arrangements for an adoption. Everything and everyone in the family was ready and so happy. The day before they were due to take the baby, the twelve-year-old mother decided to keep it.

The Other Side of the Hill

Jack and Margaret turned their attention to other things. Although Margaret's mastectomy in 1971 was successful, there had to be a question mark over the implications of parenting young children for the future. There was plenty to do. Sally got married in 1971 and John a year later. Soon the grandchildren began to appear. Jack was already on the town council and busy in community life. He and Margaret were involved in setting up and running the Oxfam shop in Goole which Margaret managed for a few years.

In 1976-1977, Jack was mayor of Snaith. It was a hard year, for that was the year the cancer returned. In all the press photographs of the functions he attended, Margaret was by his side. Only those closest to her knew how ill she was during the latter months of his term of office. There was a second operation in the spring of 1977. From then on, Jack nursed his beloved wife at home as best he could. She died in hospital in July of that same year. Jack and his "Jill" had climbed the hill of married life so happily together. Now he was left to go down the other side alone.

It took a long time for him to pass beyond his grief. Eventually he did make a new life for himself in quite unexpected ways. By 1984, he was sufficiently at peace in himself to write some simple, heartfelt verses entitled *An Old Man's Room of Memories*. He may have been an old man at seventy-one in terms of age. Nevertheless, he had fifteen active and profitable years still before him, but that is a story yet to relate. Meanwhile, he wrote a poem.

An Old Man's Room of Memories

My room is not a big room
Compared with some I know,
But size is not important
When your heart is all aglow.

It's the memories it holds for you
That fill you with delight
And make you feel how good is God
To make your life so bright.

I'm sitting here, all comfy like,
In my big, easy chair
And pondering over days gone by
And all my answered prayer.

There are photos on the mantelpiece
And photos on the wall
Of all my lovely children
And their mother, best of all.

The curtains at the windows
And covers on the chairs
Are products of her loving hands
Who guided our affairs.

We've played and joked and laughed in here
And shared each other's joys,
The treasure of a happy home
Was love and fun and noise.

I never will feel lonely
Sitting in this room of mine,
It holds such lovely memories
Of once upon a time.

Signed
Jack Punton.

April Cottage (front right)—family home
as seen from church tower.

Growing family with Sally, John, Jane and
Ruth—Simon and Joyce yet to arrive.

Rogues gallery. Taken at Ruth's wedding shortly after Jack died. Sally, John, Jane, Andrew and Ruth, Simon, Joyce.

CHAPTER 7

JACK OF ALL TRADES
or
HOW JACK MADE A LIVING

The Day of the Auction

As the day of the auction arrived, a goodly group of people gathered in the back premises of the Plough Inn. The venue was central enough for the said hostelry stands in the middle of Snaith where the Selby, Goole, and Pontefract roads meet. By the time the auctioneer, a Mr Neville Townend, entered, the room was full. He surveyed the rows of closely packed chairs and mentally registered the familiar faces in the crowd. He glanced at his notes and began.

Mr Sid Womersley had taken a seat towards the front where he could easily attract the auctioneer's attention. Mr Womersley frequented auctions. He bought things, especially run-down property, which he renovated and then sold for a profit. He had his eye on a couple of places coming up that day. He was not desperate. If they went cheaply, he would buy. If the bidding rose too high, he would let them go.

Proceedings progressed smoothly under Mr Townend's practised skill. At last, something that interested Mr Womersley came up. The auctioneer made the best of describing the premises, such as they were, then named his starting price.

"Who'll bid me £1,000 for 1 and 3, Market Place, Snaith?"

Everyone knew 1 and 3, Market Place, just across the road from the Plough Inn. It was a fine, double property comprising a tall nineteenth-century building with a mock Tudor frontage and a lower but much older and less pretentious adjoining building. There was also a cottage and sundry outbuildings at the back. The place had possibilities, but it was in disrepair and shabby.

"£1,000? Will somebody start me off at £1,000?"

Mr Townend looked round the apathetic faces before him and knew better than to persist.

"£900 then?"

The silence was stolid.

"£800?"

Not one encouraging movement could Mr Townend discern. He hurried on.

"£700?"

Not one face changed expression, and yet unbeknown to anyone, a quiet gentleman seated at the back had tensed. The quiet gentleman wondered when to make a move. He had already approached the Yorkshire Rural Community Council about those premises. He needed a loan to buy them. He had nothing of his own.

"Get a valuation and make an application," they said.

The estimated value for 1 and 3 Market Place was £700, and they had guaranteed him up to this amount. Suddenly the quiet gentleman felt hopeful. He would wait a bit longer and see what happened. Truth to tell, he was nervous. It was one thing to bid a pound or two for a few tools or a piece of furniture, but bricks and mortar and hundreds of pounds he did not have? That was something else.

"£600? £500? £400? Look, this property must go today. These are my instructions."

"£300. £200."

The descending litany droned on down to £100.

"I'll give ye half a hundred."

A laconic voice broke the deadlock of disinterest. The auctioneer acknowledged Sid Womersley's intervention with relief. The quiet person squared his shoulders.

"I'm offered £50. Is there any advance on £50?"

By now, Mr Townend had little expectation that there would be. He was all prepared to pronounce the property sold to Mr Womersley, but he had to go through the motions of proper procedure. He glanced around perfunctorily as he repeated, "Any advance on £50?"

"I'll give you £55."

A stir of interest rustled through the room. The quiet gentleman had spoken.

"£65!" said a surprised Sid.

"£70!"

"£80!" said Sid.

"£85," said the quiet gentleman.

Sid Womersley turned round. He thought he recognised the voice behind him, but he wanted to be sure. Yes. He was not exactly a close friend of the man bidding from the back, but he respected him. He sat silent.

Jack Punton had bought his shop.

Beginning at the Beginning

When Jack was demobbed, as we already know, he had a wife and baby to support with no income or savings to cushion the way. As you will also recall, his old boss in Carlton, Willie Hinsley, offered him work. Though poorly paid, it was better than nothing. Unfortunately Mr Hinsley was more interested in his pigs than his carpentry and undertaking business. Jack often found himself with little to do other than potter around with odd jobs here and there. Only one piece of work during this period seemed worthwhile.

During the war, all church bells stayed silent. Only if our shores were invaded would the bells boom out to warn of danger. In 1944, the government ban on bell ringing was lifted. It was then discovered that the three bells of St Mary's Parish Church in Carlton were in a dangerous state. They dated from the early and mid-seventeenth century. Even for victory celebrations, they must not be rung; lest a few tons of metal and masonry descend on the ringers' heads.

At the end of the war, the verger and his brother privately decided that, whatever the risk, the bells could not hang idle when their fellows were merrily jangling from one end of the land to the other. They locked themselves in the bell tower. The first anyone knew about it was when the Carlton bells pealed forth. The ringers survived; but the bells, in their parlous state, could not. The village council decided that they must be recast and rehung. If funds were available, three new bells should be added to bring the peal up to six.

Now Dr McGranahan, whom you met briefly in chapter 5, had two sons. Both fought in the war. One morning, the dreaded telegram arrived. The eldest boy had been killed. Two days later a second telegram announced the death of the second son. The doctor and his wife were in shock, and the whole community mourned on their behalf. At the end of the war, Dr and Mrs McGranahan made an offer. They would bear the cost of three new bells as a memorial to their two sons and the men of the parish who had also fallen if the council and parish would undertake the restoration of the three old bells.

The offer was accepted. That was how it came about that one of Jack's first jobs was to help rehang the peal. An old snapshot gives an idea of the task. Each bell, with the workmen standing alongside, was some four—to five-feet in height. I have no idea of their weight. On Wednesday, July 31, 1946, the new peal was dedicated.

Apart from this one interesting piece of work, Jack found himself mucking out his boss's pigs or repairing a few things like fences and outhouses. Moreover, his family and consequent financial needs were expanding. He was not happy.

"I decided," he told me, "to go it alone. Margaret was behind me. People were already privately offering me decorating and joinery jobs, but I didn't want to go behind my boss's back. In the end I gave him a month's notice. I did tell him, however, that I would not do any undertaking. That seemed only fair. He wasn't pleased. At the end of the week, he gave me my wages and told me I could finish."

In a sense, it was a relief to end so soon and yet frightening. Those were not the days when the state stood in to meet your every need. To "go it alone" meant, more or less, exactly that. The Puntons were already living from hand to mouth. Jack had hardly any tools of his own other than a few basics like a hammer, saw, and screwdriver. He had no work lined up and no way to advertise his services other than by word of mouth. As he said,

> I didn't even have a ladder. For my first job I borrowed enough to buy some paint and used borrowed brushes. I started by carrying my tools and materials on my bike. As soon as I could I bought a ladder and a few odds and ends at an auction. Then I made a hand cart.

And so it went on. Jack was reliable, honest, and pleasant. People liked him, and they employed him. Soon he was employing others to work for him. He needed a base and a workshop. When an upstairs function room became available in the former Railway Inn in Snaith, he rented it. Jack himself was surprised to see how well he was doing. His outward cheerfulness gave him an air of self-confidence which he did not always feel inside. At the same time, his easygoing exterior belied a dislike of the dead end, and he was not afraid of a risk and a challenge. None of this meant that life was easy. On the whole, he managed (just) to pay the household bills and keep the business solvent. Occasionally Margaret had to feed the family with reduced housekeeping so he could pay his workmen's wages. They had the basics, but they mostly did without the luxuries. They did not mind. They had hopes for the future.

A Proud Day

As business grew, a bike and a handcart were hardly adequate as a means of transport. Jack wanted a van. He did his sums. No, there was no way he could buy one straight out; but if the bank would give him a loan, he was sure he could pay it off in a couple of years. Accordingly, he cycled into Selby one fine day to see a bank manager. The bank manager had his job to do. Yes, he could arrange a loan, but he needed some form of security. Did Mr Punton own any property? No! What other assets did he have? In those days, nothing. Was there, then, someone who would stand security for him? Mr Punton thought there probably was. He left the bank feeling hopeful.

Now as is pointed out elsewhere in this book, this is a rich farming country. Some of the wealthiest farmers in the district were Methodists and on friendly terms with Jack. He therefore went to see the one he knew best to make his request. No, he did not want a loan, only a signature for surety. Yes, his business affairs were succeeding as everyone knew; and no, he did not foresee any problem in repaying the bank. The farmer, who was very well to do and a good Christian, looked his visitor up and down and said no. Jack felt humiliated. He would not ask elsewhere.

A few days later as he was walking down the street, he met a coal merchant acquaintance. He was a tough man who had little time for religion and who could drink and swear in plenty. That did not stop either he or Jack from enjoying a chat.

"How are things going then? I hear you're doing well."

"Yes, I've got one or two problems, but I'm managing fine."

"What are the problems, then?"

Jack explained and added, "The trouble is, I've nothing behind me, and nobody will stand security for me."

"Where's your bank?"

"Selby. Barclays."

"Fine. That's my bank too. I'm going there now. I'll have a word with the manager and sign for you."

Just like that, Jack got his loan and his van. The first thing he did was to inscribe on the side in big letters, "J. Punton. Joiner and Decorator." It was one of the proudest days of his life. The story does not quite end there. A little over a year later Jack sought out his benefactor.

"I want to tell you that I've paid off the bank. Thank you. I won't need your signature anymore."

"That's all right, Jack. I'm glad to help. Leave it there a bit longer. You might need it again for something else one day."

Setting Up Shop

Such was the way things were until the Puntons moved to April Cottage in 1956, and Jack bought 1 and 3, Market Place, early in 1958. There are only two more things to say concerning the day of the auction, for in country places associations are long and close.

When Jack was an apprentice with Fred Robinson, he did some work at a big house on the left as you leave Snaith by the Pontefract Road. Being only a lad himself, he would take time to play with a red-haired baby in a pram in the garden. That baby was Neville Townend of the auction. On reading this, John, Jack's son, was surprised. He knew Mr Townend as a black-haired gentleman. I can only pass on to you what Jack told me. I would also like to put it on record that the same Mr Townend, now retired, always used to send Jack donations for his charity walks in later life.

As for Mr Womersley, he died a year or two before Jack, and the Puntons' undertaking service looked after his funeral. I cannot say that the two men were ever close, but Jack always knew that if Sid had continued bidding on the day of the auction, his own story might have been very different.

Who would have guessed, thought Jack, that the little boy who ran errands for his mother to the dapper, moustachioed Mr Edgerton Wood's draper's shop would one day own the premises himself? But he did, and he had plans. He would open a hardware store. There were no big DIY conglomerations in those days for competition. In three weeks it was Easter. Could he make it for then? The place was dirty and down at heel, but Jack was buoyant as he surveyed his derelict kingdom. He worked early and late. Margaret helped him. How she found time to do so, no one knows. At the very last minute, he bought some stock, mostly wallpaper and paste and a bit of paint. It was all he could manage, and it was not much, but displayed to best advantage it looked good. At Easter he opened shop.

With ups and downs, the business developed. Before long Jack phased out the joinery and decorating work to concentrate on the shop. The Yorkshire Rural Community Council which had guaranteed the loan of £700, happily not needed, stepped in again. They gave Jack a course on bookkeeping and small business procedures. They were always supportive. Soon he employed a lady to handle the accounts and office work which he never liked. Then just when he was doing well, he had a large amount of money stolen which greatly set him back.

"But," said Jack, "the business gave me a living, and John too when he joined me later on."

Here I want to quote from Jane again as she wrote in 1985.

> [The store] *has changed, evolved, but it hasn't really grown, and while it has supported the family, it has rarely been in credit with the bank. How could it? A man comes in for a box of two inch nails. Dad asks him what he wants them for. The man says he's hanging pictures and needs three nails. Dad opens the box, gives him three nails—no charge—and he's stuck with an open box. A lady needs some glue to stick a handle back on a cup. Dad says, "Oh, you only need a bit; no point in buying a whole tube; I have some open. You can have this." No charge.*
>
> *He's never lost a customer. He's there to support his family and to help everyone . . . . He's the kindest, gentlest, most loving man I ever met. I'm biased but my opinion is shared by hundreds of people who know him. He's well known for many, many miles around.*

Being behind the counter had its lighter moments. Imagine, for instance, the fresh-faced lad who comes in, kitted out in new, unsoiled dungarees, and reminding Jack of his own pride in his new overalls when he started work, more years ago than he cares to recall. The boy opens a list. It is as Jack suspects. He wants a dozen sky hooks, a pound of glass nails, a rubber hammer, and a tube of gumption. The new boy's workmates are having him on. They always do.

John, who later worked with his dad in the shop, had his own moments too. One morning, the doorbell sounded and in walked a teenage girl. John was serving. What could he do for her? She was on work experience at the hairdressing salon next door. Did he, by any chance, have a long stand in stock? As she spoke, the telephone rang. The hairdresser was on the line. They had sent Emma in and would he play along with their joke for a while. Eyes twinkling, he agreed.

"Look, they're teasing you," he explained to Emma. "We'll turn the tables on them. You wait here. There's no hurry. It won't hurt to keep them guessing for a while."

John went out to the back and found a solid block of wood. He drilled a hole in the centre and inserted a broom handle. He then screwed a hook into the top of the handle and hung a coat hanger on it. Next, he prepared his account, carefully pricing all the materials used and including his own time.

"Now you take this along and see what they say."

He never did get paid for Emma's long stand. Neither did he get it back.

In a small town, everything is to hand. The shop is at one end of the main street and April Cottage, a mere two-minute walk away, at the other. It is confusing that the store is in Market Place and the house in High Street. Old Snaithites can no doubt pinpoint exactly where Market Place ends and High Street begins or vice versa. Newcomers have no idea while tradesmen and even postmen are confused. For Jack, it did not matter. He was home for meals in a few seconds. He kept a regular eye on his dearest wife in her last illness. Once, when a lady he knew came into the store with her new baby he said, "Would you mind keeping shop for five minutes, and let me take the baby home to show Margaret?"

His own children loved to come home from school then rush down the road to help their dad. While they were young, visiting grandchildren still liked nothing better than to "help" Uncle John, to play or make things at the back, and generally be around. It is still a happy, caring, family business.

Undertaking Undertaking

Behind Jack's premises was a triangle of land and some cottages. When they were condemned and demolished, he bought the land and thereby gave himself a back entry from the Pontefract Road, just where it joins the mini-roundabout and the highways to Goole and Selby. He now had access for vehicles which was a problem on the busy corner of his Market Place frontage. He also now had facilities to do something else, for which he had experience, namely, undertake undertaking. His promise so many years ago to Mr Hinsley in this respect had applied only to Carlton and no longer held.

In the country, undertaking is a sporadic rather than a full-time occupation, with quiet spells and sudden surges of busyness. There is also the tricky matter of cash flow. If the undertaker handles everything and pays all the different expenses involved, he will have an immediate outlay today of well over £1,000.

Some families pay the bill within days. Often, however, the affairs of the deceased are in the hands of a lawyer. It is then many months, even up to a year, before the estate is settled, and the undertaker is paid. Multiply this by all the other funerals concerned and you know the reason for the cash flow problem. To have two businesses, as Jack now did, means that they help each as needed and both survive.

How different is the approach of the country undertaker, who knows most of his clients, dead or alive, from that of the impersonal city firm? My dad died in Glasgow. The people we saw could not be faulted in what they did, and yet what was their solemnity but a practised act? I understood. Perhaps I was unreasonable, but to be honest, I found their show of sympathy obsequious and felt irritated. I remember how I wished they would, well, if not laugh, at least smile. My mum died in Snaith. Jack looked after her. It was a totally different experience—warm, right, and satisfying in a way impossible to put into words.

Later I learned that it always was so with Jack. He has sat through the night with distressed people, gently sharing their grief. He has held distraught mothers and bewildered widows in his arms and coaxed them to leave their homes and attend the funerals of their loved ones. He has visited and succoured the most desperate of his bereaved clients long after the funeral, helping them come to terms with their loss.

Consistent with such compassion, Jack always fully participated in every funeral service. Most undertakers will sit at the back of the church until they are required to lead the cortege out. The pall bearers, if they are working for the funeral director and have nothing to do with the deceased, go outside for a smoke and a natter. Never so Jack. He always sat discreetly behind the family and joined in all that happened. He sang "The Lord's My Shepherd" thousands of times and deserved no prize for being able to recite the funeral liturgy off by heart.

The Reverend Cyril Roberts, rector of our parish since 1986, once said to me, "I miss Jack at funerals. If he was there, I never worried about the singing. He'd keep it going."

Jack, in turn, would say to me, "Of all the vicars I've worked with," and he had worked with many, "Cyril is one of the best. He leans over backwards to fit in with arrangements, even to his own inconvenience, and he's a real pastor to the families."

Cyril and Jack worked closely together. They liked and respected each other. Cyril, in his own words, "wept like a child" when he heard of Jack's sudden passing. As for Jack, he saw his job every bit as much a Christian ministry, as any vicar would do. It was part of his way of serving God.

Today and Yesterday

Undertaking now is very different from when Jack started out. Then more people died at home than in hospital, and they lay in their own homes until the funeral. Now they lie in the undertaker's premises where refrigeration facilities are available and relatives come to say farewell in a chapel of rest. Then coffins were handmade to measure. Now they come wholesale in a selection of stock sizes. Then burials were the norm, now cremation.

When people died at home, someone had to lay them out; and often, it was neither pleasant nor easy to manage alone. Jack used to take Dolly, his sister-in-law, to help. As Ted and Dolly had no telephone, he would go round for a night call to the back of their house and tap the clothes prop on the bedroom window. One night, they drove out together to Drax. In the moonlight, frost glistened on the tree branches while rabbits scampered on rime silvered grass. Dolly was enraptured.

"Our Jack took me to Fairyland," she said.

Jack was called to Dolly's house one evening three years into our marriage. She was sitting in her chair with the fire full on as if she had felt cold. He knew she had gone the moment he saw her. At her funeral, he told the story of Dolly's visit to Fairyland.

Jack had known Dolly for almost seventy years. In his long life, he must have looked after hundreds of his old friends. It is this closeness to the people you deal with that can make the work emotionally hard. I once asked Jack how he reacted when he had a former school friend or long standing acquaintance lying in his chapel of rest.

"I feel it, sometimes deeply, and the memories come. You get used to it, you have to, especially when you're as old as I am. Whoever it is, I still have a job to do. Even dead people need some attention, and I have to check up regularly on all my 'visitors' to ensure that everything is fresh and pleasant. And yes, I'll go in, and just look at an old friend. I might even talk to them about old times as I say my own good-bye."

There was one thing I could not help wondering about and had to ask.

"How do you feel when you're alone with a dead body, especially if it's dark and you're all isolated in your rambling back premises?"

I should have guessed the answer, for Jack was neither fanciful nor highly strung.

"It's never bothered me. I try to show the same respect towards someone who has died that I do to the living. To me, the person before me is still a person. Why should I be scared?"

"But what about the supernatural experiences, ghosts and things?" I pressed on.

"No! I'm not troubled by such fears. There was only one occasion when I ever sensed anything strange. It was nothing really. It was a man I knew, and I was by myself laying him out in his own home. I suddenly got the feeling that I was not alone and that he was somewhere high up in the left corner of the room watching what I was doing. It was not at all scary and—oh, I can't explain it, but it was real."

If Jack's job was not spooky, it was often harrowing. He was always upset when a baby or a child died, and suicides distressed him too. There were other things. Whenever I drove out with him, he would point out his own personal landmarks.

"That tree over there, the police called me one morning to cut down a man who had hanged himself."

"Here in this field, a farmer was trampled to death by his own ram. He was in a terrible mess when I dealt with him."

"You see the bridge across the main line railway? A man jumped over into the path of an express train. We were picking up bits from the fields on either side. You couldn't tell if it was man or animal."

"A body was washed up along this stretch of river. It had been in the water for three weeks. It looked awful, and the stench made me feel sick. I had to take it to Hull for all the necessary examination."

I could go on. Farmers blew their own heads off with shotguns, either deliberately or by accident. Farm machinery hit overhead cables and electrocuted the drivers. Tractors overturned and crushed the driver. People perished in house fires and were mangled in road accidents. It all seemed so senseless, especially if the victim was young. Too often, Jack knew the families involved, and it was hard. Then came the day of his own tragedy.

A Personal Tragedy

Trade was slow on that grey, drizzly January morning in 1986. The doorbell shrilled. Jack glanced up with swiftly vanishing expectation as he saw not the hoped-for customer but two policemen entering his shop. Oh well! He was used to the police calling. What did they want this time? It could be anything from a body in the river to a cat locked in an empty house. He stepped forward.

"Are you Jack Punton?"

"Yes."

"Could we have a word privately?"

There was no one else around, but Jack took them into his office. One of the officers produced a wallet and a small photograph.

"Do you by any chance know this man?"

"What are you doing with that picture?" Sudden premonition made him sharp. "That's Ted, my brother."

"I'm sorry, Mr Punton. We have bad news. Your brother was knocked down by a train a short while ago. I'm afraid he died instantaneously."

Every morning Ted walked his dog down a country lane and back over a level crossing just beyond Snaith station. He had, along with myriads of locals, used that crossing thousands of times. Jack could only assume that with it being so wintry, he had pulled his anorak hood round his face, depended on sound rather than sight, failed to see or hear the train drawing out of the station, and had walked right into it. The dog was injured and had to be put down. Meanwhile, it was Jack's task to break the news to Dolly.

Dolly was a character, outgoing, outspoken, and strong; but this was a body-felling blow. Jack knew that his doughty sister-in-law would cope, but he hated to see her hurt in such a brutal way. It would be hard for her. She and Ted had shared a lifetime together. Like all married couples, they had their ups and downs and ways of handling disagreements. When they really were annoyed with each other, they stopped speaking and communicated by notes left strategically round the house. Such things were minor. The family was close. Sandria and Nicky, the two children, lived nearby. They would give their mother every support.

There were other reasons why Jack felt so deeply for Dolly. I am told that in her younger days, she was a fashionable peroxide blonde who knew everybody and everything about everybody and who, with her big heart of warm gold, would do anything for anybody. Jack and his family had cause to love Aunty Dolly and to know her worth. When Margaret lay ill at home in her last weeks of life, Jack still had to keep shop and leave her alone for long spells. Dolly, without being asked or saying a word, regularly popped in to check up on things. She made cups of tea and chatted to Margaret who, by this time, lay on a bed downstairs. When she saw Margaret tiring, she went through into the kitchen, tidied up, prepared a few vegetables for the meal later, left an apple pie on the table, and quietly slipped away.

When Margaret went upstairs, for an afternoon sleep, she often awoke to the hum of the vacuum cleaner below. Dolly was at work. By the time she came down, everything was clean; and the house was empty. After Margaret died, Dolly still called in. Jack would arrive home from the shop to find his washing up done and an apple pie on the table. He was partial to apple pies, as his sister-in-law knew. If he had introduced Dolly to Fairyland, she herself was his good fairy in his time of need. Now she had her own crisis to face.

Dolly survived her tragedy, as people do. In her last years, she lived in a row of bungalows with other elderly widows on either side. She had a heart condition and rarely went out.

"But," said Jack, "she knew everything that was happening. If I wanted to know about anything in the community, all I had to do was visit Dolly."

As for Ted, Jack never quite got over the loss of his gruff older brother. He once said to me,

> *I still miss Ted. I used to go round two or three times a week to see him, and he came to me. There were only four years between us, but he remembered things about the old days that I never knew. I often asked him about the family history of people I was looking after who had died. He liked his pint in the pub of an evening which was never my scene, but we were always very close.*

If I Were a Rich Man

A few folks felt that when I married Jack, I was doing well for myself. I was. Marrying Jack was the best thing I ever did in a happy and privileged life, albeit not in the sense that our above "few folks" thought. Like Tevye in *Fiddler on the Roof*, who sang the title song of this section, Jack was not a rich man. He worked hard to make ends meet all his life. When he retired, he had his state pension—a very small allowance from his business—and less savings in the bank than anyone might have guessed. These, he spent in visiting his daughters in California seven times. He had ample for his fairly frugal needs and no great surplus when I married him.

I am quite certain that Jack could have been, well, if not excessively rich, at least a gentleman of comfortable means. So why was he never wealthy? Also, having already made this point twice in earlier chapters, why am I doing so yet again? It is to allow me to talk about two things. Jack was honest, and he was generous.

There are many grey areas in business life where things are not clearly black or white, wrong or right. Despite such uncertainties, Jack told me that to the best of his ability, he always tried to conduct his affairs with integrity. This included pricing his goods and services reasonably and not looking for every legal loophole to get one up on the taxman.

A commercial traveller who called once presented a scheme to him. (I should explain that those were still the days when you bought your stock through "reps" that represented and sold wholesale for a firm. Nowadays, John goes into the big warehouses in Leeds and sees for himself what is on offer.) The suggested scheme involved Jack and the commercial traveller joining partnership to make something on the side for themselves. I did not understand the details. I am not sure that Jack did either. Suffice to say that it was dubious. Jack would have none of it. He took his Christianity into his business in every possible way. This also included compassion and generosity towards people as the next anecdote indicates.

The funeral was over. Jack allowed a few days to elapse before driving out to see the old lady whose husband he had just buried. He hated presenting bills at the best of times. In this case it seemed a particular intrusion, for as far as he knew, the widow had no one close to support her. The lady welcomed the caller, yet somehow Jack sensed anxiety in her demeanour. Eventually he felt in his jacket pocket saying, "I've brought your account."

The woman took it.

"I have the money here," she said, reaching for an envelope behind the clock on the mantelpiece. Jack did not miss the tremor in her hand, as she passed it to him. It had not been there when she had offered him his cup of tea. "Would you count it? I'm afraid it's not quite enough." She hurried on. "I'm sorry. Would you mind if I gave you something each week when I get my pension?"

Jack counted the money. It was short by quite a lot.

"Do you have any insurance?"

A lot of people made weekly payments into insurance policies for funeral costs. She had no insurance. She had no savings other than what the envelope in Jack's hands contained. He believed her. He knew something of her circumstances.

"Don't worry. You'll get your money. I'll give you something every week when I get the pension." She was anxious to reassure him, mistaking his silence for displeasure.

"Give me the account," he requested gently. He pulled out his pen and wrote across it firmly, "Paid." He signed and dated it and handed it back to the woman together with her envelope and its contents. "This is between you and me alone," he assured her. He was almost as close to tears as she was.

Fortunately for Jack, most of his clients did have insurance. In the case of the gentleman who did not, the relatives clubbed together to put him away decently. Came the day when Jack presented his account.

"You've made a mistake," affirmed the lady who had taken it upon herself to handle affairs.

"I don't think so." Jack was punctilious about such matters.

"It's the cars," said the lady, "we had two, and you've only charged us for one."

"That's right. I've charged you for one. There's no mistake."

Concerning the Grave

Not everyone wants to be cremated, although it has now become, perforce, the norm in cities. In the country, there is room for graveyards to expand. Snaith churchyard, for instance, is literally full to overflowing. Dig anywhere and but a few inches below the surface, you unearth loose bones. The new cemetery opened in the 1950s. It lies outside the town off the Pontefract Road and will serve a goodly time yet. Be they churchyards or corners cut out of a farmer's field, our country burial places are all part of an undertaker's life. Take grave digging for instance! At one time each parish had its own gravedigger until financial stringencies made him redundant and shunted the job over to the undertaker. It is not as simple as you might imagine.

To begin with, only experience and a measuring tape can ensure that the size of the hole is right—length, breadth, depth, and vertical slope of the walls. If you are digging what is to be the last resting place for a husband and wife, you must dig down deep to leave room above for the second coffin at a later date. There are regulations about how far below the surface a coffin must be. So there you are, at the bottom of a narrow hole; and the deeper you delve, the less room you have to manoeuvre and the higher you must throw the earth out. And how do you get out yourself at the end? An agile undertaker braces and levers himself up the sides. Otherwise a short ladder is an essential part of your equipment.

Nor is that all. Each cemetery has its own peculiarities. In Hensall, for instance, you need a pickaxe. Close below the surface lies a stratum of compacted pebbles. Once through that, you are back to sandy soil; and the rest, so to speak, is easy. In Snaith and Cowick, you might end up digging your own grave as the earth caves in. You, therefore, shore up the sides with planks as you work. In all too many places in this low-lying, flat landscape, the graves will flood. In some cases, it is enough to lay a piece of grass matting down to cover the water. If the water table is higher, the coffin and grass matting together will still float. Vicars and undertakers experienced in local matters take care to keep the mourners back from the edge, lest they be distressed by a bobbing coffin. An alternative is to dig the grave down to the water level one day, then rush out to finish the last few feet just before the funeral. It generally takes an hour or two for the water to seep in significantly.

On one bad occasion, John had to hire a pump. When the cortege approached the cemetery, he gave a signal to the person manning the pump who speedily removed all traces of his activities only minutes before the funeral group arrived. So rapid was the influx of water that even the pump could not cope and the coffin still floated. However, anxiously, you seek to observe the protocols of the event; you cannot override the forces of nature.

The Not So Grave

Jack approached his job with decorum and dignity, but that is not to say that amusing things did not happen.

The Quaker committal in Pontefract crematorium was a quiet affair where everyone sat meditating with downcast eyes. Says Jack, "I closed my eyes as well. Suddenly I came to with a jerk. How long had I been napping? The two ladies at the front, in charge of proceedings, were looking at me quizzically. Obviously time was up."

By contrast, a funeral in a Roman Catholic church in Carlton involved the long ceremonial of full requiem mass plus sundry sprinklings with holy water in the crematorium afterwards. When all was over, John (for this is one of John's stories) walked back to the cars with the priest and his acolyte.

"Father, there's some holy water left over. What shall I do with it?" asked the acolyte.

Father Maudsley looked around and espied a sturdy bloom flourishing by a wall.

"Give it to that sunflower. It looks as if it needs a drop of holy water."

Another day, Jack was in the hearse going to the crematorium. It was an old-fashioned vehicle where the front seat stretched from door to door. The vicar, who is long since gone and probably dead himself by now, was sitting in the middle between Jack and the driver. He was a large man and seated awkwardly. All three were uncomfortable. He was also a grumpy man. On and on he complained about the discomfort until suddenly Jack had had enough.

"Mr—," he said, "I'm fed up with your grumbles. You could have gone in your own car. If you don't shut up, I'm going to ask the driver to stop, and I shall get out and walk. You can deal with everything at the crematorium yourself, and I shall explain why to the family."

The vicar shut up. Later the hearse driver told Jack that he wished he had had the courage to speak first.

We all like to farewell our deceased with a flattering eulogy, no matter what kind of a so-and-so the dear departed actually was. More than once in his long career, after a spiel of fulsome praise in a full church, someone has come up to Jack with a remark such as "Hearing all that rubbish, I thought I must have got into the wrong funeral by mistake." Or, "The vicar didn't know the man (or woman) I knew." Or, "I think the vicar was talking about the archangel Gabriel, not a man."

Even relatives express their feelings with robust bluntness as when, having collected the ashes from the crematorium, Jack asked the daughter of the deceased what she would like done with them.

"I don't care," came her swift response. "Put them in a beer mug on a shelf in the D—s Arms. He'll be happy there."

I close this section with one of Jack's jokes. I believe he read it in a magazine for funeral directors, which is the correct term for undertakers today.

A businessman was invited to a luncheon. He arrived late and flustered. Gradually he composed himself, then as the food arrived, he suddenly put his hand to his mouth with a groan.

"Are you all right?" asked his neighbour with concern.

"Yes! No! You see, I came out in a hurry, and I've left my teeth in the bathroom."

"Don't panic," his companion reassured him, as he felt in a pocket and brought out a small box. "Have a look at these. Try them for size."

The businessman opened the box. Inside lay a perfect set of false teeth. He tried them.

"No! I'm afraid they're too small."

His friend sought in another pocket.

"What about these, then?"

"Sorry! They're too big."

Once more his fellow diner rummaged in his pockets. Once more he produced a box and handed it over.

"Mm! Wonderful! These are just right."

The two gentlemen began their meal.

"By the way," asked the businessman at last, "what's your job? Dentist?"

"No! Undertaker."

Two Treats

No matter how busy he was, Jack made time for his chapel. Apart from the local preaching, he held various offices and even ran the circuit youth club for a while. In addition, he loved his cricket and captained his team. It all took its toll on family life. The time had come for choices. To be fair to Margaret and the children, something had to go. It was hard, but he gave up the cricket. Sacrifices in one area brought compensations in others, and home life was always fulfilling. However, two special events always stood out for Jack. I call them treats because this is what they were. They gave him a needed break from routine and a boost in morale.

In May 1951, the Methodist church organised a lay conference in the Kingsway Hall, London, on the subject of "The Church and the Christian in the Welfare State." We take our welfare state for granted as one of our rights. In 1951, it was only three years old and still a revolutionary social experiment. Hundreds of delegates gathered to hear Christian and political leaders of the day express their views and to discuss the issues involved. There were speakers such as Anthony Eden, a former foreign minister and future Conservative Prime Minister. There was George Thomas, a Labour MP, future speaker of the House and the future Lord Tonypandy. Mr Thomas was also, of course, an active Methodist local preacher all his life, even when he was famous and at the height of his career. Having read a transcript of the proceedings, I doubt if they are of any interest to the readers of this book, although a social historian might well find the record fascinating, for I believe that it reflects the mood of thinking people in our country at that time. The real point of mentioning the conference is because Jack went, along with a younger local preacher friend called Mr Billy Darley.

Now neither Jack nor Billy had any hope of attending in normal circumstances. Financially, Jack often felt worried and under pressure, as he struggled to make a go of branching out in business alone. Then Mr Killingbeck entered the scene, a well-to-do farmer and a Methodist stalwart. He took Jack and Billy as his guests. Not only did they go to the conference, they also fitted in two days of sightseeing which included the Chelsea Flower Show. It was a wonderful experience for both men, and for Jack, it was a psychological uplift when he most needed it.

At this point I have three more of my "incidentally" remarks to add. The first is to say that since I lost Jack, this same Mr Darley often came round to see me, especially if he happened to be preaching in Snaith on a Sunday morning. The second incidentally concerns his daughter-in-law Shirley. She was one of my regular carers who helped me keep going and remain in my own home. She was one of the best. And third, it was Shirley's daughter Emma who went into Punton's DIY shop to ask for "a long stand."

The second treat was a trip to Sweden in 1962. The Yorkshire Rural Community Council had arranged a fact-finding tour for people who worked with wood. They went to Sweden for two weeks—all expenses paid—to see every aspect of the timber industry. They learned about forestry management, visited saw mills, wood pulp, and paper mills and discovered how wood chippings and sawdust were processed into chipboard and so on. They toured furniture factories and shops and finally saw how wood was exported to end up in some form or other in their own workshops or places of business.

In the sixties, sea travel was still cheaper and more frequent than by air. Accordingly, the party went by sea. It was Jack's first time abroad and in a big ship. He loved it all—the programme, the company, the scenery and sightseeing, the Swedish food, and the hotels. He bought presents for all the family. To this day, Ruth remembers her umbrella with its different coloured segments. They sailed home in a gale. Here is the traveller's diary entry for the journey.

> *I was awakened several times in the night with the ship rolling . . . . I was sure I would roll out of my bunk. I got out of bed and attempted to wash and shave but it was impossible to stand still. The wash bowl was at such an angle that the water wouldn't stay in . . . . I wasn't feeling too good but I decided to . . . go up on deck hoping the fresh air would make me feel better. It did but I couldn't shake off the unhappy feeling in my tummy. My friend, Mr Townsend, wouldn't attempt to get out of bed. He was pretty groggy. I decided that bed was the best place so I got back in.*
>
> *I stayed there until lunch time, when I decided to try a cup of coffee. I went to the dining room which was less than half full. I was just having a sip of coffee when the boat gave a terrific roll. Cups and saucers fell off the tables. This proved too much for me. I . . . made a rush for the deck. (I didn't want to disgrace myself in the dining room.) With my handkerchief acting as a stopper I just reached the deck and all my troubles went overboard, including my false teeth. That was a tragedy. I knew I should never live it down.*

He never did. When Simon and his wife, Jayne, went on a cruise to Sweden a few months ago, I asked them to look overboard in case his dad's teeth are, perchance, still floating upon the waves.

Family Fortunes

Everything Jack did, he did it for his family. He loved his shop and the business he had built up from nothing. Nevertheless, the great inspiration behind all his achievements was his wife and family. They were the centre of his life, and he was proud of them all to his dying day. It can only be fitting, therefore, to conclude this chapter by telling you what has happened to each one of them in later life.

Of all the family, Sally is most like her dad in her placid temperament and perhaps in looks as well. She is practical and capable and meets every occasion with her own quiet dignity. She went to teacher training college in Oxford where she met her husband-to-be, Kevin Johnson. They both taught for a while until Kevin took over the family garden centre and nurseries near Hull when his father died. Their four children—Stephen, Jane, Angela, and Jenny—are all grown-up and making their own way in life. It is also Sally who has spent hours typing this book for me, as I have had to write it all in longhand.

In 1999, Kevin and Sally took early retirement. They now live in their favourite place—Crackington Haven—in Bide-a-Wee, the house designed by grandfather Stephen Ward so many years long ago. Meanwhile, the garden centre is in the capable hands of a manager and son Stephen. Kevin and Sally may be at the other end of the country, but they are far from isolated. They have speedily involved themselves in local life, and Cornwall still remains a favourite holiday venue for all the Punton and Johnson clans.

As a matter of interest, when I eventually moved into residential care in May 2001, my dog Sally went to live with them in Cornwall where she settled happily. Well, any dog who gets a ride in a car—with a heated seat no less, and the occasional treat of a crispy pig's ear—has, I think, landed firmly on all four paws.

John went to college in York then taught in Chesterfield for some years before joining his father in the business. He met his wife, Jean, in Guernsey when he was on a rugby tour and she on holiday. Jean, like myself, has multiple sclerosis and is up and down in health. Their children—Mark, Nigel, Michelle, and Matthew—are all grown-up and independent.

Ever since Jack died, all John's family have kept an eye on me. Apart from handling odd jobs in the house, John was always quietly understanding of the physical and emotional crises I faced, as I struggled to cope alone with decreasing strength. John and Jean are active members of Carlton Methodist Church. I believe John continues to run the business in a way that Jack would approve.

Jane trained as a nurse in London. On a visit to America, she met her future husband Mike Daye. Sadly, Margaret died only a few months before their wedding. Jane and Mike live in Escondido, California. Their eldest son is Alex. Shortly after I met Jack, they began to foster a little boy called George and later adopted him. We understand that he may be a descendant of Rudyard Kipling who could account for his literary and dramatic talents.

Jane visited us five months before her dad died. One morning he said to me, "I've just had quite a turn. Jane came through that door, and for one moment, I thought it was Margaret."

Jane is introspective and thoughtful. She describes herself as a free thinker. According to Jack, she is the most like her mother in both looks and personality. I am so glad that I have met all four of the Daye family. Normally Jane comes home by herself because of the expense; but a few years ago, Mike, Alex, and George came with her. I wish I could see them more often and get to know them better.

Ruth followed in her mother's steps and trained as a nanny, for she is good with children. In between nannying, she has tackled a variety of jobs, including that of a driving instructor. Also like her mother, she can do anything with a needle and a piece of material and is a great organiser. Whenever she used to visit her dad, she would spend hours spring-cleaning bedrooms and tidying drawers and cupboards. After she had left, I got used to hearing Jack go round muttering, "I can't find a thing anywhere. Our Ruth's been tidying up again."

Jack always said that from childhood, Ruth was independent and self-contained, able to play for hours by herself in a world of make believe when all the others were demanding attention. Shortly after Jack died, she married Andrew Lee and they now live in Berkshire. She chairs various committees, organises things like village fetes and harvest suppers, and generally livens up the rural community.

Simon took some time to work out what he wanted to do but eventually moved high up in his profession of psychiatric nursing. To me, judging only from photographs, Simon looks like his Uncle Raymond. In fact, apart from Sally, I think all the family favour the Ward side rather than the Punton in looks. As such perceptions are very individual things, other people might disagree.

Simon met his wife, Jayne, when she was a student nurse training with Joyce. They are both practical, down-to-earth, caring people. Their children—Katie, Ross, and Jessica—are all beginning to make their way in their chosen professions. They live in Stockton, about an hour and a half's drive away. Because they used to visit every month when the children were small, I have watched the children growing up and feel very honoured when, along with the American grandchildren, they call me Granny Anne. For that matter, I also feel honoured when John calls me "the wicked stepmother."

Joyce is the youngest and the last, but never the least. She has a warm, sunny, bright personality. From a little snippet I once read about her maternal grandmother, I wonder if there is a similarity there. A young photograph of Margaret's mother may also show a likeness in appearance.

Joyce trained as a nurse and was sister in a urology ward in Bristol before she settled in America. I hope that when I reach the stage of serious nursing, I hope someone like Joyce will look after me. Her little boy Stephen Jack is Jack's youngest grandchild. He was born in America. Joyce and Stephen live with Mike and Jane, which is a happy arrangement. The two women, both nurses, plan shifts so that one of them is always at home for the family. Mike is like a father to Stephen whilst Alex and George are more like brothers to him than cousins.

It was very sad that Joyce and Stephen were booked to visit us in March 1999, and Jack died unexpectedly in February. Being the youngest, Joyce did not share much of her adult life with Margaret when the mother-daughter relationship matures into new dimensions. Consequently, she felt, as perhaps did all the family, that the bond with her father grew correspondingly deeper. Everyone else saw Jack shortly before he died. Even for Jane, it was only five months. For Joyce, it was almost two years. She was deprived of that last opportunity, and it hurt.

Jack himself had no favourites. Each child was unique and meant something special to him. He filled his walls with their pictures and his heart with happy memories. His one sadness was that their mother never lived to see how well they have done and to watch her grandchildren growing up.

Snaith Methodist Church, to which Jack gave so much of his time and love.

Rehanging the Carlton Church bells after the war.

The shop property in 2011.

The shop property, 1 and 3 Market Place, Snaith,
as it was when Jack was young.

1 and 3 Market Place, as it is today, now managed by Jack's son, John.

CHAPTER 8

JACK THE WALKING MAN
or
HOW JACK TOOK TO THE ROAD

Stormy Winds Ahead

Jack was sixty-three and at the peak of his career, for he had just been elected town mayor of Snaith and Cowick. Business was comfortable, the struggles of younger years over. Margaret was well with the scare of her mastectomy quietly receding. The children had all successfully flown the nest. Sally and John were married and had produced the first grandchildren. Jane, Ruth, Simon, and Joyce were following their chosen careers whilst still returning to home base with anticipated frequency. All was set for a calm course into predictable old age.

Then the wind changed. Margaret complained of back pain.

"It's probably arthritis," said the doctor.

"You need to take it easier," urged Jack. His wife was managing the Goole Oxfam shop by this time and working hard. "You're straining your back, humping all those heavy bags up and down stairs."

The pains worsened. The cancer had returned and was spreading. There could be no reprieve. An operation in the spring of 1977 was only ameliorative.

From then on, Margaret deteriorated rapidly. She died on July 25, 1977, aged only fifty-seven. Like her husband, she was loved and respected by everyone. Together, they had made a perfect partnership.

I would never want to minimise the grief of the family at the loss of their mother. However, their lives were still unfolding in challenge and adventure. For Jack, that was in the past. All he could see before him was a lonesome old age.

"I didn't know what to do with myself in that first year," he told me. "I kept the shop going. In the evenings, I went to meetings and anything else that was happening to fill in time. I dreaded going out, but I had to. Even just walking down the High Street, people kept stopping to ask me how I was, and all I wanted to do was burst into tears. In the house alone, I hardly dared sit down. I paced the floor from room to room for hours."

The children came often, and it helped. Apart from losing a dearly loved partner, some of the problem was that, for the first time in his life, Jack was alone. He had grown up with brothers and sisters, shared barracks in the NCC, and raised his own big brood. Now it had all gone, and Margaret too. In desperation, he considered the future. He could see no future. Who can in the early days of bereavement? He, who, with Margaret by his side, would have worked in his shop to his last breath, health, and with wifely permission granted, suddenly saw the red-letter age of sixty-five looming and made up his mind. None of his children wanted the business. He would sell up and retire. Beyond that, he dared not think.

The decision was irrational given his pride in his business, his zest for life, and his determination never to give in. Deep down he recognised this and amended it. He would tell the children what he was contemplating and get their reactions. The first one came swiftly. John was teaching in Chesterfield where he lived with his wife, Jean, and two young sons, Mark and Nigel. In a letter that expands on the homely details of baby burps and tummy upsets, John also wrote, "I can't see myself teaching for the rest of my life. How about if I come into the business with you?"

He did in July 1978. Before long Jack displayed a new sign on the shop front—J. Punton and Son. I think that was the moment when his hopelessness and some of the loneliness went.

Father and son worked well together despite a few frictions. Son came in with new ideas. Father had always done it this way and saw no need to change.

Father would go off for a few weeks on one of the jaunts you are shortly to hear about. Son took the chance to do things as he wanted to alter the layout a bit and such like. Father returned and served his first customer, only to discover that a required item was no longer in its usual place. Son suggested making a new office. Father saw nothing wrong with the old one. Father went off again. Son made the new office. Father returned and looked round dubiously before admitting, "Hm! Not bad!"

In the end Jack had to acknowledge that John's suggestions were beneficial and in keeping with modern progress. For instance, it was John who, recognising that more people were beginning to lie in the undertaker's premises than in their own homes, decided to make a chapel of rest behind the shop. Also, it was he who, realising that the old system of dealing with commercial travellers was on the way out, began going to wholesale warehouses to choose their stock.

Father and son worked happily together in more ways than one. John was able and bright. He needed to be given more of the responsibility for the day to day running of the show. As for Jack, he had unexpectedly found a new interest. He wanted freedom to follow it up.

Taking to the Road

Night after night pictures of the Cambodian refugees filled our news' screens. As always, the plight of the children touched Jack's heart. What could he do to help? Another coffee morning, or bring and buy stall in his shop? A straight donation? He had done it all. He wanted something different. He had an idea. What about a sponsored walk to Hull? Thirty-five miles in a day was not bad for a sixty-seven-year-old. He could then stay with Sally and Kevin for the night.

He planned his publicity carefully, which was not difficult, for he was already widely known. He soon had the local press and radio covering the story. To his delight, he accomplished the distance with ease, finishing up at a Hull radio station for a final interview. There, Sally was due to pick him up. When she failed to arrive on time, the interviewer put out a call.

"Would Sally Johnson please collect her father who has completed his sponsored walk from Snaith to Hull and is waiting for her?"

More day walks followed for other causes. On February 2, 1981, Jack's sixty-eighth birthday, he and Simon trudged the forty-four miles to York and back. Planning an early start, they awoke to a white world. Here the record is mixed. Each man averred that the other suggested putting it off to a better day. Each continued to aver that he was the one who refused to be daunted by a little snow. Whatever the true facts, they set off at 6:00 a.m.

It was a dreadful day. It hardly ever stopped snowing. Soon the untrodden, early white was churned brown. Every few seconds, passing traffic showered them with filthy slush. A backup car skidded into a ditch. A tractor hauled it out, but it reached our weary walkers hours late. Simon's boots were new. He developed blisters and could not complete the return journey. Jack battled on alone. His journal reads thus,

> *It was getting dark by 5:30. I arrived at Selby Toll Bridge at seven o'clock and was pleased to see John and Mark who had come to meet me. I think they would have liked to give me a ride home and was almost tempted to do so but I felt I could make it to Snaith in another two and a half hours. It was quite dark but I had a torch and was able to walk on the right hand side of the road, stepping on the grass verge when a car came towards me. Camblesforth Common seemed never ending but I cheered up when I saw the street light outside The Black Dog at Camblesforth. I reached John's house in George Street at just after 9:30 p.m.—fifteen and a half hours on the road. Jean had a good meal ready for me.*

> *This was my second sponsored walk. Although I was very tired when I went to bed I fell asleep feeling very pleased with my effort and knowing that I would have raised a few hundred pounds for York hospital. I think the final total was just under £700. I was very pleased to be invited at a later date to the launching of the new body scanner and that I had played a small part in making it possible.*

There is an interesting correlation here which anyone who pits their will against the odds will recognise. The more punishment endured in fulfilling set goals, the more impelling the urge to attempt greater heights of achievement. This challenge of physical endurance combined with his passion for children's charities soon developed into the local celebrity, Jack the Walking Man.

Once Jack had started, he could not stop. Before long a mere thirty or forty miles a day seemed trivial. The lure of longer distances beckoned, and there was no shortage of worthy causes to support. Therefore, for his first major long walk, our hero decided to attempt Snaith to Cornwall. Where else?

Cornwall, Here I Come

My husband kept diaries of all his big excursions. Here is an extract from the first day of his first long walk where he explains in his own words how it came about. He was seventy-one.

> *May 14, 1984. I got up this morning at 7:00 a.m. feeling a little bit apprehensive and wondering if I was attempting too big a task to walk three hundred and fifty miles. Towards the end of 1983 after hearing a special appeal on the TV by the NSPCC I had decided that sometime in 1984 I would do a long sponsored walk for their benefit . . . and wondered if I could do something really big.*
>
> *I thought a lot about Jesus telling his disciples to "launch out into the deep!" . . . I had done several sponsored walks varying from twenty-five to seventy-three miles. The public had . . . supported me well but I felt I needed to do something extra . . . . I had driven to Cornwall dozens of times . . . . Could I walk it? I decided, yes. At least I would try.*
>
> *So I announced it. I said I hoped to raise £1000 which could be shared between the NSPCC and Oxfam Famine Relief Appeal . . . . The newspapers gave it good publicity and many people immediately offered to support me by collecting sponsors.*

At this point I must stop to explain procedures. The walking man always planned his routes, sponsorship arrangements, and publicity with exactitude. His were no haphazard campaigns. He walked with a backpack to which he fastened a large waterproof placard bearing the name of the charity he was supporting and his destination and mileage. As much as possible, he stayed on roads with plenty of traffic but where cars could stop reasonably easily to give a donation. It worked. Much of what he received also came from people in towns he passed through or places he halted at for food and, of course, from his own home area. He had a sponsored walk account with Barclays Bank in Selby into which he regularly paid whatever cash he collected on his travels.

Other than a route and a map, he made no advance personal arrangements. He found bed-and-breakfast accommodation as he went. Always he paid his own costs. Every penny donated went to the cause. Contrary to what one might imagine, these trips were by no means cheap holidays for him. Sometimes John had a map in the shop window on which he marked the daily progress, for Jack phoned home every evening to report on his whereabouts. With this background in mind, Jack continues his record of his first day out.

I left the front of my do-it-yourself shop at 9:00 a.m., being sent on my journey with good wishes from a group of supporters . . . As I said at the beginning, I was a little bit worried wondering if I was "biting off more than I could chew." But Jesus said again to his disciples, "Once you've put your hand to the plough, don't look back." And so I was off.

Bawtry, twenty-four miles away [near Doncaster] *was my target for today . . . . The sun was shining and I soon shook off the nagging doubts . . . . A few cars gave me a friendly toot . . . . About three miles from Thorne Bill Ramsey* [Remember the lad and the butcher incident?] *was waiting for me to wish me well . . . . He gave me a can of orange juice. By the time I reached Thorne* [eight miles out] *the sun was quite hot and I began to sweat . . . . A boy ran up to me and gave me fifty pence and wished me good luck. It was so nice. It made me feel quite excited about what I was doing.*

I stopped at a small cafe and had a mug of tea and a sandwich . . . . I felt much refreshed . . . I was really feeling great . . . . A few miles on a van stopped. The driver called to me and I went across to chat with her. She gave me a pound note and wished me well . . . . Eight miles from Bawtry I went into a grass field, took off my boots, had my can of orange juice, and lay down and fell asleep. The sun burnt my face a bit but I felt better for my nap.

I arrived at Bawtry about 5:00 p.m . . . . I asked a young couple who were sitting at a table outside a wine shop if they knew where I could phone from. They gave me a glass of wine and two pounds and the owner of the shop allowed me to use his phone.

The Journey Continues

Jack stayed the night with friends and deemed his first day a success. Tuesday, the second day, was also very hot. Already he realised that he would have difficulties with his feet. Up to then he had always walked in trainers. For something this big, he decided he must have proper hiking boots. It was a mistake. His feet blistered constantly. After that he went back to trainers. Even with trainers, he experienced some problems; but considering the thousands of miles he was eventually to cover, he managed very well in that department.

Tender feet and heat notwithstanding, Tuesday was also a good day.

> *When I arrived at Blyth roundabout* [three miles from Bawtry] *there was a police van parked and about seven policemen . . . . The sergeant . . . asked if I would like some coffee . . . . They were all so nice to me and were impressed with what I was doing. When I left they loaded me with sandwiches, biscuits, chocolate, oranges, apples, cans of Coke, and £1.75. They were parked there to deal with the troubles of the miners' strike.*

The days passed, full of interest and incident. At the Axe and Compass, eleven miles from Coventry, Jack records,

> *I took a seat . . . in the dining area and took off my boots and then a customer bought me a pint of shandy. He then called the attention of the other customers to my backpack notice . . . They took a collection for me, £7, and also paid for my meal.*

I am not sure about the etiquette of removing one's boots in a public eating area. Unfortunately the hot weather was exacerbating his foot discomforts. Later, after a long thirsty slog on roads with little shade, Jack was desperate for a drink.

> *I stopped at a dairy farm and asked the man loading bottles of milk to sell me a bottle. He gave it to me.*

A few miles from Bristol, still with the sun shining and sore feet, Jack sat at the roadside at midday to eat his sandwiches.

> *I lay on the grass and went to sleep under the shade of some overhanging trees in a garden. When I awoke a fairy had been and left me a tube of soft-centred mints . . . .*

> *When I approached Bristol along Fishponds Road, I was dying for a cup of tea but there wasn't a cafe open. Then a man . . . called to me asking if I would like a drink . . . . He took me into his home and his wife made me some tea while I nursed the baby.*

At Taunton, Jack had difficulty finding a bed-and-breakfast place.

Two young girls came up to me to ask about my walk. They were impressed and put themselves about to help me . . . . They had a car and took me around until we found a very nice guest house. The girls went off and gave me £5.

On day eighteen, Jack finally arrived at Bude in Cornwall where Leonard, his brother-in-law, picked him up and took him to Crackington Haven. It was an amazing adventure, and Jack was thrilled. He ends his last diary entry with the inevitable question,

What next?

What Next Indeed?

During that first long distance trek, a pattern—often to be repeated—emerged. Wherever Jack went, he met kindness. Strangers invited him into their homes for cups of tea and ended up offering a meal and a bed for the night. Guest houses charged reduced rates or, occasionally, nothing at all and often gave a donation as well. Some of these people became his friends, and he visited them on future walks through their towns. (His Christmas card list was lengthy.) In cafes and pubs where he ordered meals, fellow diners took up collections for him and landlords waived bills.

Where possible, he contacted the local press and radio stations for publicity and met representatives of the charities he was supporting. The police were always helpful. Only once did they ever question his credentials, in a genteel sort of way. If ever he arrived very late in a town or was unable to find accommodation, he always went to them. Unfortunately, in that respect, he never realised his great ambition which was to spend the night in a police cell because nothing else was available.

Each day, Jack covered between twenty and thirty miles. Unlike some walkers, he had no backup of any kind, not even for the eight hundred and seventy-six miles of his Land's End to John o'Groats venture. If his route took him near friends, he stayed with them for the night and allowed himself a day off. He never accepted lifts. That was cheating. If someone picked him up and took him off his course, for whatever reason, he insisted on starting again where he had left off. Even in terrible weather, he battled on. He would happily sit in a workman's parked van for shelter and a hot brew up. He might even finish the day early in extreme conditions, but sooner or later, the distance must be walked. It was a point of honour.

As the catalogue of my husband's performances grew longer, he compiled a list which he sent out with his publicity material for each new exploit. With some minor editing, I now append it to this section, as it gives an idea of all that he accomplished, and most of it while he was in his seventies.

Sponsored Walks by Jack Punton

	Miles	Km
1979 Snaith to Hull	35	56
1980 Snaith to Doncaster and return	36	58
1981 Snaith to York and return	44	71
1981 Snaith to Market Weighton	25	40
1982 Snaith to Leeds	26	42
1982 Snaith to Billingham	73	117
1983 Snaith to Bridlington	54	87
1984 Snaith to Bude, Cornwall	350	563
1985 Land's End to John o'Groats	876	1,410
1986 Snaith to East and South Coast and Midlands	753	1,212
1987-1988 Hull to Hull via Coast of England and Wales	2,300	3,701
(a) Hull to Aberystwyth	24.4-3.6	1987
(b) Aberystwyth to Exmouth	24.8-1.10	1987
(c) Exmouth to Hull	20.3-22.4	1988
1988 Snaith to London and return (indirect)	500	805
1989 Snaith to Harwich plus 350 miles in Holland	550	885
1989 Bristol to Ipswich via London	250	402
1990 Snaith to London plus London Marathon	206	332
1991 Snaith to Land's End via West Coast	500	805
1992 Coast of Scotland (Record missing) Estimate	800	1,287
1995 Snaith to York	22	35
1997 London Marathon	26.2	42.2
1997 Great North Run	13	21

Walks in United States and Others

1989 "17 Mile Drive" Carmel	17	27
1989 Julian to Escondido	40	64
1991 Los Angeles Marathon	84	135
and Lyke Wake Walk (twice)		

All in all Jack walked over eight thousand miles on official distances and many, many more if you take into account his various added diversions and his training before each expedition. He raised between twenty and thirty thousand pounds for charity on his walks and through other less headline grabbing ways. He started out small. He exceeded his own hesitant expectations. He ended up a local legend known by everybody. I do not exaggerate. Recently someone visited me on business, and in passing, I mentioned my husband's name.

"Do you mean the walking man?" asked my visitor.

To this day, if you mention Jack's name in public, there are people who will immediately identify him as the "Walking Man."

Getting the Feel of Things

If all I had to draw on for this chapter were Jack's diaries alone, it would not be easy to write. It was his custom to fit a whole day's events into a little more than one side of a school jotter page, and he wrote last thing at night when he was tired. His style was factual and unemotional. He reserved his most enthusiastic comments for pots of tea, hot baths, and comfortable beds at journey's end. He could not record all that happened or describe background details. Fortunately I have gleaned my feel for events in two other ways.

Jack regularly spoke about his walks to all kinds of groups. When I was well, I always went with him. He was a good speaker. However small or large the audience, his informal style made people feel as though he were chatting to each person individually, as from an armchair in their own sitting room. He had you laughing, gasping, oohing and aahing, and even interrupting to ask questions. A friend of mind once said, "By the time he'd finished, he had them all eating from his hand."

That kind of atmosphere the diaries do not impart, and I learned much.

Later, when I was ill, it became an evening ritual for Jack to read his diaries to me as I lay in bed. He often paused to fill in some terse entry with colourful detail that made the plain record sparkle. I constantly stopped him in midflow to find out more about an incident. He had time to talk. How lovely those sessions were, and how soothing. Sometimes I dozed. Dearest man! He understood and softly read on. When I awoke, he patiently reread what I had missed. I wonder if he ever knew how much he helped me through a bad few months. I think he did. The point is that, despite the dozing, I took it in. It all stands me in good stead now as I try to give you a picture of what it was like for Jack on the road.

How then, for instance, did a typically good day go? Obviously much depended on the elements. Ideal walking weather is dry, mild, slightly overcast, and with a touch of breeze, which is why Jack never travelled in midsummer. His average daily distance was about twenty-five miles. Not many walkers maintain a four-mile-per-hour pace, but this was Jack's aim. It was a very good day if he managed it.

For walking, A roads were the most direct routes, but some were fast and dangerous and no use for soliciting donations if cars could not safely stop. Generally Jack preferred the quieter byways if he had a choice, even if they added mileage. On one occasion, he found himself on a busy A road and in danger of being whirled into the ditch, or worse, by every heavy lorry that passed. To his relief, a police car picked him up and drove him to a safer, alternative road. It was much better. Vehicles slowed down, read his placard, and stopped to give something. There were houses, farms, shops, and pubs in villages where he met people and could buy a meal or a blissful, thirst-quenching pot of tea. In the evening, he found pleasant accommodation not far off his route. That was a good day.

Most important of all for a typically good day was the cash collected for the cause. How about this example at a Happy Eater near Peterborough in 1988?

> The staff were really marvellous to me. They brought me double of what I ordered and a pot of tea. They emptied their tips' basin into my bag. Several customers gave me some money and the waiter at the cash desk screwed up my account and said forget it. I received £20 there.

It was a happy disadvantage when his money bag grew too heavy with small change. The problem was easily solved as many a shopkeeper was only too glad to exchange a couple of £10 notes for a supply of coins.

Towards the end of the Land's End to John o'Groats distance, this happened.

> *A couple of miles from Bonar Bridge a Wallace Arnold bus stopped and all the passengers waved for me to go in the bus. They gave me over £7. They were lovely and gave a cheer when they left.*

There were other bonuses, not necessarily typical, but they made a day good. I think of his satisfaction in rescuing a stray farm animal off the road and releasing a sheep whose head was caught in a fence. On one special day, Jack thrilled to the beauties of the world around him. He was somewhere near Selkirk on the same John o'Groats trek.

> *I walked down a B road. It was lovely. The sun was shining and I felt on top of the world. I walked for two and a half miles and not a single car on the road. I kept wishing I had a Methodist Hymn Book with me. Some of the great hymns kept going through my mind.*

> *"Lord, how thy wonders are displayed*
> *Where e'er I turn my eye,*
> *When I survey the ground I tread*
> *Or gaze up in the sky."*

> *There was just me and God on this road with sheep and birds. It was magic.*

Jack often communed with God and nature as he stepped it out on the highway, for the world was beautiful, and he had time to take it in. A chance passerby might see him leaning over a fence talking to some curious cows or a friendly horse and feel uplifted by this man's pleasure in country things. At the risk of breaking the spell, I now must say, take care. Do not approach. Our Jack may well be responding to a call of nature of a different kind.

Not all days were good. The British weather and the odd blister saw to that. Head winds, rain, icy temperatures, steep hills, muddy spray from traffic—all took their toll. In those conditions, waterproofs were a joke, especially for Jack. He sweated heavily with exertion and soon was as wet inside as it was outside. By contrast, hot sun with cloudless skies, no shade, and little breeze was equally hard. Apart from developing blisters on swollen, sweaty feet, thirst was a constant torment however much you drank. On isolated stretches of road, you could trudge for miles, unable to obtain water. If at the end of a bad day you had difficulty finding a bed for the night, life was truly miserable. Oh, the joy of reaching a haven where your hostess plied you with tea and food and offered to wash your soaking or sweaty clothes.

Bad days, of course, were also the days when, irrespective of weather conditions, you took little money. One entry, in the Exmouth to Hull, the final leg of the coast of England and Wales walk, is rather telling. Jack never forgot the purpose of his expeditions.

> *Not much money given away on the south and east coast . . . . Plenty of admiration but no cash. Admiration won't feed hungry kids.*

In addition to describing the typically good or bad day, I now offer a few incidents that I feel are typically Jack himself.

Typically Jack

Jack had a cap. Jack has had many caps. Jack loses his caps. Folks in Snaith see his name inside and obligingly bring the errant article back to his DIY shop. In the anonymity of the road, it is a different matter. On April 11, 1990, he was lucky. He set off that morning in pleasant conditions and left his cap behind.

> *When I got about a mile on the Nottingham road a car was in a lay-by and a man was taking a movie film of me as I walked towards them. It was one of the couples in the guest house. I discovered that I had left my cap in the bedroom . . . . A little later on they caught up with me again. They had been back and fetched my cap.*

Jack also loved football. But let me start at the beginning. In April 1987, at a bed-and-breakfast in Hawick, he made friends with Peter and Marian. As they were Dutch, I have probably spelt their names wrongly. It does not affect the story. As a result of this meeting, their home became his base when he walked round Holland in 1989. Now Marian, though only the age of Jack's own daughters, mothered him with proprietary concern. She insisted that he phone her each night to assure her that he was safe.

"We'll come and get you, wherever you are, if you need us," she promised.

Being a compliant bloke, Jack did as he was told and acknowledged her kindness. Then came the evening of the big European soccer match. He discovered in his host for the night a kindred spirit. The two men sat happily glued (forgive the cliché but there is no other word) to the television until nearly midnight. Only when it was all over did Jack remember Marian.

"Where have you been?" his anxious mentor scolded. He explained. "What? You've been watching football? And I've been worried out of my mind. I kept saying to Peter that poor Jack must be sleeping in a ditch somewhere, and he must go and look for him. And all this time you've been watching football."

Obviously Peter knew his wife and was in no hurry to go to poor Jack's rescue. Perhaps he was watching the football as well.

There was something special about Jack. To see him, even in passing, was to trust him. The incident I am about to describe happened, with variations, more than once. I know we are talking about the 1980s and that little over a decade has seen immense changes in our social climate. I still think, however, that this story pays high tribute to the man Jack was and fits appropriately into this section of typically Jack. He was heading for Hereford on the way to John o'Groats. He was walking through a residential area with no refreshment places to be seen, and he was very thirsty.

> I begged a glass of water at a house. A couple of miles further on a little girl came out of a house and asked me to go in for a cup of tea. Her mother had seen me earlier on the road and had been looking out for me. She made me a plate of sandwiches and two mugs of tea and gave me an apple and an orange. I took photos outside their house.

How many mothers today would send a little girl down the street alone to greet a total stranger?

One day, Jack was setting out towards Berwick-on-Tweed when a car with an attractive young lady drew up. The lady was interested in his walking, and he sat in her car for a long while, chatting and sharing an orange and some chocolate. He discovered that Mrs Susan Smith was a businesswoman who lived in Windsor. Her car had been stolen, and when the police found it in Berwick, she decided to fetch it and have a holiday at the same time. She would gladly have driven Jack the remaining miles into the town, but naturally, he refused the lift, and they parted. The following morning, as Jack was striding northwards out of Berwick-on-Tweed, Susie passed him again. They sat in the sun on a handy bench and again found much to talk about. Eventually Jack asked a window cleaner working nearby to take a photograph of them both on his camera. He then promised to stay in touch and said good-bye. How typical it was that this friendship, made like many other chance meetings on the road, should last for the rest of Jack's lifetime. Of itself, the encounter with Susie was very ordinary, but it had a moving sequel which will be revealed later.

Something else which was typically Jack was his pride in his walking prowess. He was never ostentatious about it, but this laconic diary entry on a day near Winchester masks much gleeful self-satisfaction.

> *I met and overtook two young men who were on a three-day walk. They were shattered and I left them, much to their amazement at my walking speed.*

"Good on you, Jack!"

Taking the Rough with the Smooth

Jack's capacity for enjoying life and people was tremendous. Here are two events from the Hull to Aberystwyth section of his coast of England and Wales walk in May 1987. They took place on the same day. The first had some consequence, the second none at all. Jack enthused equally about both.

> *I came to the village of Bolden en route for South Shields ferry, and a tall man was waiting for me near a school. He was the headmaster and he invited me to the school for a cup of tea. He let all the children come to talk to me and most of them put a small donation in my bag. I thought it was really nice of the headmaster to invite me to tell the children what I was doing . . . .*

> *Later that day I asked a lorry driver directions for South Shields ferry. He says, "Why, it's Jack Punton; I've read a lot about you. I'm from Selby." . . . I do meet some super people.*

If Jack met some super people, he also met some superb acts of kindness.

Three hundred miles round Holland in 1989 was not enough for such a veteran. He had to walk to Harwich for his ferry. Now Jack, amply generous to a cause he believed in, never spent money needlessly on himself. He therefore bought the cheapest ticket and planned to stretch out on a deck lounger for the night. Arriving at the terminal, he prepared to board ship.

"Are you Mr Punton?" enquired the lady who processed his ticket. Jack affirmed his identity. "Please wait here a minute, sir."

Shortly an official gentleman greeted him.

"We've been told about you. We think you're doing a good job, and we'd like to help you on your way. Please accept this with the compliments of the management."

"This" proved to be a first-class ticket to one of the best cabins on board.

I could go on. On the west coast of his round Scotland walk, Jack met a man and his wife who stopped their car to talk to him. As they parted, Mr Brown handed him a card.

"When you get to—, go to this hotel and give the receptionist my card. They'll be expecting you."

Jack did as instructed and found himself installed for the night in one of the best rooms in one of the best hotels in town, dinner and breakfast provided, and all for free. A couple of days later, the Browns met up with him again. He received another card with similar instructions and once more finished up in a posh hotel. Mr Brown was the manager of a chain of hotels. All in all Jack was a guest, every expense paid, in about five of them.

On other occasions, he met town mayors, bishops, and even aristocracy. He loved it all, and people loved him. At times he was as excited as a little boy about his adventures. In the end I just had to ask him, "Did you never have any nasty experiences?"

He thought about it then replied, "Not really. Perhaps one or two unfortunate things, but nothing terribly bad. I was never mugged or robbed, if that's what you mean. There was the egg, of course, and the accident and a boardinghouse in Dover. They were unpleasant little episodes rather than nasty."

Later, I found the incidents in his diaries. Here they are.

An unusual thing happened to me walking through the village of Holland [between East Grinstead and Eastbourne]. *I was on the footpath and suddenly something hit me on my right shoulder with force and really hurt. It was an egg which obviously smashed . . . . The yolk ran down my arm. Where it came from I'll never know. It must have been thrown from a car. If it had hit me in the face I would have been in a mess.*

This was Jack's only experience of deliberate hostility. The accident on the road between Hawick and Carlisle was somebody else's misfortune.

Half a mile out of Longtown a young man on a racing bike fell off and hit his head on the road knocking him unconscious . . . . I stopped a car and a lady helped me . . . . A lorry driver phoned for an ambulance. It was twenty minutes before it came. A nurse . . . stopped and helped. Two police cars came. I had to give details as I was the only one who saw it happen.

Jack never heard the outcome of that story. By coincidence, in Carlisle, the evening of the same day, another lad came off his bike. He was unhurt. I cannot help wondering if Jack was the unwitting cause of both tumbles. Were the cyclists more intent on him than on the road?

Undoubtedly our traveller's worst experience, and it was not all that bad really, was his night's lodging in Dover on the last leg of his coastal walk round England. He had no choice. It was the only place he could find. The house was dirty and stank of rancid food. The couple in charge were slatternly with alcohol on their breath. He shared a room with a man who coughed and snored all night. For Jack to record that he did not sleep well says enough about the conditions. The bedclothes were dirty. He put his money bag under the pillow for safety and covered the pillow with his shirt for hygiene. He realised he was in a place where the same bed is used twice by different people working day and night shifts.

I got out of bed at eight o'clock and washed and shaved. There was no towel . . . . I . . . went down to see about breakfast. There was no one about. I knocked on a door and a man came out looking dirty. Said he was a guest . . . said the owners weren't up. He shouted and knocked for them but no one came. I said I was not waiting . . . . I told him to tell them I had gone and if they wanted payment to send someone after me. I would be on the road to Ramsgate.

Needless to say, nobody chased him up, and Jack never did have any pangs of conscience about the unpaid bill.

A Few Funnies

Jack had a sense of humour and soon saw the funny side of things. As a matter of fact, having more than once heard the way he told the boardinghouse story, I still wonder if I should have included it in this section as a funny, rather than in the previous one as a baddie. Try this instead.

Jack was passing through London. He was having a pub meal at the Elephant and Castle where a group of smart young men stood at the bar. After a while, one of them came over to chat.

"You're doing a wonderful work. I'd like to give you something," he said as he ostentatiously signed his cheque book.

Jack thanked him and glanced at the proffered slip of paper. £50. That was great. The young chap departed. Another customer nodded pleasantly to Jack then asked casually, "Do you know who it was who gave you that cheque just now?"

Jack had no idea.

Can you recall the Guinness fraud case in the news during the eighties? One of the men who stood trial and went to prison was Ernest Saunders. Apparently Jack's benefactor was Mr Saunders's son. To Jack's disappointment, he had used his father's cheque book, and the cheque bounced.

On another occasion, when Jack walked to London to do the London Marathon, he spent a night with friends in Nottingham—Nick and Lindsay and their children. He wrote concerning the morning of his departure.

> *Nick went off to the surgery* [he is a doctor]. *Lindsay, Anna, and Tom took me to the Melton Road about 11:00 a.m. It was a cloudy morning again but dry. I found a lady's watch in my pocket and wondered where it had come from . . . . I learned later that Tom had put it there. It was Lindsay's. The young rascal.*

Another evening, when Jack was walking round Scotland, he made his routine phone call to John. John had been working behind the shop, putting in a new sink and digging down to install drainage pipes.

"Guess what I found today?" he asked his dad. Jack failed to guess. "A skeleton!"

"A what? Have you informed the police?"

"Of course. They came and took it away."

By the time the investigation was complete, Jack was home again; but their conclusions were no real surprise to him.

"It's the skeleton of a man. He died over five hundred years ago. If you find any more, put them back, and don't bother us."

It appears that way back in time, Snaith churchyard extended well beyond its present boundary. In Jack's younger days, when workmen dug up High Street and Market Place to lay water pipes and electricity cables, they unearthed human bones all over. I was disappointed that we never found any when we added our back extension to April Cottage. I feel sure there was the basis for a good "whodunit" plot in the tale of John's skeleton.

Down Memory Lane

Do you remember Reg Walker, the minister who stood by Jack all those years ago when he faced the tribunals as a conscientious objector? The two men never lost touch. It was near Liskard, on the Aberystwyth to Exmouth part of his coastal walk, that Jack passed near Reg's home. Now Reg was dying of cancer. Jack phoned Margaret, his wife, hoping to see him, only to learn that the end was close. It was not the time to call. He went on his way with bittersweet nostalgia in his heart.

On the same trip, he spent a happy evening with Phyllis Lacey. The former matron of Rawcliffe Hall had retired in Exmouth; and as with Reg, Jack remained in touch with her. She went blind but never gave in and acquired a beautiful guide dog who stole Jack's heart. A couple of years into our marriage, word came that Phyllis had died. Inevitably, if you live into your eighties, you see old friends passing and the gates of your past closing. Happily, the trips down memory lane, though tinged with sadness, were by no means all gloomy.

It was Sunday, May 25, on Jack's east-to-south coast walk. He was making for Oxford.

About 4:00 p.m., I came to the turn off to Didcot . . . . It was three miles so I decided to go . . . . Entering Didcot a man came towards me and said would I like to go to his house for some tea. He had passed me in his car earlier. His name was John McConnell and his wife, Erica. They invited me to stay the night so I just couldn't resist . . . .

I went to the service at the chapel at 6:30. Erica said she would have a meal ready for me when I came back. She also washed all my clothing. It was lovely going to chapel again where I met Margaret. It had been altered a bit.

The main street in Didcot was all built up. A health centre on Rymane field where we camped . . . . I sat talking to John and Erica until 10:30. They are Quakers and are going to Sri Lanka in July. They have a little baby boy. I'm sure there was a lot of divine guidance today.

Next morning, they sent him on his way with £20. After a walk down Lydals Road to see the nursery where Margaret had worked, Jack was off again with a full heart. He made no attempt to describe his feelings in his diary. That was not his nature. What words were adequate? A few days later, and most appropriately, he arrived at the home of Jack Ash, his old friend from those same Didcot days. Indeed, my Jack often called to see this Jack and his wife, Nell, when passing their way.

On the final stretch of the English coastal walk, another heart catching moment occurred near Arundel.

I called in a Little Chef and had a chicken salad sandwich and a pot of tea. A man and woman with five children came in and the lady was again pregnant. It reminded me of the days when our children were young and we used to parade into cafes. This lovely man and woman paid for my meal. Bless them! I had a chat with them.

Jack was happy and thoroughly enjoying life. He felt sure that God had guided him and was using him in his walking ventures. Nevertheless, deep down, he continued to miss Margaret and often wondered how the future might have worked out had she been spared for them both to journey into old age together. Moments like these above brought it all back again with poignancy.

Of Shows and Chapels

Two special loves for Jack were the theatre and his church. Finding himself near Stratford on Avon, he decided to have a day off and a treat. He was therefore disappointed to learn that all the theatres were fully booked—until, that is, a lady in the box office fell for his charm, which, being entirely unassumed, was correspondingly potent.

After pressing a few buttons on a machine and talking to someone she said, "There we are! A ticket for you in the dress circle! Romeo and Juliet! £8.50!" . . . Gosh, was I pleased . . . . What a great show . . . . Three and a half hours long . . . . Of course I was shedding a few tears before the end.

Jack went to a lot of local productions on his walks. Somehow he always managed to steal a little of the limelight by ending up receiving acclaim and donations. Take this typical example in Whitby.

I arrived at Whitby at 7:15 p.m. I saw a poster which said the local amateur operatic society were doing "Hello Dolly." . . . I hurried to see if there were any tickets . . . . I had to find accommodation also. A man saw me and said a woman in the show had a guest house not far away. He took me in his car . . . and brought me back to the theatre. He gave me a ticket. He belonged to the Whitby Lions. I was ten minutes late. The show was great.

At the interval, a lady told me that the producer had a cheque for £25 to give me from the Whitby Lions. She asked me to wait in the bar after the show. They presented me with the cheque, introduced me to members of the cast, showed me round backstage, said they would make a collection for me tomorrow night, and put the money in my account in Barclays Bank.

Regarding religious exercises, Jack tried to worship in a Methodist chapel each Sunday. Near Berwick on Tweed, he went into a chapel at 11:00 a.m.

The minister invited me to have a word with the congregation about my walks. Several people put money in my bag after the service. The minister's wife invited me to their home for dinner.

Another walk and another Sunday, he arrived in Boston at 6:30 p.m.

Enquired where Methodist church, . . . a massive church. Service in small chapel. Changed clothes in toilet. Service had begun when I went in with a gentleman who waited for me. Good service. Sacrament. Minister announced I was there. Collection was taken. Over £40. Just what I needed. Was given accommodation by two ladies. Two lovely ladies and so kind.

I need not go on, for I am sure you get the picture by now. However, considering Jack's love of the theatre, the next section follows on fittingly.

Hills Alive with Music

It is August 1981. Jack is at Crianlarich in the west of Scotland. "Not," you groan, "more free accommodation or a whip round to put something in his bag." No! This is different. The Goole Amateur Operatic and Dramatic Society, of which Jack is a longtime member, is putting on a two-night, open-air production of a well-known musical.

Mrs Doreen Chapell, the producer and director of GAODS, went to Scotland on holiday a year earlier. Moved by the splendour of moorland, mountain, and pine forest, she suddenly heard those same hills alive with the sound of music. Was it possible to stage the Von Trapp story in such a setting? Her producer's eye surveyed the landscape and rested on a small hill sloping into a natural amphitheatre alongside the holiday chalets. Behind rose the three-thousand-foot backdrop of Ben More.

Back in Goole, at the end of a rehearsal for her current show, Doreen revealed her idea.

"We won't make anything out of it. In fact, we'll have to fund-raise like mad this coming year and probably still have to dig into our own pockets at the end. We'll bring in some professional help, but we'll all have to go up early to get the site ready. It will be hard work. What do you think?"

The assembled cast knew their leader. She was a perfectionist and ruthless in attaining her required standard. She was a visionary with skill to organise. They loved and trusted her.

"You're mad," was the unanimous verdict, "and we'll do it."

The Sound of Music was to be played, courtesy of the proprietors, on the site of Portnellan Lodge chalets. Over sixty people took holidays off work, brought their families, and spent a week of hard labour transforming the area. Every skill was acceptable—cooking, sewing, carpentry, clerical. Even the children did their bit. Professional firms installed three tons of gear, including six miles of sound and lighting cable. It took £1,000 worth of timber for staging, seating, and walkways. They gave one of the chalets a makeover to give it an Austrian look. Some firms gave free loans of materials. Others reduced or even waived charges. The hired costumes cost £5 per item. The hirers knocked £2 off, and cast members donated £3 each. United Carriers transported the consignment free. In addition to all the fund-raising of the previous year, everyone involved paid £10 into the kitty.

The show played for two nights to about one thousand delighted people, many of whom were passing tourists. The local community wished it could be an annual event. As for Jack, he took his part in the chorus and doubled up as a Nazi soldier and the dignified bishop in full regalia who married the happy couple. It was, he said, one of the highlights of his life.

"We worked like slaves. We dropped into bed bone weary at night, but we loved every minute of it. Doreen is a great leader. The group rapport was tremendous."

There was only one problem—the midges. They were a torment. The village shop ran out of midge repellent. The orchestra pit was positioned over a stream, and the midges love water. It was hard to play either an instrument or a convincing part when all you wanted to do was scratch and slap the insects off. Jack's solution was to rub his skin with onion juice. It kept the midges away and, I imagine, everyone else too.

Let me end the tale with one of my "incidentallies." Doreen's husband, Arnold, was assistant head of Goole Grammar School when Jack's children were there, and they held him in high respect. Jack counted the couple as dear friends, and I know Doreen had a soft spot for him. He often popped in to see them when he was in Goole, and Doreen wrote me a beautiful letter when he died. I cannot read it without crying.

Marathon Man

The night was miserable—cold, dark, and drizzly. Jack took a cloth and walked round to the rear of the car to clean the dirty window. Deed done, he stepped away. The ground opened at his feet. He fell backwards into nothingness. Even as he lay stunned in the deep hole, he understood what had happened. They had been working under the car behind the shop that afternoon. Jack knew that the inspection pit was still open. What he did not realise was how close the car was to it. He should have been more careful.

Slowly, he sat up. The pit was deep, long, and narrow like a grave. If he had fallen at an angle, he would have hit his head on the side and broken his neck. As it was, he felt sick and shaken. His knuckles were badly grazed, and his hands were sticky with blood. Nothing seemed to be broken, but he lay pulling himself together for some time. At last, he managed to haul himself out. As he emerged, John appeared. Five minutes too late, he had come to cover the inspection pit. It was not his fault, but he was shocked. Eventually Jack said, "I'm supposed to be speaking at a meeting in Eggborough in half an hour. I think I can manage if you'll drive me there."

John took him home to clean up then transported him the five miles to Eggborough. Fortified by sympathy, sweet tea, and aspirins provided by one of the ladies, he gave his talk. John then drove him home. Next morning, he could hardly get out of bed. Apart from being bruised all over, one of his knees was swollen to twice its size; and he could not bend his leg. Ruth happened to be visiting at that time.

"Oh, Dad, do let me call the doctor," she wailed.

No! All he needed was a day in bed, and he would be fine. Ruth phoned Simon's Jayne. We all tend to do that in a medical crisis. Jayne was adamant.

"Tell him he must have it seen to. Take him to casualty."

At casualty, they checked him over, took a pint of fluid off the knee, encased it in plaster to the top of the thigh, then sent him off with crutches and firm instructions not to put any weight on the damaged limb.

"Come back in a fortnight," they advised. Jack protested.

"A fortnight today, I'm flying out to America to visit my two daughters." He added defiantly, "And three weeks after that I'm running the Los Angeles Marathon."

The doctor looked speculatively at his seventy-eight-year-old patient.

"OK! Come back in twelve days. We'll get the plaster off and see how you are. One thing's for sure. You can forget any marathons."

Twelve days later they removed the plaster, swathed the leg in bandages, and told him to keep using the crutches, and have wheelchair attention at the airport.

"I'm not taking crutches to America, and I'm not having any wheelchairs," stated Jack firmly—not to the doctor, only to his solicitous offspring.

The leg was stiff, sore, and weak. For the first few days in California, Jack pottered round the house and garden in frustrated disappointment. He had set his heart on that marathon. Oh well, if he could not take part, he would still go and watch, provided he could get his knee well enough for even that mild activity. Spurred by the thought, he began a regime of gentle exercise and short walks. At first he went only round the garden and then down to the shops two or three times a day. He increased distance and speed. The leg responded well. A week before the big day, he felt good.

"I'm going to start the marathon," he declared to his American family. "I don't have to finish it. I'll just do what I can." Deep in his heart, he silently added, *But I am going to finish it, and I'll give what it takes.*

A week later Jane and Joyce drove their dad to Los Angeles and deposited him with the thousands of other entrants lined up for the great event. Exactly six hours, thirty-three minutes, seventeen seconds from the start, he passed the finishing post. His knee was fine and his morale sky high.

The Great Reward

People often asked my husband, "What do you get out of all your walking?" It seems to me, and I may be wrong, that such a question reflects a prevalent attitude in today's society where few of us are prepared to do something for nothing; and financial benefit for oneself is the prime incentive. Such considerations aside, Jack himself once summarised his answer as follows:

My Rewards for Long Distance
Sponsored Walks for Children

1. Seeing the beautiful countryside in slow motion.
2. Meeting lots of delightful people.
3. Improving my own health and physical well-being.
4. Knowing that my efforts will help many needy and abused children.
5. And an added bonus, getting a lovely smile from a princess. [i.e., Princess Margaret. See chapter 9.]

The thing that upset Jack the most after his heart problem of 1992 was not only that his walking days were over but that his one special area of service to society was also finished. I shall never forget the tears in his eyes when he told me how much he had been asking God to open up some new sphere of usefulness and how he believed that looking after me was the answer to his prayers. Neither of us foresaw the spectacular improvement in his health. Ahead still lay a number of day walks—the London Marathon and the Great North Run half marathon. To the end of his life, God gave him purpose and usefulness.

What was it about this ordinary man that called forth so much good will and kindness? To begin with, he believed completely in what he was doing, and his enthusiasm made those who met him believe in it too. Part of his secret must be that he was so genuine. He had no side, no airs. He loved the publicity that came his way, but it never spoiled him. An important third reason was that other people mattered. He related to everyone fully and directly. Even strangers on a brief encounter recognised these qualities and responded to his warmth.

Walking in Holland. No hills to slow you down there.

2,300 miles towards the N.S.P.C.C. Humber bridge in the background.

Proud finisher of the London marathon at 85 years of age.
(Courtesy of the London Marathon)

67 years old and in his prime.

CHAPTER 9

JACK THE GIANT KILLER
or
JACK'S PHILOSOPHY OF LIFE

A Philosophy of Life

This chapter, in slang parlance, is all about what made Jack tick. What influences formed his character? What indeed was his character? Obviously you must have made your own assessment by now, but I believe that the things I am about to say are a necessary part of the picture.

The first thing to note is that, for such an easygoing man who was also a proven pacifist, his philosophy of life was unexpectedly confrontational. Jack deliberately and purposefully withstood the giants that came his way. Perhaps they were not very large giants, but such as they were, he fought them with his own weapons. Hence, I did not have to look far for the title of this chapter, which is fortunate as, apart from the inappropriate "Jack the Ripper" or "Jack in the Box," I have run out of Jack phrases for any more chapter headings.

The second point to observe is that Jack's philosophy of life was very simple. He was a Christian. It is, of course, more than likely that even had he been an atheist or an adherent of a different religion, he would still have been a man of moral principle and humanitarian ideals. In which case, he would naturally have approached such positions from a different perspective. As it was, his Christianity consisted of more than mere morality and compassion. It permeated his life, private and public, with the imperative of loving and serving Jesus. To fail to understand this is to fail to understand Jack.

Although I have already talked about my husband's relationship with Jesus earlier on, I want now to expand upon it. It means presenting you with a touch of theology and a soupcon of spirituality. Afterwards I promise to return to anecdotes plus a few rhymes and pithy sayings, and all by way of illustration.

By definition a Christian is someone who follows Jesus, the Christ. Christ is the Greek translation of the Hebrew *Messiah,* and both mean the anointed one of God. Hence, Jesus is God's own son, chosen and anointed by God for a special task. The task that Jesus came to perform was to show God's love for individual men and women and to accomplish God's rescue plan for the human race which has gone so badly wrong.

Jesus, the Son of God, lived a perfect life on earth as a man. He took the punishment for the sin of the world on his own shoulders when he died on the cross. Because that was not the end and Jesus rose to life again, anyone who comes to him repenting of their sin can know forgiveness and a renewal of inner spiritual life. Here is the essence of the Christian faith. Here the Christian experience begins. Here it finds its inspiration. To know more about what this kind of Christianity meant to Jack, there is no better place to start than the four gospels which were his prime textbook for Christian living throughout his life.

As you know, Jack committed his life to Jesus as a young man, and ever after Jesus became his great hero and role model. In my own short five years with him, four realities of his inmost life stood out. They are the reality of the cross, the reality of prayer, the pursuit of perfection, and, to borrow a title from Thomas à Kempis's classic of Christian literature, the imitation of Christ.

Four Realities

The Cross

Good Friday was for Jack the most solemn day of the year when he always closed shop and went to church. His reverence for the cross was very deep. However, it was not the day or the symbol that mattered but what they signified.

One can only say that if the remedy for sin was so radical, how terrible sin must be and how wonderful God's love for us is.

"We should never forget," Jack used to say to me each year as Good Friday drew near, "we should never forget that a real man hung there on that cross and died for us. It was a dreadful thing. Surely such love deserves a response from us."

Jack was easily moved and never tried to hide his feelings when we were alone together. At such times, his eyes moistened. Throughout his life, he believed that if Jesus had given his life for him, he must live his life to the best of his ability for Jesus. However, like many of us, Jack could be a bit obsessive about the things which touched him most closely. I include the following story to show that, however rightly motivated by his feelings, sometimes his reactions to an event were a little less than laudable and influenced by personal considerations.

For many years, Snaith Methodist Chapel had no cross in the building. This was not particularly unusual, but Jack felt the omission. At last he made a rather stark wooden cross and set it upon the communion table. It was large, purposely so, that it might be plainly seen by all. It stood there for years. One day, a minister came who decided to replace it with a small metal one, and Jack was upset. He disliked metal crosses. For him, they had to be wooden. He disliked pretty crosses. For him, it was an instrument of torture. He also disliked small crosses in public places. For him, they had to be conspicuous.

"It's the central symbol of our faith," he explained. "Remove it, make it fancy or discreet, and you lose the sense of what our salvation cost."

Certainly the fact that Jack had made this particular cross coloured his feelings. The minister, who had not expected his well-meaning suggestion to evoke such a heated response, was—it must be acknowledged—gracious. Jack's cross remained in place.

Prayer

To be aware of the reality of prayer for Jack, you had to know him intimately, for he did not display this part of his life to all and sundry. Although even I rarely saw him praying privately, I know that he did so; and of course, our daily time of prayer and Bible reading together meant a lot and drew us closer to each other.

Are you familiar with a picture of Jesus, well-known in Christian art, entitled "And Jesus turned and looked upon Peter and Peter remembered"? Jack had a framed copy hanging on his sitting room wall. He told me, "I often sit looking at this picture when I pray. I imagine Jesus is in the room, and I talk to him as if he were sitting opposite me. It helps me to concentrate." If a specific matter arose Jack would say, "I'll have a word about it with him up there."

He was not being disrespectful. He truly was on familiar terms with God, but he never lacked reverence. The thought of sudden death and being called to meet his maker held no fears. Why should it? He had been in touch with God all his life. Death would be the moment when, so to speak, he would meet his old friend face to face. That was something to look forward to, not to dread.

A couple of times, when I felt so ill I did not know what to do with myself, I asked Jack to pray for me. He did, easily and without embarrassment, using prayers from a book along with his own words. It always helped. Jack, from much practice, knew how to pray.

In Pursuit of Perfection

At this stage of my book, who could blame anyone for saying, "Did this fellow have no faults at all? He sounds too good to be true."

Of course, he did. Ask his children. Despite the fact that his family thought the world of their old Dad, children always know their parents' faults better than anyone else. As a wife, I saw some too. Nonetheless, I can still testify that living with Jack made me want to be a nicer person, less impatient, less critical, and more considerate. That was because I saw the way he worked on his own character. Early on, the words "in pursuit of perfection" settled in my mind.

It all began when I drew his attention to a matter so minor that I cannot even recall what it was. He dealt with it, and it never happened again. Time after time I noticed the same thing. Mention a propensity for scratching his ear when he gave a talk, trivial though it was, the habit was rectified. Point out that his pinstripe funeral trousers were showing threadbare on the seat, he never wore them again. Let me be critical about someone, he refused to be drawn into the discussion. Be it mundane or of significance, he tried to put it right or to respond aright.

Had I imagined my husband's fixation with self-improvement? I asked John. He too had seen it. True, the examples we were thinking of were really very minor and nothing for anyone to feel hurt or sensitive about. Even so, Jack considered them to be every bit as important as the larger character-building issues of life. Without doubt, he worked at the process of self-improvement to the end of his days. This is the attribute of a humble man.

The Imitation of Christ

Jesus was Jack's role model. If he was not sure what to do, he asked himself one question. What would Jesus have done in these circumstances? Even in specific cases, the answer could usually be deduced from the teaching of Jesus or the stories about him in the gospels. In general everyday living, certain principles emerge. For instance, Jesus had time for people. He listened to them, related to them, helped them, and often challenged or advised them. Jesus was involved with society and the issues of his day. Jesus did things. He never turned aside in lethargy or disinterest, hoping someone else would do what was needed instead. Jesus never condoned sin, but he always reached out to the sinner.

Jack took these things to heart. In his own small way, he modelled himself on his master and followed the discipline of a life lived in the "imitation of Christ." The rest of this chapter aims to show how he went about it. For now, here is an example which illustrates Jack's "imitation of Christ" better than most.

The young man was foolish rather than bad, but he was in trouble, and the police were investigating. His offence might well land him in prison. Everyone in the community knew the story. The young man stayed indoors. His family felt the shame and cringed before the ostracism of many erstwhile friends. One evening, Jack donned his jacket and said he was going out for a while. Making his way to the home of the stricken family, he rang the bell. The door opened.

"Can I come in a minute?" The face before him was wary. "I'd like to have a word with you if I may." Jack's tone was friendly. The man at the door stood aside for him to enter. "I know you're in trouble," said Jack, "but I just wanted to tell you that I care. If there's anything I can do to help, please let me know."

For Evil to Prevail

For evil to prevail it is only necessary for good men to do nothing.

The quote is from G. K. Chesterton. The concept is pure New Testament theology. The words, in firm black lettering, stood on Jack's desk.

Amongst Jack's papers, after his death, I found the following handwritten excerpt. Where it came from I cannot say, but Jack liked it enough to copy it out. Perhaps he even wrote it himself.

Our deepest need today is not to learn more and more about God, not to understand more, not to fill our brains with more and more religious ideas, but to have the courage to put a few ideas into practice in our way of living. Not to attend more and more services but to act in a Christ-like way in every circumstance in which we find ourselves.

Jack loved a quote, a rhyme, a pointed saying—especially when it summarised his own feelings about life. He wrote them down, filed them away, propped them up around the house, produced them for me to peruse, and recited them at apt moments. Some were humorous; but they were, like the next one, always telling.

Everybody was asked to do it. Everybody was sure Somebody would do it. Anybody could have done it but Nobody did it. Somebody got angry about it because it was Everybody's job. Everybody thought Anybody could do it but Nobody realised that Everybody wouldn't do it. It ended up that Everybody blamed Somebody when actually, Nobody asked Anybody.

Jack's life view is well illustrated by these three extracts. He fully believed that, whatever the issue, you could not look the other way and ignore it. If your inner life needed attention, you dealt with it. If it concerned other people, you did not say, "It's none of my business." You made it your business to help or to be involved. If it was a crisis of world dimensions, you must not be overwhelmed by the feeling that your efforts were too small to make any difference. You had to believe that if many people do their little bit to help, the accumulative impact will be meaningful. Jack was not prepared to sit back and do nothing in the hope that someone else would handle it. He never shirked involvement on the grounds of lack of interest or ability. Neither was he daunted by difficulty. Whatever the odds, he was loath to pronounce a thing impossible until he had made an attempt. If he then failed, he at least had the satisfaction of knowing he had tried.

Because of this, Jack did things. He was public spirited. He cared for the environment, took an interest in local politics, raised money for good causes, quietly ministered practical love to individuals in their needs and tragedies, and generally lived out his faith in works.

"God," Jack once said to me, "God must be the most unhappy being in all the universe."

"What do you mean?"

"Well, when he sees all the suffering, wars, disasters, and what we do to each other and to his beautiful world. We make such a mess of everything and mostly because of our selfishness and greed. It must break his heart. I often feel sorry for God. Do you understand?"

Yes, I understood. In a strange way, Jack dared to hope that his tiny efforts to better the world around him might bring some measure of comfort to God's heart.

In the Public Spirit

Jack was intensely public spirited. This covered many areas of life, both great and small. For instance, I once came across an old letter dated 1962 which thanked him, not only for being a regular blood donor himself, but also for introducing so many of his friends to the service. I later found a 1992 newspaper cutting. The Reverend Cyril Roberts had arranged a weekly series of nine-mile walks to help keep the youngsters of the parish occupied during the summer holidays. Who was in the accompanying picture but "veteran walker Jack Punton" lending his support?

If ever you passed Jack's house on the High Street, there was usually something to see in his windows. In his sitting room, between the double glazing, he displayed ornaments. We used to laugh when passersby, especially children, stopped to look, unaware of our presence a few feet away inside. In the other window beside the front door, he put up notices—a concert, a church function, a public meeting. And yes, at election time, he called upon the good citizens of Snaith to vote Labour for he was not shy of proclaiming his political allegiance.

Someone, assuming that his preferred colour was blue rather than red, once asked, "Would you let us put a 'Vote Conservative' poster in your window?"

"Certainly," came the prompt reply, "as long as you don't mind my big 'Vote Labour' poster beside it."

Early in the eighties, Jack worked hard to develop bowling and putting green on the open ground beside the sheltered housing bungalows in Eden Place. He wanted to do something for the senior citizens of the town. Sadly, not enough people used the facilities. The upkeep too was always a problem as they could not get regular funding and had to depend on volunteers. Despite Jack's efforts, the scheme fizzled out.

Another aspect of the public spirit was that Jack recycled rubbish, not only his own, but other people's. At one time he made his shop a centre for collecting old newspapers and silver foil to encourage others to be involved.

"Would you like a drive out this afternoon?" he asked.

It was a sunny April day. Having been ill, I had not been out all winter. I agreed, and we duly set off.

"Where are we going?" I wanted to know.

"Well, I've got all this rubbish for the tip."

Only then did I notice the black plastic bags in the back of the car. So on my first trip out for months, we went to the Goole recycling tip with our papers, tins, bottles, and plastic cartons. Actually, it is a fascinating place; but by the time we had finished there, I did not have strength to go much further, and we simply drove home a long way round. I never minded, as long as I was with Jack.

Municipal Matters

Being public spirited had more far-reaching consequences. Over the years, Jack became a prominent and respected figure in the community. In May 1970, he was elected to the Snaith and Cowick Town Council. Of the nine newly elected members, he received the second highest number of votes.

In view of this, it may seem strange when I state that Jack was not a political person. He never liked committee work where much the same agenda came up at every meeting, and nothing was accomplished speedily or without argument. When a local Labour MP tried to persuade him to stand for the county council, he refused without compunction. Rightly or wrongly, he did not feel that he had the necessary gifts. Neither did he believe that this was the best way to use his time. To serve on his hometown council was a different matter. That was a duty he could not shirk.

In 1976, he was elected town mayor. He now had responsibility for chairing council meetings, a job which, he admitted, scared him stiff.

"Then why let yourself in for it?" I asked.

Part of the answer lay in his first speech in his new office.

> My feelings at the moment are somewhat mixed. I can't help but feel a sense of pride at being elected town mayor. I was born in Snaith and have lived here most of my life and naturally I have a great love for this parish. I only hope I can do justice to my position as your chairman.

Jack was realistic. He did not overestimate either his leadership qualities or his administrative abilities. If anything, he underrated himself. At the same time, he knew that he was respected and that he understood local matters. He did not covet his new position, but he honestly believed that he had something to contribute to the well-being of the place that meant so much to him. Given the opportunity, it was unthinkable not to be involved.

"Think positively," he said, as he did so on any challenging situation. "There's no such word as 'can't.' If you think you can, you can."

With such an attitude and despite trepidation, Jack started his new duties with a determination to succeed.

Jack kept his copies of the minutes of the council meetings for his year of office. Such documents do not make riveting reading. A cursory glance through them shows that the business of the year was much as you would expect for any small country town. It dealt with street lighting, footpaths and bridleways, a site for a playing field, a job creation scheme, parish rates, dog fouling, street cleaning, unmanned rail crossings, sewage smells, vandalism, bus shelters (or lack of them), sale of land and property, and plans for the 1977 Queen's Silver Jubilee.

For part of the Jubilee celebrations, the young people challenged the mayor and council to a football match. With Jack at the helm, such a challenge was immediately accepted. Sadly, I cannot record that the town dignitaries won.

As mayor, Jack attended functions, opened things, and generally did the honours on public occasions. This was part of the job he enjoyed and did well. Margaret supported him throughout and was by his side as much as possible for official events even though she was not well for, by this time, the cancer had returned. She died in July 1977. Jack's term as mayor had only ended two months earlier. He did not seek reelection, and when his time on the council expired, he stood down.

Jack was only the third mayor of Snaith and Cowick since the local government reorganisation of 1974. Now although Snaith has long been classed as a town, for some reason, the mayor had no proper chain of office, only a medallion on a piece of ribbon. Jack, together with a fellow councillor, rectified this. They personally bought a mayoral chain to which new links could be added and names inscribed. Other achievements were no doubt ephemeral, that at least, and for what it is worth, is lasting. As Jack himself was fond of saying, "Such is life."

What's in a Name?

Before I leave the municipal scene for good, I have two amusing stories to relate about mistaken identity. By this time, Jack was doing the occasional "Thought for the Day" broadcast on local radio. For one of them, he told the following story. The moral is unimportant for present purposes.

A few weeks ago I attended a . . . service in a small village chapel. It was almost full when I arrived, and I took a seat next to three schoolboys in the front pew. During the service, the preacher made reference to the town mayor's presence in the congregation. As I was not known to these boys and as I was not wearing my chain of office, they immediately started looking round . . . for this notable person.

After the service a member of the congregation . . . leaned over and whispered to them, "He's sitting next to you." The boys looked at me with a mixture of disbelief and disappointment. Their image of a mayor was a fancy hat and cloak and a gold chain.

The second instance took place at Snaith chapel fete in July 1976 when Jack, as mayor, invited the Duke of Norfolk to open proceedings. Now to invite England's premier duke to an insignificant provincial event was not so presumptuous as it sounds. To explain, we must go to Carlton Towers, the big mansion and estate in Carlton.

The history of Carlton Towers reaches back to the Norman Conquest. The pedigree of the family who inherited it in the fourteenth century is complicated, but in brief, it has been for many generations the home of the Beaumont Stapleton line. Miles Francis Stapleton Fitzalan Howard, born 1915, is the twelfth Baron Beaumont. Complex relationships link most of Britain's nobility. It thus came about that when the sixteenth Duke of Norfolk died in 1975 leaving no direct heir, his cousin, Miles Francis of Carlton Towers, succeeded him as the seventeenth duke.

Plenty of local people knew the Beaumont family, if not intimately, at least in passing acquaintance. Jack had often worked at the Towers in his younger days. He found the family friendly and unostentatious. The duke occasionally came into his shop and stayed chatting. Apart from being so close in age, the two men seemed to like each other. Jack, along with others from the region around, was occasionally invited to a reception or family function. He kept the invitation cards with pride amongst his collection of memorabilia.

So it was, therefore, that the duke, responsible for organising some of our country's great state occasions, found himself opening Snaith chapel fete. Do not, however, get the wrong impression. In those days, this summer fete was quite an affair. The chapel, a fine and unspoiled example of Victorian architecture, stands in its own grounds. It is approached through wrought iron gates and a short curved driveway. To the left is about an acre of parkland, ideal for stalls, marquees, games, and strategically placed seats under shady trees.

The great day arrived. With limited parking in the drive, a gentleman named Bob Duckles was detailed to stand at the gates to keep all vehicles out except the press and the duke. Bob was a long standing friend of Jack's—his best man, a local preacher, and an insurance salesman by profession. As for Jack, it was his duty both as mayor and chapel member to meet and introduce the noble guest. Bob would let him know as soon as the duke arrived.

Time passed. They were due to open, and still His Grace had not come. Anxiously, Jack joined Bob at the gate. At last they saw him, walking up the pavement. Jack went to meet him. The duke apologised.

"I'm sorry I'm late."

"That's all right," responded Jack, "I hadn't realised you'd be walking. We could have sent a car for you."

"Oh, I did come by car, only I didn't know there'd be no parking at the chapel. I couldn't get in, so I had to go back into Snaith to find a place."

"That didn't apply to you, sir. We were watching out for you."

Jack looked across at Bob. He felt irritated. Bob, in turn, looked pink and slightly puzzled. He defended himself.

"I'm sorry, sir. I know I turned you away. I'd no idea it was you. I didn't know what you looked like. I was expecting a Rolls-Royce with a chauffeur, and you turned up driving yourself in a mini."

The duke took it in good part. He, like Jack, has probably often told the story since.

Aid and Charity

It was the time of the Ethiopian famine back in 1984-1985. Jack and Joyce were talking to a friend.

"I never give to these things," said the friend. "You never know whether your money goes to those who need it."

Jack was sharp. He felt cross.

"I'd rather risk giving a few pounds in the hope it might help a starving child than be too mean to give anything at all."

He did much more than that, as I discovered from the inevitable old newspaper cuttings. The *Goole Times* of November 22, 1984, recorded,

> *Jack has been holding coffee mornings in the back of his shop every Friday. . . . He has kept a stall selling toys and household goods, donated by Snaith people, outside his shop. Customers bring in their donations, including Mr Bill Ramsey who raised £22 at a bonfire held at his home . . . . Jack and his shop have become the nucleus of fund-raising for the Ethiopian fund in Snaith.*

In fact, Jack often made his shop a focus for his charitable efforts and ran it on very generous lines. Only recently Simon said to me, "Dad ran his shop as one big charity. He would help anyone and everything."

In January 1985, Jack organised a New Year concert in the school. With his wide contacts in the dramatic and musical world of the region, he persuaded various local celebrities to volunteer their talents. He even had a display of conjuring. The concert was deemed successful despite the fact that Jack was disappointed with the attendance. The proceeds, of course, went to the Ethiopian fund.

There was hardly a time in his postwar life that Jack was not raising money for some cause or other. When John joined him in the business, he was free to step up his efforts. Always, his favourite causes concerned children. Amongst his papers, I constantly came across letters and certificates from organisations like the National Children's Home, Save the Children, and the NSPCC acknowledging sums of money donated.

The NSPCC was his favourite charity. For many years, he was a welcome guest at the annual meetings of the South Yorkshire branch in Doncaster. In 1997, Princess Margaret, their patron, opened a new centre for abused children in Doncaster. Jack was one of those who were informally introduced to her. Later that same year, he was made an honorary member of the NSPCC National Council in recognition of his services. Two ladies from the Snaith branch drove him to Leicester where, this time, he would be officially presented to the princess and receive his badge and certificate. I was disappointed, but I was too ill to go with him.

Now Jack, though not a republican, was by no means an ardent royalist. He, whose powerful singing voice swelled any gathering, stood stubbornly silent during a rendering of the national anthem.

"Why?" I once queried when we arrived home after a Remembrance Day service.

Apparently the "send her victorious" bit offended him.

"I'm not standing there asking for Britain to have military might and victory in warfare," he grunted.

I understood. We talked about other verses, seldom printed these days, expressing the sentiment that all our enemies would be scattered and asking God to "confound their knavish tricks." I am afraid that the full version of our national anthem is rather chauvinistic in its assumption that we are always in the right and our enemies are all rogues and villains. In the end I said, "All right, but you could ask God to save our queen and give her a long, happy reign. If history is anything to go by, she's one of the best monarchs we've ever had as regards her life and character. You can close your mouth if you must at the 'victorious' line, but surely she needs our prayers."

We argued the matter a bit, but the next time we sang the national anthem, my husband offered a low-key contribution. Forgive the digression. I feel it adds to the picture of Jack's character, and it fits in here better than anywhere else. Back to Princess Margaret, Jack apparently always had a soft spot for her, and he was pleased to be seeing her again.

"I feel that life knocked her right from the start when she had to give up Group Captain Townsend. Nothing seemed to go quite right for her since."

In a tone of sudden belligerence he added, "But I'm not bowing to anybody, even if they are royalty."

In the subsequent photograph of Jack shaking hands with Her Royal Highness and receiving his membership certificate, he may not be bowing, but he is certainly bending over her with smiling deference. His explanation? "She's so petite. I couldn't believe how tiny she was. She's lovely."

A Thrifty Yorkshire Man

Jack used to dream about what he would do if he ever won the lottery, notwithstanding one vital impediment to his hopes. He never bought a lottery ticket. Still, he had it all worked out.

"I'd give my children and grandchildren a couple of hundred pounds each. That's all. A struggle to make ends meet and find your own way in life doesn't hurt anybody. Too much money isn't good for you. Oh yes, I'd maybe buy John a new car for the business. The rest I'd give to charity, every penny of it."

Come to think of it, I never heard him say that he'd give any of it to his wife. Never mind? It was only a dream, and he did enjoy allocating it all in his head. Returning to the real world, it was true when Jack said that he never worried about money—and he knew what it was like to have been very poor. He had enough to live on comfortably, and he used to say, "You can't wear two suits at once," and yes, he did possess more than one suit, but apart from his wedding outfit, the others came from charity shops.

Before I met him, he had to make choices about how he spent his money—for instance, visit his daughters in America or put in central heating. He chose the former. He only installed the heating when he received a small legacy a few years after our marriage. The rest of his legacy he spent on other people, including one of those lifting beds for me.

Often, as we watched our birds, Jack would quote the following ditty.

> Said the robin to the sparrow,
> "I should really like to know
> Why these anxious human beings
> Rush about and hurry so."
> Said the sparrow to the robin,
> "Friend, I think that it must be
> That they have no Heavenly Father
> Such as cares for you and me."

If I cannot attribute these lines to any known source, I can say that they summed up Jack's attitude to the frenetic lifestyle of today, mostly directed to the pursuit of wealth. He truly believed that God would look after him and that it was wrong to worry or get taken up with the so-called rat race.

Work hard by all means. Do your best with what you have. Never be careless or wasteful. In the end you must find a balance between the lure of the mere material and the soul ease of a relaxed and quiet spirit before God.

It is almost a paradox to say that Jack was a hoarder by nature. He kept newspaper cuttings, programmes, tickets, letters, sermons, anything of interest from his past life. It logically follows that in our throw-away society of heedless and needless waste, he believed it was wrong to dispose of anything that still worked or might come in useful one day. Once, when I first started going to his house and was looking for a pan, I noticed a shelf full of electric kettles, about five of them.

"Oh!" he assured me. "I'm going to mend them sometime."

"Jack, how many years have you been collecting this lot?"

We were not even married, and I sounded like a nagging wife, but my hints hit the target. When next I looked, the kettles had gone. I did wonder if they finished up no further than the garden shed, but I could not get there to see.

An amusing example of his reluctance to throw anything away occurred soon after we had moved into April Cottage after the renovations. Jack's TV was on its last legs.

"We'll get rid of it and start using mine," I suggested. He was not keen and protested, "It works sometimes."

It sometimes did, after a bang. It sometimes did not. He got the point eventually, after he had missed a football match that he specially wanted to see.

No doubt if you struggle in your early life, you learn of necessity never to throw anything away that might somehow be reused. When Jack did jobs around the house or garden, he produced old but serviceable pieces of wood, rusty but cleanable hinges, glass removed from some defunct object and stored away for such a time as this. He mixed leftover paint, often to good effect, the only problem being that it was impossible to match when you wanted to touch it up. His family laughed at him. So did I, but I was used to it. My own father, who also grew up poor and struggled for most of his life, did exactly the same.

Voices of the Earth

This was the title of a harvest sermon Jack once preached. Being a countryman, he valued the natural world because it spoke to him of God's power and loving provision.

It was his custom, when younger, to rise early on a Sunday morning and walk in rural byways. Little London, just beyond East Cowick, was a favoured destination, maybe because of the farmer's wife who gave him cups of tea and nice eatables. Wherever he went, he knew the stones and fallen tree trunks that made comfortable seats. There he would sit, joying in the loveliness of sight, scent, and sound, as he went through his sermon notes for later in the day.

One morning, he made his way to a special place with a pond and a copse of trees. He was horrified at what he saw.

"I sat and cried," he told me. "They had felled the trees and filled in the pond to reclaim the land. All that beauty and precious wildlife was gone, just for the sake of an extra acre of ground."

Jack believed that because our world is God's world, we must care for it. Life, even animal and plant life, is to be respected and never wantonly destroyed. This did not make him a vegetarian. Perhaps it should have done. It did make him kind. He would rescue spiders from loos and moths round lights. He avoided using harmful fertilisers and insecticides on his garden and planted bushes and shrubs to encourage wildlife. Despite all this, he had his inconsistencies. He sold such things, including mouse traps, in his shop.

On a global scale, he was genuinely concerned about environmental issues. He did his little to help by joining Greenpeace. He liked their upfront image and, it must be admitted, their belligerent stance against opposition. Rightly or wrongly, they got things done. Jack approved, and he became a paid-up member.

If he went out walking, my husband habitually returned with something for me—a minute floweret to fit into an eggcup, tall, untidy stems of pink rosebay, a cluster of purple elderberries, or, my favourite flowers, a bunch of perky yellow dandelions. As wild flowers rarely last long indoors, we learned to put them outside, just beside the back door where we could see them through the glass. There they thrived, dandelions included, even when the wind blew them over at night.

"Just look at this!" Jack had come in from a walk with Sally. He held out a perfect spray of thick, creamy, hawthorn blossom. "The hedges are full of it this year. You can't get out to see it, so I've brought some for you. Wouldn't it make a beautiful bouquet for a bride?"

"Perfect," I agreed, "Apart from the thorns." I added as an afterthought. "Jack, if we could have our wedding over again at this time of year, I'd have you going out early in the morning to pick me a spray like this for my bouquet."

When I lost him, I kept thinking to myself, if only you had died a few months later, you would have had pink and white hawthorn on your coffin, costing nothing, a gift from the prodigality of God's own garden. Never mind what people might think. You would have approved.

There is no question that Jack would have approved. Part of his job as an undertaker was to arrange for flowers and wreaths at funerals. He was appalled at the hundreds of pounds spent on ephemeral blooms whose fate was to wither within days. For his Margaret, he put wild flowers on her coffin which he gathered himself. Thereafter, each July, on the anniversary of her death, he traversed the hedgerows seeking seasonal flowers to put in the chapel for Sunday. It was things like that which made my Jack so special.

Zest for Now

During the seventies, Jack gave a series of meditations for the "Thought for the Day" slot on local radio. One talk began as follows:

> *A father turned his back garden into a playground for his two children. On a cold day in early spring, he put the finishing touches to a paddling pool and a sand pit. No sooner had he put the sand and water in than his two children were off with their shoes and socks and were splashing about in the pool. A neighbour . . . remarked, "My word, won't you . . . have some fun when summer arrives." To which one of the children replied, "Oh! We're having lots of fun now."*

The point of the story, in Jack's words, was as follows:

> *Life doesn't wait until we are ready to enjoy it. It goes on, and if we don't take what it has to offer now, it may be lost forever . . . . Life is a gift,*

and each day, each minute of our lives is a day, a minute that cannot be repeated . . . . It is foolish to throw away the gift of the present time while we wait for something we may not be destined to enjoy.

How aptly this sums up Jack's outlook on life. Each morning, he awoke looking forward to a new day with all its promise. This attitude had two practical outworking.

First, you tackled the tasks of the day with a will, cheerfully and unshirkingly—unless (and here comes an inconsistency again) it happened to mean making up beds and preparing a room for a visitor. My beloved husband, in his eighties, could labour all day in the garden—repairing fences, digging, hauling heavy paving stones around, and so on.

"You must be whacked, darling," I would say with wifely solicitude when he came in for a break.

"No! I'm fine. I'm enjoying myself. Hard work does me good."

The next day, he might spend a couple of hours with the vacuum and sorting out a guest bedroom than collapse into a chair declaring exhaustion.

As regards the second outworking of this attitude, he never fretted unduly about the future, especially concerning probable eventualities that might never happen. He did not appreciate it when my imagination went into overdrive as I looked ahead, as this trivial story illustrates.

We had just decided to move from my bungalow and back to Jack's house and were discussing what renovations and building extension we wanted. Then I began to work out the actual move and sundry associated details. Jack went quiet.

"You're not listening," I accused.

"No! You can't plan that far ahead. We haven't even got an architect or applied for planning permission, yet, and here you are, sorting out the move. It's silly. We've got to go step by step, day at a time."

How right he was. Without being careless about tomorrow, it was always today that was most important for him.

Jack broadcast his "Now Is the Time" talk a mere two months after Margaret's death. His life had crumbled round him, and yet he could still say, and mean it,

> Now is the time to love. Now is the time to laugh. Now is the time to serve.

Despite his grief, he never opted out of life. If anything, he became more involved. Most circuit events saw him in attendance. He took up his sponsored walking. He started a popular Sunday night Songs of Praise. He threw himself into the performances of Goole Amateur Operatic and Dramatic Society. Although his inner sadness lasted for years, his great zest for life survived and helped to pull him through. Above all, he never lost his humour and sense of fun.

> We don't stop playing because we grow old; we grow old because we stop playing.

I can happily report that my octogenarian husband never grew old and never stopped playing. He had these words pinned up on his sitting room wall. They were part of his creed, encouraging him to live his life to the full.

For instance, Jack enjoyed dressing up. He had a trunk full of clothes and props and a shelf of fancy hats, bowlers, Stetsons, golfing hats, and so on. He dressed up as Maurice Chevalier when he sang "Thank Heaven for Little Girls"! He caused a laugh when he came over and bowed to me as he declared that little girls, "they grow up in the most delightful way." We were just newly engaged. Once, for a fancy dress parade at the chapel fete, he dressed up as Billie Jean King, the then Wimbledon champion. He loved any excuse for rummaging through his trunk for the gear to fit a part.

Jack's zest for living also included a sense of the ridiculous and the ability to laugh at himself. One year, he had to dye his hair black for his part in *The King and I.* The lady who did it assured him brightly, "Don't worry. It'll wash out."

He thought one wash would do it. To his horror, it took some weeks. He kept his cap on whenever he went out; he felt so self-conscious. Came the day when a regular customer entered his shop.

"I had my cap off. I could see him looking me up and down," said Jack, "and trying to work me out."

Finally the man solved the problem.

"I come in here a lot, but I don't believe I've met you before. You must be Jack Punton's younger brother."

On another occasion, he entered the egg-and-spoon race at the chapel fete. As everyone stepped gently forwards balancing their delicate cargo, Jack took off with a dash towards the winning tape. The spectators gazed in amazement until someone observed that he was running with his spoon upside down and the egg still firmly in place. It was stuck to the spoon. He never said whether he got the prize for cheek or was disqualified for cheating.

I am afraid that despite his youthful approach to life, my husband did grow deaf, and it was a trial. I tried to help him when he failed to catch what those around him were saying. Privately we had a few laughs ourselves at some of his mishearings.

"I'm thirsty," I declared. His back was to me, and he did not see my lips. "I think I'm going to have a drink of Coke."

He turned a puzzled face.

"What's happening on Thursday that you don't think you'll be able to cope?"

Life with Jack was never boring. Humour and pathos moved hand in hand, as the next three incidents will illustrate.

The Personal Touch

On several occasions, Leeds Royal Infirmary hosted a day symposium on "Infant Death." Midwives, consultant obstetricians, social workers, all presented papers. Jack was approached to speak at the last session on the role of the undertaker. He did not accept the assignment lightly, and yet to refuse because he was scared was unthinkable, especially when he believed he had a contribution to make.

"I could hardly sleep for weeks," he admitted, "I was so nervous. By the time I'd heard the morning's lectures, I was in a state. Here were all these high-powered people using technical terms I couldn't understand. How could

I follow them? When my turn came, I felt physically sick. I was trembling and my notes fluttered. I couldn't hide it."

Jack was well prepared which, once you get going, is one antidote to nervousness. He spoke factually and from experience. His own daughter Jane had lost a baby at birth. He described how he personally related to distraught parents and tried to help them handle their grief over the funeral period. Being Jack, he was perfectly capable of putting his arms around someone, especially if it was someone he knew and he felt that was what was needed. He told moving stories of mothers who phoned him to ask how their babies were—if they were comfortable, if they were warm. He understood. Nothing distressed him as much as a child's death, particularly a baby. He could, in some strange way, reassure them. He always looked after the little ones in his care with great tenderness.

Soon he relaxed. He sensed that his audience was with him. When he finished, there was absolute silence. More than one surreptitious hand could be seen wiping a misty eye. It hardly seemed appropriate for applause, yet when it came, it was not perfunctory. One of the consultants approached him later.

"I saw your knees knocking, but you'd no need to be nervous. I was bored for most of the day until you got up to speak. We were all clever and technical. Even I didn't understand what some people were talking about. Then you brought us all down to earth and made us face the fact that we were dealing with human tragedy, not just statistics and medical case histories."

Jack spoke again at subsequent courses. Although he never completely lost his nervousness and a feeling of intellectual inferiority in such company, he always knew that he had insights to offer and that he could move his hearers to tears.

There were only two occasions when I heard Jack express real anger. The first I mentioned in chapter 6 in connection with a certain lawyer. Here is the second. It too is a case where Jack's personal touch is evident.

In Snaith lived a lady, slightly eccentric, independent, and not overly trusting of strangers. She rarely answered the door to callers, and few people ever gained entry to her house. Jack knew her because she came into his shop for gas and paraffin, which he used to deliver for her. He made an effort to win her trust and soon was privileged to be invited into her home. He quickly realised that she needed help. He gained her confidence sufficiently to persuade her to allow him to approach the social services on her behalf. In setting events in motion for a visit from a social worker, he made one thing very clear.

"It's this," he said. "The lady never answers her door and never lets anyone into her house, but she trusts me. Would you let me know when someone is coming and I'll be there to meet them. It's very important. You won't get in otherwise."

Time passed. No one turned up. Jack phoned. Why had nobody visited?

"Oh, we did. Twice. We got no answer."

Jack was furious—a word one never normally associates with him. The powers that be, having decided that they knew best, were not keen to cooperate with him. He made a fuss, something else not habitually in his nature. I believe he even wrote to the papers deploring awkward attitudes and incompetence in the department concerned. Sadly, subsequent events made his anger worse in retrospect.

One day, a policeman came into the shop. "There's been an accident. We understand you know the lady involved. We wondered if you could help us and perhaps identify the body." Jack accompanied the policeman round to the lady's house. As they approached, the officer warned, "I'm afraid it's not a pretty sight. Will you be OK?"

"I'm an undertaker. I'm used to unpleasant sights. I'll be all right."

Inside the house, there had been a fire. It had not spread. Rather, it had smouldered then burnt itself out. It looked as if the lady's clothes had caught on the gas fire. In her effort to beat out the flames, she had rolled across the carpet and lay huddled under the table.

As Jack told me the story so many years later, his distress was evident.

"That upset me terribly. It still does. It never should have happened."

In his mind, he somehow linked the tragedy with the failure of the social services and in part blamed them. No doubt he was probably wrong to do this. I have to put it on record that I never discovered whether they proved helpful in the end or not. I certainly do not wish to malign an excellent institution needlessly, but I must tell you how Jack felt.

"Poor soul," he said. "She didn't deserve to go like that."

The last story illustrating Jack's personal touch concerns Joyce and her son Stephen who lived with Jack for six months when Stephen was a toddler. First thing each morning, Jack came downstairs and prepared his breakfast: cereal and a banana. Jack's descent was Stephen's cue. Leaving his mum in bed, he would negotiate the stairs on his bottom to join his grandpa below. Together they had breakfast which, for Stephen, meant eating his granddad's banana. A lovely bond grew between the elderly man in his late seventies and the little boy.

In the end Joyce felt it right to go back to America where Stephen was born and bring him up there. It was a sad day for Jack when they left, not because, Joyce told me, she herself was leaving but because her dad would lose his youngest grandchild with whom he was so close.

Before they left, Jack handed Joyce a letter. She must not open it until she was on the plane. In it he told her not to be sad at leaving him. She had her own life to live and Stephen's future to consider. He would be all right, and he loved them both very much. How typical of him to think of them and not himself. Yes, it reassured and comforted Joyce while, at the same, she said, "It broke my heart."

No Soft Touch

How loving and caring this man always was. Anyone could appeal to his compassion and evoke a response. If there were times when people took advantage of his tender heart, that was preferable to Jack, rather than risk turning aside from someone who genuinely needed his good will. Having said all this, Jack was by no means a soft touch.

He had the courage of his convictions, as we saw from his attitude to the war. He carried this through into later life. He continued to hate physical violence and refused to retaliate when it was threatened. Once, he and another man had a disagreement. It must have been pretty heated, for suddenly the man concerned squared up to him, ready for a fight. Jack stood his ground, put his hands to his sides, faced his opponent and said, "OK! Come on then. Hit me."

Totally unprepared for such a reaction, the man stood nonplussed. After a few seconds, he dropped his fists and turned away.

Jack also had a sense of his own worth. In as much as he respected other people, he thereby expected them to show respect towards him in return. When, for some reason, another man gave him a mouthful of foul language and abuse, he responded sharply, "Don't talk to me like that."

This man, like the other, was brought up baffled. Neither had he anticipated such a firm reaction from the mild Jack Punton. His eyes fell. He likewise walked away.

What few people realised was that although Jack was so gentle, his feelings could be aroused, not only to anger but even to aggression. Rarely did anyone see this side of his character, for it was not dominant; and he always held himself well in control. One evening, however, he attended a chapel business meeting—never one of his favourite duties. Partway through, he arose and, without a word, walked out.

"Were you all right?" asked Bill Ramsey later.

"Yes, but I couldn't sit there any longer. That chairman made me so mad. If I hadn't got up and left, I would have got up and hit him."

To this day, I am afraid I do not know wherein the hapless chairman transgressed.

The more I have discovered about Jack, both as his wife and from others who knew him well, the more I realise why he was so highly esteemed in the community. Not everyone liked him. Some folks were jealous of his success and popularity, but they were in the minority, and even those who resented him were reluctantly obliged to accord him their regard.

Interlude from the Past

The following story is a piece of wartime history, unimportant to all but those concerned and yet worth recording. It tells of so-styled enemies reaching out to each other in recognition of their intrinsic value as human beings. I have thought much about where to place it. I have decided that, although it is different, it is entirely within the spirit of the present chapter to include it here.

One Sunday in February 1993, my mother and I went to chapel as usual. During coffee in the vestry, Jack came up to us with a pleasant-looking gentleman.

"I'd like you to meet a friend from Germany, Mr Harry Poeschke."

The two men had not seen each other for many years, but Harry had decided to visit for a special reason. At my request, he wrote to me after Jack died to give me more of the background.

Harry was born in Berlin in 1925. At eighteen, he was called up for army training in Russia. Fortunately, as he felt it, he was sent to Guernsey instead. During his twenty-two months there, he had a happy relationship with the islanders. Even when the islands returned to British jurisdiction in 1945 and he became a POW, he could still walk about freely and visit friends. He tells how at this time the Guernsey Council wrote two letters. The first thanked the German soldiers for their understanding through difficult times. The second, to the king, asked that the German POWs be treated as well as they had treated the islanders during the occupation.

Thus, it was that in spring 1946 Harry found himself in a POW camp of nine hundred men in Brayton near Selby. By 1947, they were allowed to leave the camp during the day if they were not working. They were also encouraged to organise their own social life. They had a good football team and an orchestra of fifteen, mostly professional musicians playing on borrowed instruments. The camp chaplain arranged with a local minister to hold a Christmas concert in his church. This was so successful that it was repeated in Goole, Snaith, and elsewhere. At first the orchestra played Christmas music. Later, it changed to items from operas by Beethoven, Mozart, Puccini, and others. Because his English was good, Harry was compere at these concerts. He did, however, make the occasional error of pronunciation. Jack was amused when he announced with a flourish the aria from *La Boheme*, "Your Tinny Hand Is Frozen." To continue, in Harry's own words,

> *After . . . Snaith . . . Jack wanted a concert in Carlton in his church. But he got some trouble in his congregation because some members had lost relations during the war . . . and they didn't want a concert by German POWs. Jack could overcome this opposition.*

How Jack did so is not explained, only that he successfully persuaded the erstwhile reluctants to attend, and with a happy outcome. Says Harry,

> *The phenomenon . . . was that in the tea time after the concert, some of the people who had been against . . . said, "People who have such a music and can perform it so perfect[ly] can't be so bad as we thought." And some of them invited young POWs into their homes.*

Naturally Jack and Margaret showed hospitality too. Harry, especially, was often in their house. Sally was two and John, six months. Harry would take Sally for walks whilst he and a young lady called Olive Ridley regularly babysat together. The Ridleys owned a grocer's shop opposite Carlton chapel. All the family were musical. Olive's mother was a chapel organist, and one or other of the daughters often accompanied Jack when he sang solos. Mr Ridley was an evangelist. Jack held him in high respect. One day, Harry had what he calls "a nice adventure." He arrived on his bike to see the Ridleys. Finding nobody at home, he prepared to go.

> *At the moment I left the yard they came . . . . They said, "If you come again and we are not here you will stay here. You know where the key is and where the food is you know too."*

Each Saturday, Jack played cricket. One afternoon, he asked Harry to go with him.

> *He introduced me to his friends and I waited at the side of the field. The team . . . stood in a circle but in the direction where I stood was a gap . . . . A ball [came] in my direction. I . . . threw it back . . . . At last I learned to play as batter and as bowler (this was the difficult part).*

In June 1948, Harry was repatriated. Before he left, he had to return a violin to its owner who had moved to Withernsea on the east coast between Bridlington and Spurn Head. It meant a train journey and a long day out. Olive was to accompany Harry, but he had a problem. He had nothing to wear other than his POW garb. It was soon solved. Jack gave him a jacket, and he made the outing with pride as a civilian.

I am glad I can say that Harry, in his own words, "felt well in England and nearly at home." I like to feel that it was, in part, because of the kindness of people like Jack and the Ridleys. After his repatriation, he and Jack kept in touch, and this brings the story full circle and back to the starting point of introductions in the chapel.

Towards the end of 1992, Ruth began planning for her dad's eightieth birthday. Surreptitiously, she consulted his address book and wrote to all his friends asking for any interesting memories of Jack. She was compiling a "This Is Your Life" book for the occasion. Harry obliged beyond expectation.

> *I made a sheet and did send it to her. But in the same moment I had the idea to make him a surprise . . . . Nobody should know it. I would visit him on this day. And so I booked a flight to Leeds. The difficulty was my wife has on the same day birthday as Jack—the second of February—but she said it would be all right.*

In the end Harry wondered if it was wise to arrive completely unannounced. He took the precaution of confiding in a delighted Ruth. She met him at the airport and arranged an overnight stay in the Brewers Arms. Harry takes up.

> *Next morning . . . Ruth and John fetched me . . . to the house. When I came in the kitchen Jack stood in the door to the living room. He looked and said, "Harry!" BBC Hull made a report for the family time in the afternoon. The next days Jack and Ruth drove me about to Brayton, Selby, York, Hull to Sally where I met Olive Ridley.*

Harry left, but how important friendship and these echoes of the past were to both him and Jack.

Am I a Sham?

While still in his fifties Jack wrote,

> *A few years ago when I was at the synod, I was one of about three hundred leaders of Methodism in the Hull and York district. All committed followers of Jesus Christ we had met to talk about our work in the world . . . . The thought came to me as I stood amongst all these people . . . . If only we had a single spark of the Holy Spirit in each of us we could change the life of Britain . . . . I thought, just how committed are we to this man whose life was so full of self-sacrifice, was so full of love for all types and conditions of men? I got a guilty feeling that I was a sham.*

How often could we all say that about ourselves if we are honest? Nevertheless, it was moments like this which, from early years, inspired Jack to be the man he was.

One evening, Jack and I were taking the Harvest Festival service at Camblesforth Methodist Chapel. During proceedings, a presentation was made to an elderly gentleman called Bob Price. Bob was shortly to go into a home, and after a lifetime of local preaching, he was simultaneously being honoured and farewelled. This lovely man came up to me afterwards.

"I'd like to tell you a story," he said.

Many years previously, he and his wife had come to live in the area. Needing some bits and pieces for their new home, Bob decided to pay a visit to the DIY shop in Snaith. As he made his purchases, he also had a pleasant chat with the proprietor who, at the end, insisted on carrying the heavier items out to Bob's car. That was all. It was enough, however, for Bob to feel the atmosphere. He went home to his wife and said, "I'm sure that man is a Christian."

If your faith radiates to others in such a way that they sense that you are different and if fellow Christians feel a response of recognition in their own hearts, then I do not believe that you are a sham.

Mayor Jack Punton and Duke of Norfolk
at Snaith Methodist Chapel summer fete.
(Courtesy of the Selby Times)

"These shoes were made for walking."
(Courtesy of The Goole Times)

Opening a children's playground.

Princess Margaret honours Jack for his contribution towards the children of the nation. (Courtesy of the N.S.P.C.C.)

CHAPTER 10

WELL DONE, JACK!
or
JACK'S LAST WALK

The Walking Man Again

"Well done, Jack!"

The voice was English although this was Amsterdam. In the final stages of his walk around Holland, Jack was striding through the streets of the city, which, truth to tell, he had entered with some trepidation. A Dutch friend at home had told him that Amsterdam was a dangerous place where you ran a high risk of being stabbed in the back for your money. He had heard of its reputation for drugs, sex, and sleaze; and he had entered its precincts warily. However, none of this was in evidence as he walked along the pavement on this beautiful sunny afternoon in June 1989. Passersby looked at the placard he carried on his backpack proclaiming his activity of walking round Holland to raise money for children's charities. Many smiled and exchanged the time of day. Some stopped to question him further then handed him a little something for his funds.

One solid lady, on a likewise solid bike, drew up and asked him where he was making for. As he was looking for a monastery on the outskirts of the city where he had been promised accommodation for the night, he in turn asked for directions. She told him then offered, "Would you like a lift?"

Jack looked dubiously at the seat over the back wheel.

"It's very kind, but no thanks. I never take lifts if I can walk."

However sturdy both the lady and the bike, he was glad he could in good faith refuse. He continued his way, enjoying Amsterdam and the knowledge that the great metropolis, despite its reputation, was by no means all bad. What place or, for that matter, what person ever is?

"Well done, Jack!"

Passing pedestrians heard the words and looked and smiled. Jack turned to look too. The lady of the English voice drew near, and they walked on together. She was a journalist over from London to cover a story. She expected to fly back that night. Before they parted, she gave him her address and telephone number and hoped he would get in touch when he got home. I believe he did when he was next in London. They went their separate ways with her. "Well done, Jack!" repeated yet again in farewell.

Ten years later Jack heard those words again. It was a freezing February evening. He was walking along the pavement of his beloved hometown, a path he had traversed many times on most days of his long life. None of the people who fetched blankets to cover the recumbent figure on the flagstones, who phoned for an ambulance or who anxiously felt for a pulse that had ceased to beat, none of these heard the voice, "Well done, Jack!"

Only Jack heard and turned to greet the caller.

"Well done, Jack, my good and faithful old friend. Come on in into the presence of your Lord."

Jack's longest walk had ended. He was home.

Walking for Whizz Kidz

And so I lost him. Despite the shock, I was not entirely unprepared. If you marry a man twenty-six years your senior and already eighty-one on your wedding day, what can you expect? However fit and youthful he might be, and Jack was fit and youthful all our married life, you cannot help but know that every hour you have together is a bonus. We did know that, both of us. Many times a day we would tell each other how much we loved each other. We never took one, single second for granted. We consciously enjoyed every moment that we had together and daily thanked God for our happiness.

I sometimes contemplated, with a frisson of dread, how I might eventually lose him. I puzzled often, and still do, about how two wives, both greatly beloved, will relate to one husband in heaven. It should be enough to believe that up there it is all going to be far better than down here. No doubt I am silly, but I cannot avoid wondering. I digress. Let me return and set the stage for that final scene.

It was a bright spring morning in May 1998. We had just finished breakfast and our time of prayer and Bible reading together. We were talking and laughing at the birds in the garden. In the post had come Jack's runners' magazine. He was flicking through it.

"What do you think of this?"

A note of excitement in his voice alerted me to full attention.

"What would you feel about me doing the New York Marathon in November?"

What would I feel? He had done the London Marathon a year earlier and the Half Marathon Great North Run six months later. They had tired him, and his times were slower than he had hoped for. Even so, he was none the worse for the experiences. He travelled home the day after the London race, and the day after that he was speaking at a meeting way out in the country about the event. Apart from the inevitable stiffness, which everyone feels and which takes a few days to clear, he was fine after a good night's sleep.

Only two weeks previous to our conversation, he had walked his own private marathon less than two miles. He had trudged all day in driving rain and wind and had then come home to entertain two old friends who were visiting Snaith for the weekend. Yes, he was eighty-five, but he would surely manage it with no ill effects. I said, "Tell me more."

"There's this group called Whizz Kidz. It's a charity providing mobility aids for children who'll never walk."

I thought that the health service might have done that, but apparently, with seventy thousand such children in the UK, the health service could offer no more than basic equipment; and some children had nothing at all. Whizz Kidz filled the gaps and even gave the little extras. He went on, "They'll guarantee a place in the New York Marathon for anyone who'll raise money for their organisation."

His big heart was touched, as he thought of the children, always his particular care in all his fund-raising work. Here was a cause he longed to do something about. At the same time, I could almost see the adrenaline start to flow as he contemplated another marathon. It is strange how these things get into the blood once you start doing them, almost like an addiction.

"All right," I responded finally, "if you feel you can manage it, I'll back you. At least you can find out more before you decide for sure."

I have never stood in the way of the things Jack wanted to do. As you know, I come from a family of fell walkers, campers, cyclists, youth hostellers, climbers, and so on, and did my share when I was young. My brother runs marathons and ultra distances and goes on expeditions in Arctic and Antarctic zones. That is how I know about the addictive adrenaline phenomenon. Like Jack, I liked a challenge. We therefore did find out more. Jack duly applied and was accepted to be a Whizz Kidz runner. Nonetheless, we both knew that Jack's decision had really been made the moment he saw the advert.

The deal offered various options. Some people had no alternative but to fit the event into a long weekend. I encouraged Jack to go for a week which gave him easy days before and after the run as well as an opportunity to book on some tours round New York. He had visited his daughters in California many times but had never been on the east side before.

There was one thing we were not happy about with Whizz Kidz, although it is common practice with most charities which offer guaranteed places at such events. If you raise a specified amount of money for them, they will pay entrance fees, travel, and accommodation costs. In this case, a helicopter ride over New York was included. Whatever Jack has done, he has always paid his own costs. Every penny of sponsorship money has gone directly to the cause. We made it clear that we were paying all Jack's expenses ourselves.

Marathon Mania

Only one thing had precedence in our house during the summer, the New York Marathon. The extension which we had added to the back of April Cottage was not long completed. We had moved in with a fair amount of decorating and touching-up jobs to do in various parts of the house. I knew that much would have to wait until the great adventure was over before Jack would turn his attention to the bigger tasks. Who minded? We both agreed that life was made up of more than paint, wallpaper, and new stair carpets.

Believe it or not, these sponsored efforts involve a lot of paper work. Jack wrote letters, some photocopied but many personal and by hand, to friends near and far, advertising his latest ploy. He prepared notices and sponsor forms. He telephoned local papers, radio, and TV stations. He had no difficulty getting coverage, for he was, as you are already aware, well-known from previous exploits. As money came in, he kept careful accounts.

Following the advice from his magazine, Jack prepared his long-term training schedule which aimed to build up speed, stamina, and distance to a peak shortly before the great day. There are plenty of quiet roads suitable for training roundabout, and Jack enjoyed planning routes. Whenever he had sponsorship money to bank in Selby, he would take the bus through and walk the seven miles back at speed. On warm days he arrived home dripping with sweat but always in high spirits.

"I feel great," he used to say. "That's done me good."

Dehydration is a real danger in hot weather, but we were already producing specially formulated fruit juice-based drinks to increase energy and replace lost body salts. You could buy a brand called iso-something or other. I never could remember the name. I called it his fill up with Esso. Our diet also took on a high pasta content. Apparently there is nothing like it for producing glycogen in the body, and as athletes know, glycogen in turn boosts high and sustained levels of energy. All in all we felt encouraged.

There was something else to do. I phoned my friend in Suffolk, Antoinette.

"What are you doing early in November? The thing is, Jack's planning another marathon. Can you spare a week to come and look after me while he's in New York?"

She could. It was important. My MS was active, and I had been quite ill for most of three years. Jack would never leave me alone for long. I always had to encourage him to go for a day's outing with his men's group or to have a day out with John at Headingly for the cricket. He would never leave me at night. That was non-negotiable.

The summer progressed, and so did the training, though not quite so well as hoped. Jack wanted to do the marathon at an average walking speed of four miles per hour, which is good going. We both realised he must settle for less but as he said, "Even if I take eight hours or more, I'll be satisfied as long as I finish it."

There was, incidentally, no question of his actually running. An old football injury to a knee, plus a certain amount of wear and tear due to age, saw to that. If he ran or jogged, he risked jarring the limb. Better to walk and stay the course than damage the knee and have to withdraw partway through.

The Best-Laid Plans . . .

In September, Jack's daughter Jane visited from America and made her base with us. They managed a walking weekend in Cornwall together which was very special for both of them. Then early in October, John and Jack took Jane to Doncaster to catch a train south. It was farewell and the end of her holiday. On the way back, John dropped his dad off at a place called Askern, for him to walk the ten miles home to Snaith. That was the turning point. Jack arrived home cold, ill, and weak. He filled in the story. Halfway back, on an isolated and exposed stretch of road, he suddenly felt cold inside, although he was sweating. Then he went weak all across his upper body. Actually, it was a cold day with a chilly wind; and he only had thin summer clothes on.

"You've probably got a chill in your tummy," I suggested, desperately hoping that that was it.

He had then struggled on to Pollington, some two to three miles from Snaith. I scolded a little, but he knew how concerned I was and how helpless I felt because I could not even make him a cup of tea in his need.

"Darling, why on earth didn't you go to someone's house and phone John to come for you? Umpteen people would have been delighted to sit you down and give you a hot drink and even drive you home themselves."

No! It was not my dogged husband's way to admit defeat. He leaned against a fence and rested, then finally pulled himself together and dragged himself on. He was a great believer in the strength of will power to overcome obstacles. Somewhere he kept a picture of hill walkers wearily trekking upwards to a distant summit. The caption stated, "They can because they think they can." He also treasured a framed verse that I once bought him entitled *Don't Quit*. The sentiment summed him up perfectly.

Regarding his physical endeavours, Jack never failed to assure me that he would be sensible. If he felt ill, he would stop. At first I believed him. As I learned to understand his inner motivations better, I was not so sure. Meeting the challenge, overcoming the odds, completing the task—all irrespective of personal pain and cost—these were not theoretical ideals. They had, over a lifetime, become part of the fabric of his very character. They could not be jettisoned at a moment of crisis. Indeed, it was in the moment of crisis that they came into play like an automatic reflex. No! Jack would have collapsed on that journey rather than give up. Foolish, you may say, yet in such moments, we see the truth of the old paradoxical insight that our greatest strengths are often our greatest weakness.

All this happened exactly one month before Jack was due to fly out to America.

Doctor's Verdict

A week later Jack was no better. By this time, he should have been approaching the peak of his training. It was all going wrong, and we were worried. He saw the doctor. She wondered about a virus that was going round. I get the feeling that there are always viruses going round to explain any unaccountable malaise. At the same time, she checked him over and took blood samples. The results showed a slight anaemia. Now this too is a risk for athletes, especially runners. I have read that it has something to do with the constant pounding of the feet, breaking down the blood corpuscles. We worked out another diet, this time high in iron. Subsequent blood tests revealed that the anaemia was clearing up, but the doctor was not satisfied; and Jack, though improving, was by no means fit. One week before he was due to fly out to New York, we were cancelling the trip and presenting our claim to the insurance company which, I may add, was met fully and speedily.

Two new young lady doctors had recently joined the practice. I already knew of more than one elderly gentleman who was chuffed to be treated by them, for they were capable as well as charming. My dear husband was no exception when he found himself under the care of Dr Susie Foster. Dr Susie, he affectionately called her.

"She's lovely," he used to enthuse. "It makes me feel better just to see her."

Dr Susie was not only nice, she was also thorough. We had no complaints about delays. Everything progressed steadily, but it does take time to run tests and establish a diagnosis. Meanwhile, there were things to do.

Jack was not well and had to take life quietly, but he never completely stopped. He tidied the garden for winter. He did the occasional stint in the shop when John was busy. As always he was involved in all the funerals that came in. He kept the house running. Such tasks caused him little trouble. It was walking, even just the short distance to his shop, that started the weakness and the ill feeling.

He also set about informing all his supporters and sponsors that the marathon was off. By this time, he had received some. Over the years, she had regularly sponsored his walks. On this occasion, she had contacted her business associates and was promising £1,000 to come. Now Jack was obliged to offer all this money back. Happily, nobody wanted it back. Why deprive Whizz Kidz children just because someone was ill? That would have been mean. In the long run, most people who had promised money also paid up, and we were glad.

By the time Jack had the final test at Christmas, he was feeling a little better. We realised the significance of the results.

"You have a leaking heart valve," the doctor told him. We already knew that he had a heart problem. "There's no question of an operation. We can help you with tablets."

They did help him. He started new medication, and by the end of January, he was a different person and walking was easier. In such fashion, we come to the day of the voice, Tuesday, February 9, 1999. It was exactly one week after his eighty-sixth birthday.

The Day of the Voice

On the Monday evening, Jack was a bit snuffly.

"I feel OK. Surely I'm not starting a cold?"

"Have some garlic," I suggested, and not inconsequentially. We had both found garlic helpful in staving off or easing an imminent cold, though preferably taken with a meal. This was nearly bedtime. Understandably, he declined. Normally we would lie in bed for a few minutes holding hands and saying silly, loving things to each other. This night we did not. If I get a cold, it affects the MS and causes problems. It was wise to avoid unnecessary close contact. He turned away from me and remained that way all night. I reached out to touch his head. We exchanged one of our funny code phrases and said good night.

The next day Jack was due to sing a duet at the funeral of an old friend.

"Don't you think you ought to cancel it, stay in, and keep warm?" I asked at breakfast. It was very wintry outside.

"I don't think it is a cold. Whatever it was, it seems to have gone now. Let's see how the morning goes."

He did truly appear to be all right and in excellent spirits. The routine household chores were punctuated with snatches of song, as he tested out his voice. From time to time, he struck an operatic pose which fitted not incongruously with the words of "How Great Thou Art," the duet in question. He kept looking to me for approval. We laughed, as I dutifully applauded his antics.

"If you go on like this, you'll soon be taking Sally for walks again."

He responded emphatically.

"I will do that, and it won't be long now."

I had in mind something short, just round the block to begin with. He was thinking big, Dor Lane or the riverbank for instance. It did my heart good to hear it. How worried I had been.

"I'm only waiting for a warmer day, and I'll be in the garden." After a pause he added, "I do hope it snows." Snow was forecast, and Jack loved snow. Even so, his next words surprised me. "If it does, I'm going to build a snowman."

Well, even if you do not feel wonderful, dogs want exercise, and gardens need attention; but nobody is ever obliged to go out building snowmen. My dearest Jack really was on the mend. I could have sung and gestured my way through a rousing operatic aria myself.

Jack went to the funeral and sang his duet. He noticed something amusing. Even funerals, as you will have gathered from an earlier chapter, have their lighter moments. We laughed about it together when he got home and told me. There was snooker on the TV which we always enjoyed. Some of the games were tense. We had our tea as we watched.

When the news ended at 7:00 p.m., he suddenly remembered that he had left the car standing on the double yellow lines outside our front door. They were a nuisance. He often risked it but not usually for so long. At night, he parked behind his shop which, being so near, was no great inconvenience. It was an icy evening and beginning to freeze. He decided to deal with it at once.

"Why don't you phone John and ask him to put the car away later?"

John had often done that while his dad was ill, although we liked to trouble him.

"No! I'm feeling absolutely fine. I won't bother John when I can manage."

Obviously he was not struggling to cope. If anything, he sounded fairly jaunty, but still I worried.

"Darling, it's a bitter night. Your cold hasn't developed, but you don't want to start it up again. If it went to your chest, a cough would put needless strain on your heart."

"I hear what you're saying, but I'll wrap up warmly. Honestly, I'm OK."

Even as we spoke, he was donning a thick anorak along with his cap and scarf. To emphasise the point, he now pulled on his gloves. He went. I did not notice the time, but it was not much after 7:00 p.m.

"I won't be long."

The cow bells above the inner door jangled loudly, as he pulled it closed. The outer door slammed, and the house shook, as it usually did when he came and went. He was quiet and gentle, but his actions were vigorous, and he did not know his own strength.

He went. He did not come back.

A Hard Waiting

At first I thought he had stopped for petrol and was talking to someone. Perhaps he had seen a light in the shop, found John working late, and was chatting to him. I phoned the shop. Only the answer phone responded. I called John's house. Only the engaged signal sounded.

The minutes passed. He had been gone over half an hour. I gave up hope of getting John. Who else could I try? Someone from the chapel? Eventually I rang a number and got an answer. It was Audrey, one of our chapel members. Her husband was at work with their car. She would walk round. She came. Yes, the car was duly parked at the shop. The security lights had come on. There was no one slumped behind the wheel or lying on the ground. Jack had disappeared.

Still, I could not get John. Audrey went round on foot. Over an hour had passed. Suddenly John's line was clear. I learned later that his boys had been on the Internet. John made a little joke.

"Perhaps he's gone into the Black Lion for a pint."

It did not greatly ease the tension. We both knew that something was wrong. Within seconds of my ringing off, John's phone shrilled again. It was from Goole. Jack had been brought into casualty and pronounced dead on arrival.

There was no way to break the news gently. John came round with his son Nigel. As he entered the door, he said baldly, "He's dead."

He came over to me. We held hands tightly. We remained silent, still holding hands, and trying to absorb the dreadful news.

View from the Hilltop

Have you ever felt, in a few seconds, a whole range of thoughts flood your mind which would take many minutes to articulate? Have you ever stood on a hilltop on a cloudless day and gazed at the vista stretching out below? In one glance you take in the entire scene; yet simultaneously, you are aware of the separate units which comprise the whole—fields, a river, a wood, a church steeple, a miniature moving train, black dots of grazing cows. You see it all.

In the few moments that John and I sat comforting each other, I saw consciously and clearly the tiny details of that desolate landscape of loss so harshly thrust to view. Only later could they be examined in depth. You must understand this as I now try to describe them to you.

1. The first landmark thought in my awareness was, strangely enough, a sense of relief. The moment I had always dreaded had come. Thank God, it had come quickly and easily. Jack had not lain semiconscious behind the car, hidden from view in the shop yard, and in danger of catching pneumonia in the cold. Nor would he ever lie incapacitated in a hospital bed with me unable to visit him and then unable to look after him if he recovered sufficiently to come home.

He died without suffering and unaware of what was about to happen. I had always said that I never wanted to see anyone I loved die a slow, painful death with cancer. Sadly, both my parents did. I know that none of Jack's family would have wanted to see him linger in sickness. However devastating the shock was for us, Jack had gone, as both he and all of us would have wanted.

2. Closely alongside this firstly perceived landmark thought stood a second. Jack was ready to go at any time. He often said to me, "I'm not afraid to die. I love life, but even if I knew that it would be tonight, I would not worry."

Brave words? I think not. Jack believed in life beyond the grave. He believed in heaven. He loved and served God all his life. What lay beyond might be a mystery, but it was real, and it was good, and God would be there.

3. My third landmark thought was this. Jack had been taken first. Despite his age, he was very strong. I, on the other hand, was quite ill during the previous three years. We could not assume that I, though so much younger,

would outlive him. We all felt, irrationally of course, that he would live forever, or at least long enough to receive the royal telegram. He himself often said, "To ninety-two!"

It was a family joke. He mimicked an old man's quivery voice and took on a tottery pose. We always laughed. He seemed so invincible.

Selfishly, I often hoped that he would be spared to look after me to my end. It was selfish. Jack had already seen his beloved Margaret go. He spoke of her often but not of his grief, for he never found it easy to bare his soul of his deepest feelings. However, he shared with me something of what he went through at that time, and it was hard. Would he feel the same if God took me too? I was not sure until one evening, during our silly moments before sleep, he burst forth with unexpected passion, "I don't know what I would do if I lost you, Anne. I don't know how I'd live without you."

At that moment, I realised that I loved Jack too much to ever want him to experience for me even a shadow of what he endured on losing Margaret. I could only be glad that God had opened his arms to Jack first.

4. A fourth landmark thought loomed large. God was in control. Despite the unanswerable *whys*, this assurance held me. God had taken the most precious thing I possessed. I felt bereft and alone, yet never once did I doubt that God had called my dearest one home either one moment sooner or one moment later than accorded with his purposes. Although my life had fallen apart, the foundations were firm.

Not then but many times since, the words of a little poem by Charlotte Bickersteth Ward came to mind. It has often brought comfort in hard times, especially line three.

> *Child of my love, "Lean hard,"*
> *And let me feel the pressure of thy care.*
> *I know thy burden, child; I shaped it,*
> *Poised it in Mine own hand, made no proportion*
> *Of its weight to thine unaided strength;*
> *For even as I laid it on I said—*
> *"For I shall be near, and while she leans on Me,*
> *This burden shall be Mine, not hers.*
> *So shall I keep My child within the circling arms*
> *Of Mine own love."*

5. I call the fifth thought the landmark in the shade. It was definitely there, but I only focused on it later.

We had sat together one evening, each quietly occupied and not speaking. I looked across to Jack. I looked again. It is hard to describe what I saw, for I had never seen it before. Was it a touch of frailty? My big, robust husband always filled his chair with vital health. Had he shrunk into it a little? He moved slightly. The impression went, all was as usual. Some days later it happened again, only this time he was standing at the sink. What was this? A hint of vulnerability in that strong frame? He had not lost weight, I was sure. Was there a trace of transparency in the features? Again he moved, and all was as before.

This happened about four times in January, and each time it caught me by surprise. The new tablets were working, and he was so obviously improving. At the same time, he had struggled for the past three months. Had those months left their mark? I knew I was not imagining it; but, I reasoned, these transient signs of illness would go, as he got built up again. I never told him what I had seen. I was not going to make him anxious needlessly, but deep down it troubled me. Only in the days following Jack's death did I discover the full implications of leaking heart valves and realise that there was a significance in what I had so fleetingly glimpsed.

Jack was not going to get better. In spite of medication and temporary alleviation, the symptoms would eventually return. A doctor friend told me that he might have looked forward to a few years of reasonable quality of life, but on the whole, the long-term outlook was not favourable. I often wonder if the improvement Jack felt in January and early February was fast reaching its peak. Perhaps within a few weeks or months, he would have started to go down again. There is no knowing. Was God gracious in taking Jack as and when he did?

6. This brings us to the sixth and related landmark thought. Oddly enough, it has to do with pride—mine, Jack's, and his family's.

Jack was a modest man, but that did not stop him from being rightfully proud of his good health and his achievements. Had he survived the heart attack of that February evening suddenly to become old and ill, it would have been a blow to his pride and to ours too. I am glad that nobody will ever be able to say, "Have you seen Jack Punton recently? No more marathons for him! What a shame after all he's done."

Such remarks, be they ever so sympathetically made, would, if overheard, have hurt unbearably. As it is, everyone remembers him as he always was—active and fit.

7. My seventh landmark thought followed swiftly on. Even as I thanked God that Jack would never now face a lingering decline in health, I briefly recalled the person who had said, "Oh, Jack would never take it well if he became sick and housebound."

My first response to that is, "Who would?"

In fact, Jack was adaptable. He would have taken it better than most people I know. We were both ready to accept that the days of big exploits were over, for even though he appeared to be improving, we had had a fright. Already he was planning what to do with a quieter lifestyle. He told Dr Susie, "My first priority is Anne. All I want to do now is to look after her."

Bless him! He had much more than that worked out. There were old friends in the area to visit, neglected jobs in the house to finish, and, of course, the occasional help for John in the business. He brought out dozens of tiny, curling, snapshots of the children when young and taken with a cheap Brownie box camera. He started to sort and stick them into albums. They lay there, littering the table, the day after he died. He decided to turn an upstairs room into a picture gallery for his more important photographs and certificates for this and that. I had a few items of my own to add. He never even started the project. One thing was sure, a quieter lifestyle did not include the option of sitting around idle.

Of course, had he become too incapacitated for even simple tasks, he would have felt as frustrated as anyone else; but there are four things to say about that.

First, Jack did not complain. Once, even when he must have been in agony from a wrenched shoulder and heavy internal bleeding down the arm, he never grumbled, got short tempered, or acted sorry for himself. I see no reason why he should have responded any differently in the circumstances we are now positing.

Second, Jack knew where to find help. His spiritual and devotional life was never on showcase display. Nonetheless, he "talked to God," as he phrased it, all the time. God would have enabled him to cope with more than human power.

Third, Jack had a favourite saying, "Such is life." He used it often to express his acceptance of the vagaries of existence. His children grew up with it. It was their cue to add in chorus, "Life is what you make it." I could have talked about this saying in the previous chapter, for it was very much part of Jack's philosophy of life. It fits better here.

Jack expected no preferential treatment from life. It ebbs and flows, independent of human control, with ups and downs for everyone. You must take what comes. What you can do something about is *how* you take what comes. If you grumble over misfortune and allow it to make you miserable or bitter, that is up to you. If you fight against defeatism, resentment, and feeling sorry for yourself and work through the hard times as cheerfully and positively as you can, that also is up to you; and you will be the one to benefit in the end. From youth, Jack had worked on the principle that "such is life, but life is what you make it." He would not abandon it in the ultimate crisis.

Fourth, Jack would have seen such trials as the last great challenge of his life. Whatever the inevitable, momentary lapses into self-pity, discouragement, or irritability, he would, metaphorically, have leaned on the fence, pulled himself together, and then struggled on. Oh yes! Had he been put to the test, I knew that my husband had the resources to come through with grace and dignity.

8. The eighth landmark thought was very prominent in the picture. I was afraid. How would I manage without Jack who did so much for me? I knew that we could arrange for carers to come in through the social services, but Jack's loving support was irreplaceable. I asked myself later if I mourned more for Jack himself or for my own predicament. It was a reasonable question given the circumstances. All grief has an element of preoccupation with the self. This is natural, and it is not bad. Neither is the whole story. However complex an emotion grief is, I now know that the focal point of my loss was always centred in the very essence of who and what Jack was.

My fifty-four single years were happily fulfilled and privileged beyond measure, although there were struggles, and I never found singleness easy. The five years I shared with Jack were blissful—there is no other word to use. However adequately the social services and the care of friends and family might meet my practical needs, nothing could replace the happiness of being with Jack. I felt this then. I am sure of it now.

9. My ninth landmark concerned Jack's family. They all thought the world of their dad. There was no way to soften the shock, and on John lay the responsibility of informing them all and making funeral arrangements. It was a blow for each of them and an especially heavy burden for John to carry. They were all in my mind.

10. There is a tenth and final landmark thought. To get to the back of the shop, Jack had to drive a short distance down the High Street and along the busy Pontefract Road. Had his heart attack occurred only three or four minutes earlier, it could have caused a dreadful accident involving other people.

Oh yes! Even in my grief and shock, I thanked God for the way it had happened and instinctively knew that these landmark thoughts would shortly be my solace.

Last Moments

Meanwhile, John and I still sat, hands tightly gripped, although probably no more than two minutes passed before we moved apart. Already there were things to do.

It was not long before we pieced together the course of events. Jack had parked the car and was walking home. He collapsed outside Priory Stores, a hundred yards from his own front door. He died as he fell from a fatal heart attack. The Priory Stores' lady was lovely. She fetched blankets and wrapped Jack up as he lay on the pavement. She then sat stroking his head until the ambulance arrived. Some young people milling around, as was their wont, on the square before the fire station, came across to try to help. Someone who was responsible for first aid at nearby Drax, Europe's largest power station, did what he could but to no avail. There was no pulse.

The Priory Stores' lady thought it was Jack because of his clothes, but nobody could be certain. As often happens in such cases, the face was suffused and distorted beyond recognition. One thing is sure, and it is such a comfort, if Jack felt any lingering sense of awareness in those last moments, he knew that he was being looked after.

At first John wondered if he could act as undertaker for his own dad. This was understandable. Of all the family, he was the one who had worked with him daily for over twenty years, and they were close. Then Simon arrived with a week off work. Together, Jack's two sons, of whom he was so proud, brought their dad home and laid him in his own chapel of rest. Jack would have been happy. Indeed, could we have discussed the arrangements with him, I am sure he would have been pleased with all that we did.

The family gathered, including Jane and Joyce from California. They lovingly supported me. I had not realised until then how much they had all taken me to their hearts. We were not miserable. It was a time for recalling childhood memories, especially of their father and mother together. It was a time for laughing at their dad's idiosyncrasies, of which he had his share, and amusing stories from his past. He would have laughed too had he been with us. There was healing in the humour.

If you are a musician, you will know what a ground bass is. The same short musical phrase is repeatedly sounded in the bass clef while other melodies and harmonies fill the higher registers. During this time, whatever the activity around me, my own internal ground bass played on ceaselessly.

"You didn't come home, beloved, you didn't come home. You went, and you didn't come home."

In the end he did. We felt it fitting that Jack should lie in the Methodist chapel overnight before the funeral. The place filled a major part of his whole life. On the way there, John and Simon brought him home to April Cottage.

They wheeled him in, so lovingly and beautifully laid out in his narrow resting place. All the disfigurement of sudden death had left his face. There was no sense of frailty here. How big and strong he looked, and yet I almost recoiled. Strange as it may seem, I hardly recognised him. On the few occasions I have had close contact with death, it always seems so empty. This was no exception. Wherever Jack was, and I firmly believe that he was somewhere, living and vital, he was not there before me. It did not matter. I said good-bye very tenderly to that dear form which had housed his great spirit for eighty-six years. An out-of-context line from a Wordsworth sonnet summed it up: "And all that mighty heart is lying still."

I moved away. John and Simon took him out. The cowbells at the inner door tinkled gently. The outer door closed quietly. It always does now.

The Funeral

I was not strong enough to go to the funeral. Jack, more than anyone else, knew my physical difficulties and would have understood. All I could do to make my presence felt was to write a tribute for someone else to read. As the family left the house that morning, I was alone in privacy for the first time since Jack had gone. I needed that space.

In moments of need, some Christians open their Bible at random, seeking an appropriate message for their problem. I prefer to follow my daily Bible reading plan and have found God speaking to my condition from the most unlikely passages. On this morning, whilst the public farewell to Jack took place elsewhere, I made my private farewell at home. I decided to depart from my normal practice. How about a random glance at the Psalms? If anything speaks to every facet of the human experience, the Psalms do.

My Bible opened roughly in the middle where the Psalms are, only I had gone too far. I flicked back—Isaiah 60, Isaiah 16, Song of Songs, Ecclesiastes. No! What was that? Back to the Song of Songs, a book for brides and weddings. What had I glimpsed? There—chapter 5, verse 1. I read it slowly. No mistake, God was speaking to me. More than that. In the words of the bridegroom to his bride, it was as if Jack himself spoke directly to me in the following lovely words.

> *I have entered my garden, my sweetheart, my bride. I am gathering my spices and myrrh; I am eating my honeycomb; I am drinking my wine and milk.*

Almost I heard Jack add in his deep, rich voice, "Don't grieve for me, my love. Be glad for me. I'm happy here."

It should have been enough, but I was greedy for more. My eyes moved down the page. Yes, verse 6 expressed my pain exactly.

> *I opened the door for my lover but he had already gone. How I wanted to hear his voice! I looked for him but couldn't find him. I called to him but heard no answer.*

Was there more? It came in chapter 6 verses 2 and 3. As it recalled those earlier words, but now echoed by the bride, I felt the achieving of a great resolution to my sadness.

My lover has gone to his garden where the balsam trees grow. He is feeding his flock in the garden and gathering lilies. My lover is mine and I am his; he feeds his flock among the lilies.

Forget all theological understandings of life after death. Forget the principles of biblical interpretation. In these words, revealed for my consolation, was all that I needed to know about Jack's future life. He is in a place of beauty where all senses are satisfied and appetites sated. It is not a place of oblivion nor even of suspended consciousness but rather of joyful awareness in idyllic surroundings. It is not a place of idleness and subsequent boredom. There are allotted tasks and pleasurable pastimes. I even dare to believe that the memory and value of earthly relationships lingers on. Moreover, Jack's personality does not change. The man who cared for others and carried responsibility in this world is entrusted with a responsible, caring job in his new world.

Make of all this what you will, whenever my sorrow feels overwhelming, I hear the words,

I have entered my garden, my sweetheart, my bride.

Jack is happy, and I must be happy too. Apart from anything else, no one likes a misery.

Requiem in Pace

There is not much else to say. I ought to mention that Jack's nephew Nicky, who helped in the business, conducted the funeral as undertaker, thus freeing John to be one of the mourners. Four of his grandsons were bearers—Stephen, Mark, Nigel, and Matthew. How pleased Jack would have been. Family and friends gathered from distant parts of the country for the funeral. We were so touched when Susie Smith unexpectedly arrived. We had all heard much about her, but none of us had met her. It was a privilege to do so for, as Jack himself would have phrased it, "She was lovely."

Jack was cremated. His ashes went to Cornwall to lie in the small windswept cemetery overlooking vale and sea at Crackington Haven. This is where Margaret is buried and where I shall go too. Jack wanted us both beside him.

Tributes came in from all over the world. Jack had so many friends. I was very touched when one couple, a George and Lily Aikens, arranged for a requiem mass to be said on his behalf. Donations to the NSPCC, given at the funeral, topped the £1,150 mark. The final total raised for Whizz Kidz was just short of £3,000.

Let me add one more thing. Snaith commemorates its better-known citizens in its street names. A select new housing estate has been built on the edges of our town, and the main road into the estate is called "Punton Walk." We are all delighted.

We all loved him deeply. We have wonderful memories, and I cannot close this book on a sad note. Jack was, and is, a happy man. I simply end with the deserved accolade, WELL DONE, JACK!

Old friends reunited. Harry Poeschke, former prisoner of war makes surprise visit to Jack on his 70th birthday.

At home with one of his grandchildren.

Final resting place in Crackington Haven, Cornwall.

"I have entered my garden." Jack as I often saw him, pottering in his April Cottage garden.

Punton Walk, Snaith. A lasting memorial.

INDEX

A

Abu El Assal, Riach, 25
Aikens, George, 267
Aikens, Lily, 267
Ash, Jack, 98, 109–10, 208
Aylward, Gladys, 155

B

Baden-Powell, 58
Bayo (Nigerian foster son), 123–27, 137
Beevers, George "Golly," 55
Bower, John Mellor, 43, 46

C

Chapell, Doreen, 210
Chappell (doctor), 70–71
Clayton, Ernie, 72
Clayton, George "Codge," 72
Clitheroe Kid, The, 145
CMJ (Church's Ministry amongst the Jewish People), 21–22, 24, 26–27, 39
Coldwell, Ronnie, 70

D

Daisy (pet donkey), 121, 147
Dapo (Nigerian foster son), 123–27, 137
Darley, Billy, 181
Daye, Mike, 183
Dexter, William, 15
Dolly (Jack's sister-in-law), 48, 171, 174, 209
Dorothy (Jack's sister), 47–48, 52
Duckles, Bob, 228

E

Eadon (owner of the Lodge), 56, 122
Earl (owner of fire station), 56
Eastam, Alice, 60
Eden, Anthony, 181
Edgar (Fred's brother), 65
Elsie (Anne's sister-in-law), 47
Elwiss (old lady), 151–52
Emma (Shirley's daughter), 168–69, 181
Ethelreda, Saint, 78

F

Field (teacher), 70
Foster, Susie, 255
Frank (Anne's uncle), 31

G

Gandhi, Mohandas Karamchand, 82, 88
Georgie (foster child), 155–56
Goole Amateur Operatic and Dramatic
    Society, 210, 236
Granny (Anne's grandmother), 19
Granny Golton, 50–51
Greenwood, Phyllis, 73
Grove Street Institute, 20

H

Haigh, Bob, 71
Harari, Huguette, 24
Heppie (family friend), 144–45
Hepworth. *See* Heppie
Hilda (founder of Whitby monastery), 78
Hinsley, Willie, 94, 164
Hodgeson, Billy, 71
Horner, Gerald, 97, 99, 101, 103–4, 107
Howard, Miles Francis Stapleton
    Fitzalan, 227
Howard, Norwood, 11, 59

I

Isaiah 22:22, *22*
Isakoff, Jo, 24

J

Jane (Jack's daughter), 11, 34, 37, 118–
    22, 124, 127, 134–36, 138, 140–44,
    147, 149, 153, 159–60, 183–85, 253

Jayne (Jack's daughter-in-law), 34,
    37–38, 182, 184, 212
Jean (Jack's daughter-in-law), 34, 46,
    183, 190, 192, 236
Jessica (Jack's granddaughter), 38,
    184
Jessie (Anne's caretaker), 72
Jessop, Gordon, 26
Jock (Scot), 150–51
Joyce (Jack's daughter), 34, 37, 115–16,
    118, 122, 125, 130, 145–46, 148,
    159–60, 184–85, 189, 213, 228,
    240

K

Karno, Fred, 98
Kathryn (Dapo and Bayo's mother), 124,
    127
Katie (Jack's granddaughter), 38, 184
Kenneth (Jack's nephew), 47
Kevin (Jack's son-in-law), 34, 140, 183,
    191
Killingbeck (Methodist farmer), 181
Kirby, Frank, 50

L

Lacey, Phyllis, 207
Lamentations 3:22–23, *26*
Laurence (Anne's brother), 11, 16, 18–
    19, 23, 32, 70, 78, 122
Law, Mary, 11, 115
Laycock, Thomas, 64
Leaver (Jehovah's Witness), 95–96
Leonard (Jack's brother-in-law), 112,
    114, 138–39, 196
Lizzie (Jack's sister), 46, 57
Longdon (headmaster), 52
Lorna (Anne's niece), 38
Loxam, Arnold, 97

M

Macdonald, John, 17
Margaret, Princess, 150, 214, 229–30
Marian (Jack's friend), 201–2
Marsden (scoutmaster), 60
Marsden, Margaret, 59
McConnell, Erica, 208
McConnell, John, 208
McGranahan (doctor), 120, 164
Merritt (old lady), 152
Methodist covenant statement, 20
Miller, Arnold, 58
Miller, Gordon, 57–58
Mitchell, Mary, 52
Moore, Bob, 17, 19
Moore, Kathleen, 17, 19, 69
Moore, Mina, 17, 19
Moxley, Canon, 80

N

Nicky (Jack's nephew), 33–34, 47–48,
    174, 267
North, Kath (Mrs. Arnold Miller), 58

O

Old Charlie. *See* Sandoe (headmaster)
"Old Man's Room of Memories, An"
    (Punton, Jack), 157
Overall, Pete, 104–5

P

Pellett, Julia, 39
Peter (Jack's friend), 201–2, 220
Plewstots, 64
Poeschke, Harry, 11, 242, 269
Powell, Enoch, 124
Price, Bob, 245

Punton, Ada
    working as a school caretaker, 45
    working as a washerwoman, 45
    working in the mill, 44, 48, 67–68
    working on the farm, 45
Punton, Anne
    attending secondary school, 16
    attending university, 20
    being engaged to Jack, 35
    birth of, 15
    breaking up with Seth, 21
    dating Seth, 20
    death of the mother of, 30
    going to Israel, 23
    having multiple sclerosis, 26
    having tea at Jack's, 34
    living in a manse, 16
    marrying Jack, 38
    meeting Jack, 30
    moving into a new house with mother, 27
    retiring from CMJ, 27
    spending time with family, 18
    View the Land, 25
    working in a hospital, 20
    World That Jesus Knew, The, 25
Punton, Jack
    attending the annual festival, 57
    being a foster parent, 124
    being a mayor of Snaith, 157
    being an apprentice, 65
    bidding for his shop, 161
    celebrating Chistmas, 57
    celebrating Chistmas with family, 136
    celebrating Easter with family, 135
    celebrating summer with family, 138
    childhood of, 49
    death of, 249
    disciplining children, 142
    establishing a new business with son, 190
    experiences as an undertaker, 171, 178
    experiences while walking, 202

facing the death of Margaret, 157
falling into an inspection pit, 212
getting into an accident
    while biking, 69
    while in the NCC, 101
    while working, 65, 68
having a medical, 96
imitating Christ, 221
joining the Rawcliffe Musical Society,
    72
joining the Scouts, 58
life in the NCC of, 97, 105
list of sponsored walks accomplished,
    197
losing blood after a tooth extraction, 68
making a cross for Snaith Methodist
    Chapel, 219
marrying Margaret, 110
moving into a new house
    after marriage, 117
    with family, 122
"Old Man's Room of Memories, An,"
    157
playing football, 54, 73, 102
playing pranks, 56
quitting smoking, 106
rehanging the bells, 164
reporting for duty with the Non-
    Combatant Corps, 96
securing a loan from the bank, 165
sermon on the topic
    "The Lifting Up of the Son of Man,"
    82
    "The Word Became Flesh and Lived
    among Us," 82
setting up a play in the army, 103
speaking for a symposium on infant
    death, 237
sponsoring a walk for Cambodian
    refugees, 191
starting a dance band, 71

starting a family with Margaret, 118
starting an Ethiopian fund, 228
starting his sponsored walks, 192
starting his undertaking business, 169
starting school, 52
traveling to Sweden, 182
visiting Rawcliffe Hall with family, 154
walking to Cornwall, 193
working in the clogmill, 68
Punton, Jimmy, 41–42, 44
Punton, Margaret (nee Ward), 6–7,
    34–35, 47, 59–60, 110–17, 119–30,
    134–35, 138–48, 150–52, 154–57,
    165, 174, 183–85, 189–90, 207–9

R

Ramsey, Bill, 50, 194, 229, 241
Ramsey, William, 50
Raymond (Jack's uncle), 121, 184
Richardson, Wilf, 87
Ridley, Olive, 243–44
Roberts, Cyril, 170, 223
Robinson, Fred, 65, 167
Ronnie (Anne's aunt), 31
Ross (Jack's grandson), 38, 184
Ross, Janette, 21
Ruth (Jack's daughter), 31, 34, 118, 120–
    22, 135–36, 140, 143, 145, 147,
    155, 159–60, 182, 184, 212, 244
R——y (welfare department
    representative), 126

S

Sally (dog), 11, 32–34, 53, 90, 148, 183,
    234, 256
Sally (Jack's daughter), 11, 34, 113–14,
    116, 118, 120–21, 123–24, 128,
    135, 140–42, 146, 154–56, 182–84,
    191, 243–44

Sandoe (headmaster), 53
Sandria (Jack's niece), 48, 174
Sangster, William, 88
Saunders, Ernest, 206
Scytha, Saint, 78
Seth (Anne's boyfriend), 20–21
Shearburn (squire), 54
Sheena (Anne's sister-in-law), 32
Shirley (Anne's caretaker), 181
Sim (doctor), 33, 37
Simon (Jack's son), 34, 37–39, 118,
        123, 125, 127, 143, 145, 152, 155,
        159–60, 182, 184, 192, 265
Six-Day War, 25
Smith (dog owner), 32
Smith, Ernest, 86
Smith, Susan, 202
Smith, Susie, 267
Smithson (choirmaster), 87
Snaith
    geography of, 75
    history of, 78
    market history of, 77
    war coming to, 91
Snow, Dorothy Barter, 22
Solheim (pastor), 24
Soper, Donald, 88
Sound of Music, The, 211
Stacey (old lady), 51
Steele, Herbert, 71
Stella Carmel, 23–24
Stewart (judge), 94–95
St. Laurence Church, 78, 122
St. Michael's House, 22
Sykes, Bessie, 20
Sykes, Seth, 20

T

Ted (Jack's brother), 48, 69, 171, 173–75
Thomas, George, 181

Thomson, John, 17
Thornham (cowman), 51
Tinkerbell (kitten), 97
Tommy (tortoise), 148
Topsy Lou (dog), 147
Townend, Neville, 161, 167
Tune, Eileen, 144
Twybill (Fred's grandfather), 65

U

Uncle George (old man), 149–50

V

Vicky (fox), 148
View the Land (Punton, Anne), 25

W

Walker, Albert, 55
Walker, Arthur, 55
Walker, Reg, 87, 90, 94, 207
Ward, Edith "Edie," 113
Ward, Stephen, 111–12, 183
Wetherhead, Leslie, 88
Whitehead, Russ, 71
Whittaker (owner of the paper shop), 56
Womersley, Sid, 161, 163
Wood, Edgerton, 51, 167
World That Jesus Knew, The (Punton,
        Anne), 25
Wurmbrand (pastor), 24

Y

Yom Kippur War, 25
Yorke, Ted, 21

Lightning Source UK Ltd.
Milton Keynes UK
UKOW031610051012

200094UK00001B/48/P